The Diasporan Self

Unbreaking the Circle in Western Black Novels

J. Lee Greene

University of Virginia Press
Charlottesville and London

University of Virginia Press

Printed in the United States of America on acid-free paper

First published 2008

9 8 7 6 5 4 3 2 1

LIBRARY OF CONGRESS CATALOGING-IN-PUBLICATION DATA

Greene, J. Lee, 1944–

The diasporan self : unbreaking the circle in western Black novels / J. Lee Greene.

p. cm.

Includes bibliographical references and index.

ISBN 978-0-8139-2739-8 (acid-free paper) — ISBN 978-0-8139-2740-4 (pbk. : acid-free paper)

1. American fiction—African American authors—History and criticism. 2. Slavery in literature. 3. African diaspora in literature. 4. Blacks in literature. 5. African Americans in literature. 6. Self in literature. 7. American fiction—20th century—History and criticism. 8. Fiction—Black authors—History and criticism.—I. Title.

PS374.S58G74 2008

813′.5409352625—dc22 2008003088

The Diasporan Self

For the African American teachers in the public schools
of Rutherford County, North Carolina, 1951–63,
who nurtured my mind, body, and soul

Contents

Acknowledgments

I thank the Institute for the Arts and Humanities at the University of North Carolina at Chapel Hill. A one-semester research fellowship the Institute provided started me on the track to this final product. I also thank the graduate students in my classes at the University of North Carolina at Chapel Hill whose probing questions and insightful observations helped me to refine my thoughts. For their assistance in retrieving research materials when I was physically unable to do so, I am very grateful to John Hannah and Robin Vander.

The Diasporan Self

Introduction
Mythography and the Western Black Imaginary

In several imaginative and scholarly texts published since the mid-1970s, the historical phenomenon known as the black African diaspora occupies a prominent place. This is especially the case in a group of Western black novels that I call contemporary fictional slave narratives. The authors of these novels typically use the African diaspora as context to interrogate identity formation. They often refer to their respective centered subject as a diasporan self, a diasporan soul, a diasporan subject, or some similar appellation. At times metaphorically and at times literally, the novelists represent (Phyllis Alesia Perry is an example) or imagine (John Edgar Wideman is an example) the primordial form of the diasporan self as an unbroken circle. They posit that the diaspora fractured the primordial Self/circle and created a Western self whose ruling passion is to regain a pre-diasporan state of Being (wholeness). Through a variety of fictive devices, contemporary fictional slave narratives indicate that the process of a subject regaining a pre-diasporan state of Being is one not of merely mending but of unbreaking the circle. To unbreak the circle, the subject must psychospiritually sojourn back in time and space to a point before the circle was broken.

Contemporary fictional slave narratives are among the most critically acclaimed and commercially successful Western black novels published since the mid-1970s. Salient aspects of their form, content, and meaning are anchored in the formal conventions of the nonfiction slave narrative, and the black African diaspora as a historical event frames many of their thematic concerns. Some of these novels are set entirely in the antebellum period, such as Charles Johnson's *Oxherding Tale* (1982), and a few of these use the northern United States in the eighteenth century as setting (Maryse Condé's *I, Tituba, Black Witch of Salem* [1986; 1992] is one). Others, such as Toni Morrison's *Beloved* (1987), use an early postbellum setting as frame for a novel whose generative action is in the antebellum period. Another group, which includes Phyllis Alesia Perry's *Stigmata* (1998), uses primarily a twentieth-century setting and interpolates a slave's narrative that is integral to the respective novel's form, content, and meaning. Still another group, to which Caryl Phillips's *Higher Ground* (1989) belongs, interpolates a slave's narrative that is set in Africa before the slave is transported to the West and connects the meaning of this slave's life to narratives of the lives of Western blacks (and sometimes nonblacks) in the twentieth century. Indeed, contemporary black novelists use the nonfiction slave narrative formally and the African diaspora thematically in a variety of ways in their novels. Western black novelists since the early 1970s have returned repeatedly and increasingly to the nonfiction slave narrative as a model for their contemporary novels; and some others have been influenced more directly by their contemporaries' revision of this antebellum model.[1]

This study focuses on a small group of representative English-language novels, mainly ones by writers from the United States but also ones from Europe and the Caribbean. The novelists—literary mythographers—generate components of what this study identifies as the diasporan myth, the morphological features of which I delineate in chapter 1.[2] This foundational myth narrates the origin, history, and nature of the Western black. Embedded in the myth is a theory of Western black Being. Several authors of contemporary fictional slave narratives and other diasporan novels collectively generate components of this origin myth and its corollary theory of black Being as narrative content within their texts. The myth and its theory of Being significantly control theme and salient aspects of form in these novels, and thus they are integral to both the production and interpretation of these texts.

Figurations of the Form

The earliest novels published by blacks from the United States—Brown's *Clotel* (1853), Webb's *The Garies* (1857), Wilson's *Our Nig* (1859), and Delany's serialized *Blake* (1861–62)—are fictional slave narratives that incorporate many of the nonfiction slave narrative's discursive conventions. Many African American novels published from the early 1860s through the end of the nineteenth century also are fictional slave narratives; Howard's *Bond and Free* (1886) and Harper's *Iola Leroy* (1893) are among the best-known ones. Though several African American novelists at the turn of the twentieth century use the era's concept of the "new slavery" as context—Chesnutt's *The Marrow of Tradition* (1901), Dunbar's *The Sport of the Gods* (1902), and Griggs's *The Hindered Hand* (1905), among others—this study does not consider such novels as fictional slave narratives. In fact, during the first three quarters of the twentieth century, African American novelists published relatively few fictional slave narratives, though many used selective narrative conventions of both the nonfiction and the fictional slave narrative. Paynter's *Fugitives of the Pearl* (1930), Bontemps's *Black Thunder* (1936), Turpin's *The Rootless* (1957), Walker's *Jubilee* (1966), and Gaines's *Jane Pittman* (1971) are among the pre-1975 African American novels that this study defines as fictional slave narratives because they center on the life of a slave or former slave and employ several narrative conventions of the nonfiction slave narrative. In the United States the novelistic form dates at least as far back as Richard Hildreth's *The Slave, or Memoirs of Archy Moore* (1836) and Harriet Beecher Stowe's *Uncle Tom's Cabin* (1852), both by white writers and both anchored in what became the conventions of the authentic, nonfiction slave narrative.[3]

Though *neoslave narrative* and *neo-slave narrative* remain the standard neologisms for novels that I call *fictional slave narratives*, some critics utilize other rubrics under which to discuss particular thematic and formal features of novels within this subgenre.[4] For the novels with which my study is concerned, I choose the term *contemporary fictional slave narrative*. In part, this is to distinguish between pre-1975 (rather traditional linear and historical narratives that I call "modern") and post-1975 versions of the form (many of which are narratologically experimental). It also is to distinguish between the form and functions of fictional slave narratives published since 1975.

This study posits that an essential criterion of a contemporary fictional slave narrative is that it includes a narrative (whether extended or abbreviated) about a slave or a former slave. In the extended narrative, the slave or former slave is the novel's focal subject, as is the case in most fictional slave narratives published before the mid-1970s and in several published after that (*Beloved* and *Oxherding Tale* are examples). When the narrative is abbreviated (usually incorporated as an interpolation) in a post-1975 novel, the slave or former slave typically is not the novel's focal subject, but his or her narrative (and thus Being) is inextricably bound to the meaning of the life of the novel's focal subject (or its focal subjects) and therefore to the configuration of the novel's form. Moreover, the novel's centered subject, who is born after the end of slavery, is an extension[5] of the slave or former slave. They are components of the same Being. In some instances the novel's author is also a component of this Being. Thus, the twentieth-century focal subject's story is a continuation of the slave subject's story; it is, therefore, the slave's narrative. Perry states the premise in *Stigmata:* the "events" that Lizzie, the twentieth-century subject, (re)lives are "replays of things that have already happened" to Ayo, the former slave from whom Lizzie is genetically extended. It is the formation of the centered subject as a plural Self, therefore, that I use as the quintessential criterion of a contemporary fictional slave narrative. In novels such as these, the nexus between the centered subject and the slave or former slave is in some instances genetic, as in Gayl Jones's *Corregidora* (1975), and in other instances it is sociogenic, as in Gloria Naylor's *Linden Hills* (1985). (I include below other characteristics of the contemporary fictional slave narrative.)

The novels focused in this study include ones that are female-authored and female-centered (the concern of chapter 3), ones that are male-authored and male-centered (foregrounded in chapter 4), and ones that combine and usually balance key features from these two gendered discourses (discussed in chapter 5). This study gives concentrated attention to two diasporan novels that do not possess its principal criterion for a contemporary fictional slave narrative, Paule Marshall's *Praisesong for the Widow* (1983) and Erna Brodber's *Louisiana* (1994). Both include significant components of the diasporan myth's theory of Western black Being and thus are integral to this study's focus on novelistic mythography and the Western black imaginary.

From Begging the Question to Begging the Pardon: The Function of the Form

Another principal defining criterion of the contemporary fictional slave narrative is that it utilizes and often formulates components of the diasporan myth. In her essay "The Black Writer and His Role" (1969), literary critic Carolyn F. Gerald astutely articulates significant changes that African American literature was undergoing in the late 1960s and early 1970s. One of her observations most relevant to this study is her statement that "the [black] writer is the myth-maker of his people" (375).[6] In this and other ways, Gerald's essay echoes one Richard Wright published a generation earlier in which he challenges the black writer to become the myth-maker of his people.

In configuring its generic plot, the contemporary fictional slave narrative in effect builds from Wright's prescription in his 1937 essay "Blueprint for Negro Writing." Wright characterizes black writing prior to the 1940s as largely "begging the question of the Negroes' humanity" (56), as "a curtsying to show [white America] that the Negro was not inferior" (53). He challenges black writers to move beyond this curtsying, and he suggests that a "fruitful point of departure . . . is [a]n emphasis upon tendency and experiment, a view of society as something becoming rather than as something fixed" (55).

Authors of the novels included in this study are among those who in effect respond to Wright's call by producing fictions whose narrative techniques are in part experimental. They create black subjects who are groping toward an ideal state of black Being (identified with pre-diasporan, primordial Africa) rather than remaining fixed within a Western white-controlled notion of black Being. Under the conceptual rubric of the plural black Self, they construct subjects who are components of a collective (primordial African) Self, which in some ways is similar to what Wright refers to as a black "nationalism" (58) and a black consciousness shared among writers and among blacks generally (64–65).

Wright calls for black writers to make fuller use of black folklore, "which rose out of a unified sense of a common life and a common fate" (57), and to "*create the myths* and symbols that inspire a faith in life" (59; emphasis added). Authors of contemporary fictional slave narratives respond to this call by creating the diasporan myth and using it to refigure the Western black as literary subject and the novelistic techniques that envelope this subject. Their creation of the diasporan myth and their production of texts that generate or utilize it, much like Wright predicted, "[restore] to the writer his lost heritage, that is, his role as a creator of the world in which he lives, and as a creator of himself" (60). According to Wright, when black writers create out of a "consciousness" that nourishes the "culture from which they were torn in Africa," when they embrace "the long, complex (and for the most part, unconscious) struggle to regain in some form and under alien conditions of life a *whole* culture again," they will produce some of the finest of Western literary art (63; Wright's emphasis).

The "theme for [these] Negro writers," according to Wright, "will rise from understanding the meaning of their being transplanted from a 'savage' to a 'civilized' culture in all of its social, political, economic, and emotional implications" (62–63). This theme "will emerge when they have begun to feel *the meaning of the history of their race as though they in one life time had lived it themselves throughout all the long centuries*" (63; emphasis added). The response to Wright's call in this instance is borne out in the relationship between author and centered subject in several post-1975 fictional slave narratives as well as between a centered subject and his or her slave ancestor. Through powers of the e-motion, Morrison, Sherley Anne Williams, and other womanist writers reconstruct their female centered subjects' lives as though the authors themselves had lived these lives. Through the powers of the imaginative intellect, Johnson, Reed, and other masculinist writers do the same. Wideman's narratological explorations of time, space, and Being establish a nexus between author and centered subject in which the author indeed lives the lives of his subjects "throughout all the long centuries." For some centered subjects, living across centuries and continents is a literal part of plot structure, as in Tananarive Due's *My Soul to Keep* (1997) and *The Living Blood* (2001) as well as in Perry's *Stigmata*.

Narratological technique in most contemporary fictional slave narratives validates Wright's contention that "the relationship between reality and the artistic image is not always direct and simple. The imaginative conception of a historical period will not be a carbon copy of reality. Image and emotion possess a logic of their own" (63). Morrison seems to concur with Wright in her essay "The Site of Memory" (114–20), in which she recounts the indirect and rather complex "route" to her writing of *Beloved*. She speaks of her creative process in this instance as "emotional memory"

(119), which allowed her access not only to the interior life of Margaret Garner but to her own interior life. Beginning with an "image" and moving to a "text," Morrison does not reconstruct a carbon copy of the world Margaret Garner inhabited. Rather, the image is her "route to a reconstruction of [an imagined] world, to an exploration of an interior life that was not written and to the revelation of a kind of truth" (115).

From "image" to "text" is an apt description of part of the narrative technique of Jean Toomer's *Cane* (1923). Several post-1970 novelists, including authors of contemporary fictional slave narratives, directly or indirectly acknowledge Toomer as one of their most influential literary ancestors, which is the focus of chapter 2. The diasporan myth's theory of Being has close affinities with Toomer's theory of Being as contained in his philosophical, theoretical, and literary texts and in his dramatization of his theory in *Cane*. Shortly after the publication of *Cane*, Toomer wrote in his notebook (12 December 1923) a poem that succinctly expresses the complementary functions the emotion and the intellect have in shaping a black author's literary consciousness:[7]

> I am of a consciousness whose earth-eye is my body
> I am of a consciousness which is beyond me.
> My intellect is its brilliance in the third dimension:
> My emotions are its glow.

Toni Morrison in effect states a kind of corollary to Toomer's poem when she says that "the deliberate effort, on the part of the artist, [is] to get a visceral, emotional response as well as an intellectual response as he or she communicates with the audience" ("Rootedness" 343). Fifty years after *Cane*'s publication, the interrelation of these concepts significantly shaped subject formation in contemporary fictional slave narratives and, consequently, helped formulate a theory of narrative applicable to these and other contemporary Western black novels.

In Wright's view, the route (or narratological technique) a writer uses to reconstruct a world is a matter of "perspective." In individual contemporary fictional slave narratives, this perspective is primarily emotive, primarily intellectual, or a balance of the two. The intellectual and emotive spaces from which contemporary black authors view the slave past allows them to approach their subjects and subject matter, as Wright suggests, "from a thousand angles, with no limit to technical and stylistic freedom"

(62). Collectively, the novels included in this study (and particularly Johnson's) manifest Wright's directive that "every iota of gain in human thought and sensibility should be ready grist for [the black writer's] mill, no matter how far-fetched they may seem in their immediate implications" (60). The technical and stylistic dimensions of contemporary fictional slave narratives help signify the subgenre's shift from begging the question to begging the pardon.

In Marshall's *Praisesong for the Widow*, a community of blacks in the Caribbean annually engages in a ritual to remember its African and Western black ancestors and to atone for ever having forgotten these forebears and the ordeal they endured during the Middle Passage and its aftermath. Called "The Beg Pardon" (211), it is a ritual of singing and dancing in which the "supplicants" are "pleading and petitioning not only for themselves and for the friends and neighbors present in the yard, but for all their far-flung kin as well—the sons and daughters, grands and great-grands in Trinidad, Toronto, New York, London . . ." (236), and other geographic spaces in the West. As one of the characters (Lebert Joseph) states, "We must give them [the ancestors] their remembrance" (166).

In Perry's *Stigmata*, a former slave, Ayo, dictates the narrative of her life to her daughter, Joy. Ayo's narrative is intended for her descendants, but it also is a remembrance for those who died during the Middle Passage: "This is for those whose bones lie in the heart of mother ocean for those who tomorrows I never knew who groaned and died in the damp dark beside me. You rite this daughter for me and for them" (17). Ayo's statement is a clear echo of what Morrison considers her (and other African Americans') "responsibility" to remember and to re-member those Africans in the Middle Passage who "died en route" to the New World (Darling 247).

Indeed, as an author Ayo shares purpose with authors of contemporary fictional slave narratives. As Wideman explains, the purpose is to give voice to "an encompassing silence forgetting . . . the countless passings of so many" who almost have been lost to memory (*Cattle Killing* 13). Charles Johnson characterizes several post-1970 African American novelists as "Novelists of Memory" and their novels as "quasi-biographical" in intent. This certainly is the case with authors of contemporary fictional slave narratives. Johnson contends that many African American authors "believe that one service they can—in fact, *must*—perform is telling stories about black people who have been written out of history. Their hope," as Johnson sees it, "is to honor their predecessors. . . . It is an effort to keep them alive, perhaps even to enshrine the meaning of their lives. . . . Such writers have a moral obligation to remember" (*Being and Race* 74; Johnson's emphasis).

I appropriate the term "Beg Pardon" as an apt description of one of the functions of contemporary fictional slave narratives in the West. For black authors of these fictions, remembering and re-membering in fictive discourse those African and Western black ancestors who almost have been lost to historical memory are, in effect, the authors' ways of begging the ancestors' pardon. Morrison suggests that black writers (and black people in general) who assume the "responsibility" of remembering and re-membering these ancestors can effect individual and collective healing (Darling 247–48). Thus, the production of these texts is a begging pardon and an atonement not only for the authors but also for all blacks in the West. (The atonement theme is also one of the plot anchors in Perry's *Stigmata.*)

It is notable that most of the black-authored fictional slave narratives are not about well-known blacks who were enslaved. Frederick Douglass, Nat Turner, Sojourner Truth, Harriet Tubman, Oladauh Equiano, William Wells Brown, Harriet Jacobs, Cinqué, and several others whose lived-worlds have been re-membered and preserved in oral and written American cultural history typically are not the focal subjects of blacks' fictional slave narratives or their other novels. The exceptions, such as Gabriel Prosser (Bontemps's *Black Thunder*), Sally Hemings (Chase-Riboud's *Sally Hemings* [1979] and *The President's Daughter* [1994]), Richard Allen, to some extent (Wideman's *Cattle Killing*), and Cinqué (Chase-Riboud's *Echo of Lions* [1989]) are rare. This is not to say that black novelists exclude well-known slaves and ex-slaves from their novels, for indeed practically all of them are referenced in the genre. In addition, nonblack authors have written novels that center several of these historical figures as subjects—Tubman and Turner, among others.[8]

It is those whose lives usually are not recorded in historical texts, not sung in literary texts, and almost lost to the common and historical memories of whom black authors of contemporary fictional slave narratives beg pardon by writing them back into the common and historical memories and into Being. Some of them are reinscriptions of identifiable historical figures (*Dessa Rose*'s title character and *Beloved*'s Sethe are examples) and others are constructed from and representative of generic persons lost to written history (*Flight to Canada*'s Raven Quickskill and *Oxherding Tale*'s Andrew Hawkins are examples).

To be sure, production of the contemporary fictional slave narrative is a form of begging the ancestors' pardon, not only by re-membering and remembering them but also, in an ironic twist, by re-commodifying them. As Wideman demonstrates in *The Cattle Killing*, fictive discourse is the site on which the contemporary author and the historical ancestor reunite (with others) as one Self/Being. He also asserts in this novel the inextricable union of story and Being (207–8). By thematizing point of view in *Dessa Rose,* Williams also establishes that author and ancestor are components of the same Self and, further, that the fictional text is, therefore, also the ancestor's production. Through his parodic installation of Karl Marx as a character in *Oxherding Tale* (79–88), Johnson in effect refutes Marxist literary theorists and posits instead that the literary text, like the slave, is a commodity. Paul Smith states the point succinctly when he writes that "'literary production' needs to be understood primarily as an activity of labor whose result can be designated as a commodity. It is in this sense that one can talk of the production of texts which are, after all, produced for exchange—in systems both of economic and of cultural capital—by the labor of one who sits down to write" (26). Certainly, some of the contemporary fictional slave narratives have garnered enormous economic and cultural capital, of which Morrison's *Beloved* is perhaps most representative. The African diaspora fragmented the African Self into Western selves, commodified these selves, used them up, discarded them, and forgot them. In begging the ancestors' pardon, the novelists reconstitute the black Self (fuse author, ancestor, story) and, somewhat ironically, the production of these texts is a re-commodification of the ancestors. As Sherley Anne Williams assesses part of the situation, black personhood is a commodity that is now self-owned (*Dessa Rose* 260).

Subject Formation and Attendant Fictive Devices

This study contends that formation of the centered subject within the context of the diasporan myth and its theory of Being is key to defining the contemporary fictional slave narrative as form and to distinguishing it from other novelistic narratives of slavery. Like the nonfiction slave narrative, the fictional slave narrative prior to the mid-1970s argues for the humanness and humanity of the slave and of blacks in general by forming black subjects whose subjectivity testifies to these qualities. Ishmael Reed no doubt has this centuries-old controversy in mind when he has one of his white characters in *Flight to Canada* tell a fugitive slave that "it's not even been determined whether you're a human being" (146). With the publication of *Flight to Canada* in 1976, the fictional slave narrative (in general) shifted its focus on black subjectivity from an argument that blacks indeed are fully human to a formulation of a theory of black Being. This shift from a sociology of black subjectivity to a philosophy of black Being refigured discourse in this subgenre in dramatic ways. The shift produced narratological explorations—especially in subject formation, setting, and point of view—that moved most works in the subgenre out of the realm of literary realism (as Wright defined the term in his essay, cited above [59]) and into the realm of what I here call *literary diaspority.*

Briefly defined for the purposes of this study, literary diaspority is a form of imaginative discourse (novelistic, in this instance) that draws upon and reflects the various fissures, ruptures, and erasures in language, geography, ontology, epistemology, religion, and other cultural forms that the diaspora effected for Africans who were brought to the West. It also draws upon and reflects New World Africans' and their descendants' incorporation of European cultural forms and the ontological, epistemological, and cultural hybridizations that resulted to produce the Western black self. Literary diaspority, therefore, refers to a specific approach a writer takes to his or her subject matter. Diasporan novels inscribe various forms and degrees of literary diaspority.

In the diasporan novel (which includes the contemporary fictional slave narrative), diaspority controls the novelist's formation of the centered subject and the novel's attendant themes and meanings. The novelist constructs this subject as more than merely a person of African descent in the West. The diasporan subject inhabits or comes to inhabit a psychological space configured by a set of historical and cultural experiences the diaspora induced. Whether consciously or subconsciously, the subject embraces (usually a developmental process in the text) a worldview anchored in the worldview of the African ancestral past. Therefore, all centered subjects (or other black characters) in the Western black novel are not constructed as diasporan subjects, and thus all black novels or even all post-1975 fictional slave narratives in the West are not diasporan novels.

Most fictional slave narratives published between 1853 and 1975 situate the narrative of one slave's experience within Eurocentric definitions of time and geographic space. Reed's *Flight to Canada* heralds the subgenre's liberation from prescriptive and restrictive notions of setting. Most of the novels included in this study follow suit, and their revisions to standard Eurocentric notions of novelistic time and space interface with their formation of the centered subject as a plural Self. Setting in the contemporary fictional slave narrative, therefore, often is not confined to events that, from a Western perspective, realistically can occur within Western boundaries of time and space.

Commensurate with the contemporary form's revisions to subject formation and setting is its revision to point of view. Johnson's *Oxherding Tale* articulates changes in the subgenre's focal character from an individual self to a plural Self and, in Johnson's words, manumits the form's first-person point of view. First person is the standard point of view in the nonfiction slave narrative as well as in several pre-1975 and a few post-1975 fictional slave narratives. Point of view in contemporary fictional slave narratives usually blends first and third persons, as in Williams's *Dessa Rose.* Sometimes it is confined to first person, as in Johnson's *Middle Passage,* and occasionally it fuses first, second, and third persons, as in Wideman's *The Cattle Killing.* Whatever the case, novelists working in this form typically thematize point of view (Sherley Anne Williams is exemplary).

Having liberated the antecedent form from the strictures of subject formation, setting, and point of view, the novelists modify other fictive devices. For example, patterns of allusions (referentiality) expand to include persons, events, ideas, and texts not only from the past and present of the novel's focal setting but also from the future. The generic "plot" of these novels turns on the respective centered subject's desire and efforts to (re)-gain "freedom" by returning "home"—that is, re-turning to an ideal state of Being. When "home" in these novels is Africa, Africa more often is metaphoric than literal. Because the novels typically do not adhere strictly to standard Eurocentric notions of time, space, and Being, the subject's return to geographic Africa is more a journey or sojourn to a psychospiritual space than to a geographic place, as in *Middle Passage* and *Crossing the River.*

Sacred Geometry and Black African Diaspority

Formation of the centered subject and attendant fictive devices in a representative contemporary fictional slave narrative align with precepts of sacred geometry. I use sacred geometry as a rubric to overarch most of the chapters in this study. Mythoforms that Western black artists adopt, adapt, or appropriate from other cultures and mythologies or ones they create are integral to the sacred geometry evident in a variety of genres in black expressive culture.[9] Such mythoforms are pervasive in contemporary fictional slave narratives. For example, in *The Cattle Killing,* Wideman adopts the oroboros (149), adapts the symbolic circle (149 and elsewhere), appropriates Josiah Wedgwood's "commemorative plate" (105), and creates linguistic mythoforms that are triads (such as "do do do," "Shoes. Shoes. Shoes," "laugh, laugh, laugh") and that are interspersed throughout the text (70, 71, for example), all of which he integrates into his formulation and application of the diasporan myth and its theory of Being.

As I and others use the term, *sacred geometry* (often referred to as *sacred science*) associates spiritual and philosophical properties with shapes and numbers, and it is inclusive of more specialized terms such as *sacred mathematics, sacred arithmetic,* and *sacred geography.* In the main, the term sacred geometry is associated with studies of ancient Egypt. The novelists, therefore, incorporate aspects of ancient Egyptian culture (that is, sacred geometry) into their formulation of the diasporan myth and its theory of black Being.[10]

The contemporary fictional slave narrative aligns with and often incorporates other forms of Western black expressive culture, especially ones that use sacred geometry in their form, content, and meaning to treat aspects of black diaspority. For example, the circle is a primary geometric shape that conveys spiritual and philosophical meaning in literary and other black art forms. Several texts in these black art forms use the circle, the triangle, and other geometric shapes to express philosophical meanings and historical formations aligned with the diasporan myth. Chief among these nonliterary forms is black painting, and the works of painters Aaron Douglas, Eldzier Cortor, Romare Bearden, Jacob Lawrence, John Biggers, and Jimmy Biggers are exemplary. For example, the circle is a signature feature of Aaron Douglas's works, particularly those with narratives about the Middle Passage and its aftermath. The triangle is a signature feature of Jacob Lawrence's works, as is evident in his visual (re)presentations of slave narratives about Frederick Douglass and Harriet Tubman and in his works that chronicle the migration of blacks within the United States. Pointillism (the dot or line) is the feature that distinguishes the works of Ghanaian-American artist Sami Bentil. Circularity, angularity, and pointillism are all geometric expressions of pempamsie (unity, strength, and harmony), and pempamsie is a concept aligned with those of Unity (Oneness), completeness, and wholeness in sacred geometry.

Visual artist Jimmy Biggers, nephew of artist John Biggers, pointed out in a conversation with me in the spring of 1998 that he and his uncle read widely in the works of Egyptologists and that what they read significantly shaped the philosophical and technical dimensions of their visual representations of Western (and occasionally non-Western) black life. It is evident that sacred geometry is a distinct feature in the production and thus in the interpretation of their visual art works.

Indeed, sacred geometry and the diasporan myth are complementary contexts and intertexts that control the configuration of texts in a variety of Western black forms of expressive culture and often are threads that intertextually and referentially connect one art form to the others. For example, several black paintings (such as ones by Romare Bearden) and literary texts (such as Ralph Ellison's *Invisible Man* [1952]) can appropriately be designated as jazz compositions or defined according to some other black musical mode.[11] Also, several black musical texts inscribe as form and content properties and philosophical meanings associated with visual and literary arts. For example, Gil Scott-Heron's *Secrets* LP (1978) installs parts of Jean Toomer's *Cane* as an intertext, making *Cane*'s sacred geometry a part of this musical text; the Sounds of Blackness's *From Africa to America* incorporates literary texts by Langston Hughes and other writers, includes ideas associated with the diasporan myth, and directly references the sacred geometry of ancient Egyptians.

Paintings from a variety of schools and cultures are integral to Melvin Tolson's poetic composition *Harlem Gallery: Book I: The Curator* (1965), certainly one of the most artistically sophisticated and complex of black diasporan poetic texts. Philosophical premises aligned with the African diasporan myth and with sacred geometry also are present in poems by Lucille Clifton (such as "the thirty-eighth year"), Etheridge Knight (such as "The Idea of Ancestry"), and several other contemporary poets. Morphological features of the diasporan myth can be found in the works of Négritude poets, such as Aimé Césaire's *Cahier d'un retour au pays natal* (1994), and in the works of later Caribbean poets, such as Derek Walcott's *Omeros* (1990).

Sacred geometry is also a salient aspect of some black music, though it is manifested differently in music than in literature or in painting. Jazz and blues are cases in point, for thematically and formally the ideas of fragmentation, wholeness, and unity are inherent in much jazz and blues music. The same is true for black sacred music. Several compositions in spiritual and gospel incorporate into their form aspects of sacred geometry and into their themes features of the black African diaspora. Certainly, many forms and genres of black expressive culture are intertwined. Some authors of contemporary fictional slave narratives incorporate other literary forms into their texts, such as the poems *Beloved* and *Flight to Canada* install. In other instances, a contemporary fictional slave narrative will include another art form as reference, intertext, or theme. The painting of a diasporan text is subject matter in *Stigmata*, which also includes a reference to Romare Bearden. *The Cattle Killing* includes painting as subject matter as well as a diasporan text of visual art and visual artists as characters. *My Soul to Keep* and *Crossing the River* reference several post-1960 musical artists and musical texts.

Among contemporary fictional slave narratives, this intertwining (either as referentiality or intertextuality) is expressed forthrightly in what functions as the epilogue to Phillips's *Crossing the River*. The epilogue blends a variety of voices, texts, and artistic genres into what Phillips calls "the many-tongued chorus of the common memory" (235).

Metafictionality and the Self-Theorizing Text

During a panel discussion of his works at the University of North Carolina at Chapel Hill (March 2001), John Edgar Wideman said, "In my novels I tell the reader how to read them." The validity of his statement certainly is evident in *The Cattle Killing*. It also is applicable to other black novelists and their (meta)fictional slave narratives. Indeed, an earmark of contemporary fictional slave narratives is metafictionality, though the amount of metafictional content varies among the novels. When the African American novel as genre began in the nineteenth century, the earliest novelists, whose novels typically maintained a close fidelity to black social reality, inserted authorial commentary that spoke directly to the form and function of their texts. This practice became more prevalent and more sophisticated in African American novels published during the first half of the twentieth century, and the current generation of Western black novelists has produced an impressive list of novels that can appropriately be characterized as metafictional—that is, novels that contain comments about the writing of fiction.[12]

Praxis in contemporary fictional slave narratives—that is, the novels' representations of blacks' lived-world—is increasingly aligned with the novels' intratextual formulation of theories of black narrative. In some instances the novelist inserts metafictional statements principally in the novel's front matter and end matter, as in *Dessa Rose* and *The Cattle Killing.* In other instances the novelist inserts metafictional statements into the text's narrative content, as in *Oxherding Tale* and *Flight to Canada.* Whatever the case, contemporary works in the subgenre typically conjoin theory and praxis. This study's observations and conclusions about the conjuncture of theory and praxis in contemporary Western black novels are not exclusive to the specific texts it examines, to contemporary fictional slave narratives, or even to contemporary novels.

Not only do contemporary fictional slave narratives tell the readers how to read the texts, they also provide terminology for an interpretative analysis of these texts. This study extracts from these novels, from other contemporary diasporan novels, and from black-authored nonfiction texts most of the key terms and concepts that it employs in its discussion of the texts it includes. Though some of these terms and concepts already are part of the current vocabulary of Western critical and literary theory, their meanings are slightly different when black novelists use them and when critics employ them for interpretative analyses of these novelists' texts.

1 Mythopoeic Realities

Vernacular explanations (especially in the forms of etiological folktales and aphorisms) about Western blacks' origin and subjectivity are centuries old. Since the late nineteenth century, black writers from the United States have incorporated etiological tales and aphorisms into their literature to embellish various aspects of their texts' form and meaning. In the mid-1970s a group of black writers from the Americas and Europe began to generate (mainly within their texts) the diasporan myth, a foundational myth that explains the origin and subjectivity of the Western black. This myth interfaces with factual and historical contexts and helps define the thematic and formal contours of contemporary fictional slave narratives.

John Edgar Wideman articulates as well as any writer the formulation, form, and function of this mythopoeic discourse: "For African American people I am in the business of inventing reality—that stands on its own feet, that gives a different perspective on history, on crime, on art, on love. I'm very actively deconstructing the given formulas and definitions of African American culture and life, and trying to put in their place those that seem more reasonable, more real, more lively, more potentially positive. In my mind, I can't think of anything more important" (L. Baker 264–65).

Toni Morrison expresses a similar sentiment about the mythopoeic nature of her works when explaining that she incorporates "unorthodox novelistic characteristics" into the "traditional genre [of the] novel." Speaking specifically of her *Song of Solomon*, she explains that she "blend[s] the acceptance of the supernatural and a profound rootedness in the real world at the same time with neither taking precedence over the other. It is indicative of the cosmology, the way in which Black people looked at the world" ("Rootedness" 342). The same process of production applies to *Beloved*, her fictional slave narrative, as well as to the fictional slave narratives and other diasporan novels on which this study focuses.

The myth and the folktale[1] as narrative forms share several elements, and writers and critics alike at times use the terms interchangeably. This study uses *myth* to refer to a narrative that speaks comprehensively about the existence (past, present, and future) of a people and that people's place in and relationship to the universe. It uses *folktale* to refer generally to a narrative concerned with a specific aspect of an individual's or a relatively small group's earthly existence and within temporal and spatial boundaries. Different segments (or stories) within a myth can be self-contained, but all are integrated into and reciprocally interrelated in the collective whole. Different folktales, such as etiological tales, also may be interrelated to form a whole, but the whole these collective tales form is not as comprehensive about the totality of a people's existence as is the myth. Another distinction this study notes is that a myth generally has more religious or spiritual dimensions than a typical folktale.

Before the current generation, Western black writers who incorporated myths into their literature drew principally from Judeo-Christian and Greco-Roman mythologies. Western black writers continue to utilize black vernacular tales as well as Judeo-Christian, Greco-Roman, and other mythologies. However, several of them, particularly novelists who thematically or formally treat the black African diaspora and the ordeal of slavery, also draw heavily from traditional African mythologies to help explain the history and nature of Western blacks and to help configure form and meaning in their texts.

As Western black writers thus far have formulated it in their imaginative and critical texts, the diasporan myth tells who the Western black subject is (Being) and how this subject came to be (Becoming). Briefly stated, I use the term *Being* in this study to refer to the totality of a person's (sometimes an object's) essence and existence, to a person's (or object's) spiritual connection to all things in the universe—animate and inanimate, past, present, and future.

Several philosophers and theorists, from the ancients to the moderns, have postulated about the nature and the process of Becoming.[2] A traditional view on Becoming, such as that found in Aristotle's *Metaphysics*, posits a link between Becoming and Being. A modern view on Becoming, such as that Xavier Zubiri proposes in *Dynamic Structure of Reality*, dissolves "the traditional linkage between becoming and being" and takes issue with "Aristotle's and many others' identification of becoming with changing" (xiii). To survey the philosophical debate about the nature and process of Becoming is outside the scope of this study. Nevertheless, this study's use of *Becoming* as a philosophical, theoretical, and critical term is aligned more with the ancients than with the moderns, but it draws from premises of both. Consistent with the ancients' view, Becoming as this study employs it is directly linked to Being and involves changes (dynamism) in the subject. Therefore, it is directly linked to ontology, a premise that Zubiri disputes by asserting that Becoming "is a problem of reality and not of being," that it is "a problem of structure and not of a subject" (26). In his discussion of African philosophy, Innocent Onyewuenyi distinguishes between Western (white) and African (black) concepts of being and posits that in "African philosophical thought, being is dynamic" (40). Charles Johnson includes a narrative formation in *Oxherding Tale* that aligns with Onyewuenyi's comments about distinctions between Western and African concepts of being, of reality: "Life . . . is *process*" (25; Johnson's emphasis).

John Edgar Wideman's observation about diasporan subjectivity speaks to the inextricable link between Being and Becoming that this study argues. According to Wideman, "What we are mainly is the spirit, something that is not defined, not reducible to something else, something that is *always in the process of being constructed*, like gas. We have these immense possibilities of making something of ourselves, but we get sidetracked, by being a man, by being a woman, or being black, being white. All the dichotomies that western thinking pushes us into" (L. Miller 7–8; emphasis added).

As this study employs the term and concept, Becoming as a process involves the collapsing of temporal units, a re-ordering or partial erasure of standard Eurocentric notions of the separation of past, present, and future. Becoming is a movement toward authentic black Being and thus is an epistemological and an ontological process. It is a systematic movement from the present to the past to the future while at the same time it erases rigid boundaries between these temporalities. In one respect, it is not a movement toward a "new" self, as Elizabeth Grosz seems to use the concept of moving toward the new (15–20), but it is actually a movement toward the old, toward the authentic or primordial self. More accurately, it is a movement toward a renewed self. Memory is often the vehicle that facilitates this movement, and thus epistemology evolves into or fuses with ontology. In this regard, the present becomes the past and the future. That is, the subject in the present (a false self) undergoes a process of Becoming that is triggered by memories of the primordial past (of the primordial self/Self), and the process changes the subject from a false self (what Jean Toomer calls "false nature") to an authentic self (what Toomer calls "true nature"). This authentic self is located in primordial Time and in epistemology. The authentic self of the past becomes the authentic self of the future, and this past-future self replaces the false self of the present. Therefore, the present becomes the past (old self) *and* the future (new self).

Authors of contemporary fictional slave narratives vary in their inscriptions of the components of Becoming, but the overall process applies generally to this subgenre. Exemplary of the subgenre is the innominate Christian preacher's Becoming in Wideman's *The Cattle Killing*. The novel's narrative structure begins with the preacher as a false self in the present, a self the West invented. Once the process of Becoming activates, the preacher's primordial memory gives him knowledge of his primordial, authentic self from the past and thus knowledge of the future self (a renewed past self) that he can become. His epistemological and ontological movement is, therefore, toward this past-future self, which he begins the process of assuming in the present. His rejection of the West's Christianity and embracing of African spirituality, his fusion with the other male selves of his Being, and his desire and intent to fuse with the plural female patient at his narrative's end are among the signifiers of his Becoming, of his movement toward the authenticity of his Being.

Through their formulation of the diasporan myth, post-1975 black novels revise the traditional black novelistic Being-Becoming construct by including the mythic origins of the Western black subject.[3] Beginning in primordial Time and proceeding through historical time, the diasporan myth narrates how a large segment of Western black reality and certain human behavior and psychology endemic to Western blacks came into existence.[4]

With its firm grounding in historical phenomena, the diasporan myth conforms largely to Mircea Eliade's definition of myth in *Myth and Reality* as an "extremely complex cultural reality" that "narrates a sacred history, . . . relates an event that took place in primordial Time, . . . [and] relates how something was produced, began to *be*. . . . In other words, myth tells how, through the deeds of Supernatural Beings, a reality came into existence, be it the whole of reality, the Cosmos, or only a fragment of reality—an island, a species of plant, a particular kind of human behavior, an institution." Eliade states further that "the myth is regarded as a sacred story, and hence a 'true history,' because it always deals with *realities*" (5–6; Eliade's emphasis). Eliade's statement in this instance aligns well with Wideman's contention that "all stories are true" (L. Miller 12).[5] This is especially applicable to *The Cattle Killing*, which deals with mythopoeic realities.

As a myth, then, the African diasporan myth does not conform to modern distinctions between "history" as fact and "myth" as fabulation. Instead, its construction in black texts proffers an intimate relation between fact and fabulation. Borrowing an operational definition from Roland Barthes and applying it to a context different from what Barthes uses, this study contends that the African diasporan myth "transforms history into [human] nature" (Barthes 129) as well as transforming human nature into history. As black writers have constructed it in their texts, the diasporan myth utilizes official Western history to discern the nature of Western blacks and at the same time uses the nature of Western blacks to (re)write their history.[6]

The African diasporan myth is not, per se, a cosmogonic or creation myth. Like black African myths of human origin that "invariably" begin with mankind already in a social organization, appearing "as a group, in company" (Setiloane 9), the diasporan myth begins not with the creation of the first man and woman but with mankind already functioning in a social organization.[7] In this respect, salient features of the diasporan myth align with portions of the compact narrative of "the nature of man and the history of it" that Aristophanes provides in Plato's *Symposium* (85–86), with elements of human origin myths from several black African ethnic groups, and with features in the religious mythologies of other non-Western ethnic groups.

Several Western black writers certainly were familiar with Plato's dialogues and probably with *Symposium*. For example, Charles Johnson in *Being and Race* quotes directly from *The Republic*, and in *Oxherding Tale* he references Plato several times. Toni Morrison's Beloved as novel, as character, and as concept echoes some ideas Aristophanes posits in *Symposium* about love, the lover, and the beloved.[8] The same is true for Wideman's *Cattle Killing*, in which storytelling is a curative that heals and restores the Western black self to his/her ancient nature (compare to *Symposium* 89). This is not to assert that any black writers consciously appropriate Aristophanes's narrative from *Symposium* in order to construct the diasporan myth. It is to acknowledge the similarity of origin myths across cultures, as John Mbiti illustrates well in *African Religions and Philosophy* by showing affinal parallels between the religious philosophies of African and European societies.

Key features of the history and nature of the Western black as black novelists inscribe them in mythopoeic narrative form have close parallels to segments of black African religious philosophies and origin myths, which works such as Mbiti's *African Religions and Philosophy*, Setiloane's *African Theology*, and Brain's *Friends and Lovers* reveal. One example is that the novelists' construction of the Western black subject has close parallels to myths about the origin and nature of twins among cultural groups such as the Bangwa and the Dogon and the "creation" of humans in the plural rather than in the singular.

From among non-Western (and non-African) ethnic groups, Charles Johnson (*Oxherding Tale*), Paule Marshall (*Praisesong for the Widow*), and Wideman (*Cattle Killing*), for example, reference elements of the Hindu religious philosophy in their texts.[9] Elements of ancient Egyptian religious philosophy and religious anthropology are mainstays in the diasporan myth as black novelists collectively formulate it. In effect, Wideman's centered subject in *The Cattle Killing* speaks for contemporary black authors of diasporan novels when in a vision he states that "all the fabled scenes [that is, myths] he'd ever imagined were accessible to him"—African, European, Native American, and Asian—"and a multitude of others whose existence had been hidden until the walls of the church [that is, the dominance of Judeo-Christian religious mythology] fell away" (68).

Several of the diasporan myth's morphological features that the novels (as well as diasporan poems and plays) generate have analogical parallels in (or actually are drawn from) discourses in history, sociology, anthropology, religious studies, and cultural studies, among other disciplines. In Western black novels, discursive formations that are predicated on those segments of the myth that belong to primordial memory (the period preceding the transatlantic slave trade) typically find verification in nonfiction works such as Snowden's *Blacks in Antiquity*, Williams's *The Destruction of Black Civilization*, Van Sertima's *They Came before Columbus*, and Bernal's *Black Athena*, among several others. Discursive formations predicated on segments of the myth that are a part of historical memory (the beginning of the transatlantic slave trade to the present) have corroborative sources in scholarly texts from a variety of disciplines.

The kind of scholarly research authors of contemporary fictional slave narratives conduct for the production of their texts is evident especially in the referentiality and intertextuality of the male-centered texts. If they were to provide a bibliography for their novels, as Ishmael Reed does for his novel *Mumbo Jumbo* (not a fictional slave narrative), their research would be even more readily apparent. To inform their texts with research gleaned from scholarly disciplines and from nonscholarly sources seems to be standard practice for authors of contemporary fictional slave narratives. As Morrison states, "I did research about a lot of things in this book [*Beloved*] . . . but I did not do much research on Margaret Garner . . . because I wanted to invent her life" (Darling 248). Though the content of *Beloved* does not identify Morrison's research sources as a typical masculinist novel in the subgenre does, her comment bespeaks the typical male-centered text's *invention* of its centered subject's life. Charles Johnson's comments about the research he conducted for writing *Middle Passage* no doubt are typical for several other authors and their texts (such as Wideman's *Cattle Killing* and Phillips's *Crossing the River*).[10]

While it is true that Western black writers have drawn from scholarly studies of traditional and modern African societies,[11] it is also true that they have drawn from the collective memory of blacks in the West (Marshall in *Praisesong for the Widow*, for example). Speaking of myth generally and African myths in particular, Gabriel Setiloane notes that "in myth there is something of a communal memory of the group as it has grappled with the questions of its and all human origins, life on this earth, being (what is the human person?) and even the hereafter" (3). It is credible that some trace of an oral myth's morphological feature from a traditional African society remained in the communal memory of Western blacks, was passed down and was modified (through contact with European culture and as a consequence of Western conditions) from one generation to another, and is reinscribed in the texts of Western black writers. Traces of origin and creation myths that survived among diasporan blacks in the

West were transformed and enriched over the ages as a consequence of the Western experience and more recently, as this study maintains, through the creative imagination of gifted Western black writers (compare to Eliade 4). Toni Morrison speaks directly to the conjunction of "memory" and "the act of the imagination" as integral to her creative process ("Site of Memory" 111–19).

When one extracts and synthesizes components of the African diasporan myth from the imaginative, critical, theoretical, and historical works of Western blacks and supplements these components with ones from works in other disciplines, what emerges is a rather complete narrative about the origin and nature of the Western black.

Narrativizing the African Diasporan Myth

According to the diasporan myth, humans originated in Africa and Africa was the site of the first social organization. This general premise can be found in history, anthropology, archaeology, and religious studies texts. In this first social organization, humankind consisted of three genders—male (born of the sun), female (sharing spiritual affinities with the earth), and manwoman (an androgynous third gender associated with the moon). Each gender was globular in shape, had two faces, and in other ways was physiologically different from the human form as it now exists (see *Symposium* 86). The globular or circular shape is a signification of humans' primordial wholeness, perfection, and divine nature (Schneider 2; Perry, *Stigmata* 7, 17, 93–94). The humans also varied in certain physiological features, the most prominent of which was skin color: some were white, some black, some brown, some red, and some yellow.[12] No two humans were exactly alike, yet the concept of individuality or a separate identity initially was not a part of human consciousness in the first social organization (*Middle Passage* 65, 61; Mbiti 141; Onyewuenyi 40–41; Tempels 58; see also Setiloane 9).[13] The humans possessed a physical form distinct from their gods and in other ways lacked the deities' powers and privileges (*Symposium* 86). For example, gods could assume the form of a human as well as a variety of other animate and inanimate forms (*Middle Passage* 101, 167, 168). Humans, though they possessed many of the gods' spiritual qualities, did not have this shape-shifting capability. Spirits, however, who hierarchically were situated between gods and humans (Mbiti 119; Onyewuenyi 40), did have this capability (*Praisesong* 238–39; *Cattle Killing* 75–76). Despite the distinctions that privileged gods and spirits over humans, the thread that tied humans to these other entities and all to the Primordial Soul (the Supreme Being) remained unbroken for many centuries. As it pertained to humankind, this intersubjectivity largely defined the African Self—what Mbiti calls "the corporate or social man" (141).

This was the period of primordial Time, which Wideman refers to as "the founding time, the ancestral time," and "a place of myth"; it was a place and "a time when the earth was ruled by [black] people like you—people who looked like you, who held your values" (L. Baker 268; Muhammad 111–22). For countless years during this primordial period, the human groups lived harmoniously with each other and with the Supreme Being, the gods, and the spirits (see Mbiti 124). In fact, different human groups (based on skin color) took turns governing the first human social organization (*Middle Passage* 65; compare to Muhammad 111–22). This harmony was shattered, however, when the group of humans with white skin became jealous of the gods' powers, began to challenge the gods' privileged status, and garnered the support of other humans in a rebellion against the social order.[14] This jealousy also created a rift between the human groups, drawing into consciousness physiological and other distinctions between the groups and resulting in the social construction of what is known now as the races or tribes of man, a categorization based largely on differences in skin color.[15]

Angered over the humans' rebellion, the Supreme Being ordered the bisection of each rebellious human into a self and an other, a division that diminished their strength and energy and therefore rendered each an incomplete self. One consequence of this literal cutting in half was that death became a part of humankind's reality because a human could not survive with only half of its self. When one of the halves died, the other half sought its complement in another divided self: the bisected male sought another bisected male; the bisected female sought another bisected female; and the bisected third gender sought whatever half was missing—the male half sought the female half and the female half sought the male half (*Symposium* 86–87; Toomer, "Split Men" and "Sing Yes!").[16] In other words, what now are heterosexual males and females came from the manwoman (third or common) gender, and what now are homosexual males and females came primarily and respectively from the original male and female genders. When unsuccessful in their pursuit to reunite the two halves into one whole self, the humans perished. Out of pity for their plight, the Supreme

Being reformatted their bodies in a way that allowed for heterosexual unions and the propagation of humankind as well as homosexual unions and psychic satisfaction (*Symposium* 87). This never-ending desire for propagation is a quest for the original state of Being, for a reunion of those selves (and their respective extensions) severed from the African Self.[17]

Another punishment the humans suffered for their rebellion was the dissolution of their social organization. Following this dissolution, the Supreme Being dispersed humans to different parts of the world—the yellow tribe to Asia, the brown tribe to the South Pacific, the white tribe to Europe, and the red tribe to the Americas, though small remnants of each of these tribes dispersed within Africa.[18] The black tribe remained in (though some dispersed to different parts of) Africa. A core group of the black tribe from the original social organization who did not participate in the rebellion remained intact as a nation and retained the epistemological and ontological powers endemic to humankind before the rebellion. These included the ability to transfer one's soul or spirit to another human host or to an inanimate object (*Oxherding Tale*, *Stigmata*, *Louisiana*), to *know* the lived experience of another human (*Beloved*, *Stigmata*, *Cattle Killing*, *Louisiana*, "Sing Yes!"), to be here and there at the same time (*Cattle Killing*, *Louisiana*), and to make the body light enough to walk on water (*Praisesong*) or to fly exceptionally long distances (*Salt*).[19] For centuries this group lived in a space "between Cape Lopez and the Congo River" (*Middle Passage* 67–68). This sacred space, circular in its geographic design, was the chosen place for a timeless, eternal, and "forever people" (*Stigmata* 7); and the symbols for the perfection of the human Self and the World were the circle and the oroboros (*Stigmata* 7, 17; Schneider 2–8; *Cattle Killing* 149).[20] In his works Charles Johnson calls this nation the Allmuseri, a name this study will use hereafter when referring to this group. In their new social spaces, the dispersed tribes further subdivided into separate social organizations (ethnopolitical units known as clans or nations), a subdivision based principally on religious orientation and common physiological features among members within each tribe, including the blacks in Africa. (In *Praisesong for the Widow* [238–39 and elsewhere], Paule Marshall refers to these African ethnic groups as "nations," a term this study will use hereafter.) Except the Allmuseri, the tribes and their nations created new societies and new gods and continued the religious and cultural rivalry between tribes and nations that began with humans' rebellion against the first social order.

From the works of Charles Johnson and Jean Toomer, both of whom blend fact (official history) and fabulation (mythic history), one can construct an abbreviated narrative history of the Allmuseri, "the Ur-tribe of humanity itself" (*Middle Passage* 61), from before 1,000 BC to the era of the Middle Passage (the 1500s to the mid-1800s AD). In *Middle Passage*, Johnson begins the narrative in primordial memory and continues it into historical memory. After the original human social organization separated into different tribes who relocated to different parts of the world, the Allmuseri nation became a highly developed civilization while other tribes and nations developed much more slowly (61, 76–78; Muhammad 119; Onyewuenyi 33). This Ur-tribe became "a seafaring people" during antiquity and left marks of its "ageless culture" in India, Central America, South America, and other parts of the world (76–78).[21] "Their globe-spanning travels" occurred long before the Asian, the European, and other tribes and their nations gained knowledge of where the different tribes had relocated and of the civilizations and cultures the other tribes and their nations had built. The Allmuseri continued to develop for centuries until the European tribe perfected its seafaring skills to the point of being able to venture into other parts of the world. Having developed into both a seafaring and a warring people, the European tribe's exploits into Africa, significantly escalating the historical Middle Passage in the seventeenth century, threatened the sociocultural survival of the black tribe, which already had been weakened by conflicts between its nations.

During this same period (from antiquity to the seventeenth century), the tribe of white skins, most of whom had removed to Europe, declared itself superior to the original human form and to the other tribes (see Yakub's story in Muhammad 110–19). Most of the nations of the European tribe eventually abandoned the religious systems they had created, appropriated and transformed the religious system of a nation (the Hebrews) from another tribe, renamed that religion's chief deity God, made God a rival to the Primordial Soul, and under this religious rubric nations from this tribe perpetrated atrocities against the other tribes and especially against nations of the black tribe.

In the seventeenth century some western European nations and their American extensions, now united under the rubrics of race and religion, escalated their aggression against black African nations as part of their campaign to conquer the African Self (the forms of humans and gods as well as the Primordial Soul). The principal event in this campaign, which lasted for over two centuries (and which is one of the anchors of plot in Johnson's *Middle Passage*), is what we know now as the Middle Passage. It was not only the forced removal of African subjects and their gods from their native lands and their relocation to the West (see *Middle Passage*[22])—that is, the black African diaspora—but also a deformation of the original African Self (see *Beloved* 210–17; *Middle Passage* 124–25; *Cattle Killing* 185–86).

In *Cane*, Toomer picks up this narrative of historical memory in 1619, the year the first diasporan Africans arrived in what is now the United States. *Cane* contains one of the most succinct and complete narratives of how the Middle Passage created the primal parent (the originating Western ancestor of Western blacks, a concept explained more fully in sections that follow) and his/her progeny. The character King Barlo provides this information in the sketch "Esther." Lapsing into a trance and couching his narrative of this androgynous primal parent in the frame of Judeo-Christian discourse, Barlo, a vernacular preacher, situates this segment of the myth within the context of the Middle Passage and locates this primal parent in memory, vision, and history. To a captive audience of blacks and whites, Barlo recapitulates the primal parent's capture in his native Africa, his transportation across the Atlantic, his enslavement in the Americas, and to some extent the biocultural conditions that transformed him from African to African American: "I saw a vision. I saw a man arise, and he was big an black an powerful . . . but his head was caught up in th clouds. An while he was agazin at th heavens, heart filled up with th Lord, some little white ant biddies came an tied his feet to chains. They led him t th coast, they led him t th sea, they led him across th ocean an they didnt set him free. The old coast didnt miss him, an th new coast wasnt free, he left the old coast brother, t give birth t you an me. O Lord, great God almighty, t give birth t you an me" (38–39).

In the West the deformation (diasporization) of the original African Self included various mechanisms to dissolve the spiritism that linked humans to humans, gods to gods, humans to spirits and gods, and all to the Primordial Soul (compare the transatlantic voyage in Johnson's *Middle Passage*). One mechanism was psychobiological—the act and consequences of miscegenation—and it created a partitioned black self by effecting an imbalance between the body, soul, mind, emotions, and other parts of the self.[23] While typically it rendered ineffectual the link between the self's soul and the Primordial Soul, it did not (could not) destroy every trace of this link.

The psychobiological mechanism was so successful that over time it produced a new tribe ("race") of humans in the Americas and in Europe.[24] This new tribe of biological and cultural hybrids became known variously as New World Africans, coloreds, and Negroes, among other appellations, including ones imposed on the tribe and ones generated within it. (This new tribe also was further subdivided into "nations," the largest of which were known as American Negroes, West Indians, and Afro-Brazilians; groups among the West Indians were further distinguished by the geopolitical space each inhabited within the Caribbean.)[25] The deformation process altered these humans' form to an extent that many physiologically resembled both Africans and Europeans. It effected changes in their psychology so severe that practically all eventually lost the original language that allowed them to communicate with their gods, most lost knowledge of their gods (see Reed's *Flight to Canada* 9–10 and Phillips's *Higher Ground* 15), and thus practically all were transformed from intersubjective Beings to partitioned selves (see *Cattle Killing* 158). This newly created tribe of partitioned selves became defined principally by their desire to reposition themselves in the unity of Being—that is, a desire for "wholeness" and "complete wholeness" (Jean Toomer's terms; explained below).

There were many African Selves (what Charles Johnson calls "Ur-tribesmen") transported to the West who remained untransformed psychologically and in other ways resisted diasporization (see *Salt* 5–7). The resistance assumed several forms—in Africa, during the Atlantic crossing, and in the West. Numerous captives committed suicide and infanticide rather than be transported to the West or to subject themselves or their progeny to diasporization (see Reyes's chapter 1). Among those who arrived in the West, some whose special powers remained basically intact walked or flew back to Africa.[26] Others found a variety of ways to undermine the diasporization process. This defiant group of Africans, some of whom also remained untransformed physiologically, retained knowledge of and thus the means for reestablishing the original African state of Being, which they passed down to subsequent generations of Western blacks and which remains active today (see *Salt* 3). This knowledge and the relatively few subjects who actively possessed it constituted a vehicle for the entire tribe of partitioned selves to reverse the deformation process. Western black literary texts that utilize the diasporan myth, particularly contemporary fictional slave narratives and the writings of Jean Toomer (such as "Split Men"), often offer a blueprint for Western black subjects to restore themselves to an African primordial state of Being.

Self-Theorizing Diasporan Novels

In what functions as a preface to *The Cattle Killing*, John Edgar Wideman in effect cautions critics ("the narratologists") and other readers that standard literary concepts and terms are not fully adequate for a critical or interpretative analysis of this novel (8). He calls this novel a "hybrid" text, and he explains that some of its formal features might resemble but are not exactly the same as some formal features one identifies with the works of writers such as Sherwood Anderson and William Faulkner. Indeed, in some instances the novel adheres to and in other instances it radically departs from standard novelistic praxis (8). Two instances of this departure are the novel's formation of its centered subject and its point of view. Charles Johnson states a similar caution for critics and readers of his novel *Oxherding Tale*. On two occasions Johnson interrupts the first-person narrative of *Oxherding Tale* to clarify for critics and readers "the *form* of this Narrative" (118; Johnson's emphasis). In his second authorial interruption he explains this novel's emendation to standard notions of point of view and its liberation of subject formation in narratives (152–53). Both Wideman and Johnson emphasize a nonstandard formation of the subject who is centered in their novels. What Wideman and Johnson state implicitly in their novels about the link between the production and critical analysis of their mythopoeic texts, Morrison states explicitly in one of her essays: "I don't like to find my books condemned as bad or praised as good, when that condemnation or that praise is based on criteria from other paradigms. I would much prefer that they were dismissed or embraced based on the success of their accomplishment within the culture out of which I write" ("Rootedness" 342).

The comments from these three writers bespeak a stance representative of many more contemporary black writers, their texts, and critical analyses of these texts. Wideman's caution in particular also echoes one by an earlier black writer, Zora Neale Hurston. Hurston's observations about blacks' spoken language are applicable to the written texts this study examines. An appropriation of Hurston's comments for an application to the black novelist reads thus: "Frequently the [black novelist], even with detached words in his vocabulary—not evolved in him but transplanted on his tongue by contact—must [emendate this vocabulary] to make it do" ("Characteristics of Negro Expression" 24).

Karla Holloway in *Moorings and Metaphors* makes a similar statement that is applicable particularly to readers and critics. Though she is speaking specifically about "literature produced by black women writers" (61), Holloway's observations about the applicability of standard "critical language" to black women's texts are valid for critical analyses of a broader range of black texts. Her observations certainly are germane to a critical analysis of contemporary fictional slave narratives. In both imaginative and critical black writing, several terms and concepts in the received critical vocabulary undergo what Holloway identifies as a shifting and bending to make them fit the nuances of meaning in a black text. As Holloway explains, "Shift happens when the textual language 'bends' in an acknowledgment of 'experience and value' that are not Western" (62). To appropriate one of Holloway's statements, one can say that "a critical language that does not acknowledge the bend or is itself inflexible and monolithic" (62) is not fully adequate for a critical analysis of certain salient features of most black-authored contemporary fictional slave narratives. In many instances, contemporary black authors' own bending and shifting of standard critical terminology and concepts occur within the narrative content of their fictional slave narratives. In other instances the authors introduce terms and concepts in their novels' narrative content that are integral to the production and interpretation of these texts.

Embedded in the African diasporan myth is a theory of black Being. The theory's basic premises can be extracted and synthesized from praxis in novels that generate the myth. Because this theory significantly shapes the contours of the novels' formal properties, it also functions as a theory of narrative and has its own specialized terms and concepts (a combination of standard ones that have been bent and shifted, hybridized ones, and new ones). Some of the theoretical terms and concepts that black novelists use to describe and inscribe aspects of Western black Being can be found in fictional, theoretical, and philosophical works by nonblack writers. However, in most instances the concepts these terms designate are not exactly the same concepts one finds in works by nonblack writers. In addition, terms for the same or a very similar concept in diasporan novels vary among the writers.[27]

Most of the critical and theoretical terms in this study come directly from the fiction and nonfiction texts of contemporary black writers. "Rememory" is from *Beloved*, "reinvention" is from *Oxherding Tale*, and "womanist" is from Alice Walker's *In Search of Our Mothers' Gardens* (1983). Several of the terms related to states of Being and Becoming come from or are based on the works of Jean Toomer. These are Western terms that the authors of contemporary fictional slave narratives employ, typically within the content of their novels. The concepts these terms name are largely African ones or they have strong parallels in traditional societies from western, central, and southern Africa. The novelists bend and shift these African concepts (if ever so slightly) to make them fit the nuances of a Western black experience.

As in the nonfiction slave narrative, the principal theme in a representative post-1975 fictional slave narrative is the diasporan subject's liberation.[28] Yet the subject's liberation in these novels is not exactly the same as the subject's liberation in the master text (the nonfiction slave narrative). Contemporary fictional slave narratives are not concerned primarily with the black subject's liberation from slavery's physical debilitations or from the oppressive social and political constraints of slavery's legacy. These and other diasporan novels focus on the subject's liberation from the spiritually crippling effects of diasporization, including slavery and its aftermath—on what Morrison refers to as the subjects' "interior life" ("Site of Memory" 110, 115).

In "Song of the Son" (*Cane* 21), Toomer calls Western black subjects "souls of slavery"; and in *Crossing the River*, Phillips calls them "diasporan souls" (236). Some other novelists (Phillips, *Higher Ground* 57, and Johnson, *Middle Passage* 188, 202, among them) refer to these subjects simply as "survivors" (of the Middle Passage), which in part means that diasporization might have muted but did not destroy the spiritual nature of their Being. Such terms foreground the inherent spirituality of Western black subjects, as do contemporary fictional slave narratives and other diasporan novels in which these subjects are situated. *Diasporan subject* and *diasporan self*, then, are apt critical terms to name these subjects. Though the terms used to describe and inscribe Western black ontology and to emphasize Western blacks' inherent spiritual nature often differ among the novelists, they nevertheless bespeak the same concept.

The diasporan myth posits that before the humans rebelled against the social order, generic man was an active component of what Charles Johnson calls the "unity of Being" (*Middle Passage* 65). The "unity of Being" is a concept integral to the novelists' formation of diasporan subjects. The unity of Being means that through the soul all things in the universe (past, present, and future) are spiritually linked one to another and all to the Primordial Soul. This linkage may be active or inactive. A subject who is actively positioned in this spiritual matrix is, according to Jean Toomer, a "*complete* whole" subject (*Wayward* 426; Toomer's emphasis). Johnson calls such a subject a palimpsestic Self, which he defines as a self who is "interwoven with everything—literally everything—that can be thought or felt" (*Oxherding Tale* 152; for another perspective on the concept, see his *Being and Race* 39). Though he does not use the term, Wideman inscribes the concept of the palimpsestic Self in *The Cattle Killing* when he posits the conjunction of story and being (207–8). Thus, he draws directly upon the lexical meaning of the palimpsest as a manuscript that has been written on more than once without completely effacing the previous inscriptions. From a synthesis of the different descriptions and inscriptions of the concept, the *palimpsestic Self* is an appropriate term to refer to a subject's spiritual connection (active or inactive) to all things—animate and inanimate, in the past, the present, and the future.

As a concept, the unity of Being is very similar to what Vincent Mulago and Gabriel Setiloane identify as the nature of Being in traditional African societies.[29] It is "a relationship of being and life" that interconnects "each individual" with "his antecedents," with "his descendants," with his clansmen, and "with God, the ultimate source of all life" (Mulago 138). Mulago calls this concept the "unity of life," "vital union," "the totality of being," and "vital participation" (138, 140). According to Mulago, "Participation is the element of connection . . . which unites different beings as beings, as *substances*, without confusing them. It is the pivot of the relationships between members of the same community, the link which binds together individuals and groups, the ultimate meaning, not only of the unity which is personal to each man [person], but of that unity in multiplicity, that totality, that concentric and harmonic unity of the visible and the invisible worlds" (145; Mulago's emphasis).

Setiloane, who agrees with Mulago, notes that "the essence of being is 'participation' in which humans are always interlocked with one another" (14). What connects one human to other subjects and objects in this bond of Being is what Setiloane calls "Seriti," which he defines as a "vital force" that is "calculated to promote and participate in relationship with the external world, human, animal, animate, inanimate, and even spiritual, like an antenna, charged and sensitive" (14). "It is like an aura around the human person, an invisible shadow or cloud or mist forming something like a magnetic or radar field. . . . While physically its seat is understood to be inside the human body, in the blood, its source is beyond and outside of the human physical body" (13). The transmissible and genetic nature of what Mulago and Setiloane call "vital force" can be identified in subject formations and narrative formations in novels such as Tananarive Due's *My Soul to Keep* and *The Living Blood*, Marshall's *Praisesong for the Widow*, and Perry's *Stigmata*. Quite similar to what Setiloane defines as Seriti is the "pulse of red light" that emanates from the presence of the character Beloved (*Beloved* 8, 18) and the "density of air" or "charge" that emanates from the Allmuseri's god (*Middle Passage* 68, 167).

A spirit-double or shadow self is part of the belief system in some traditional African cultures, such as Yoruba and Egyptian, as well as in some non-African cultures.[30] However, the particulars of this concept vary among traditional and nontraditional societies, as they do among the several Western black writers who employ the concept. Ishmael Reed's term "Etheric Double" (*Flight* 8) means essentially the same as *spirit-double* in traditional African societies—"a person's second . . . who accompanies him in thought, word and deed" (Oduyọye 273). Toomer's concept of the shadowed Self limits a subject's conscious or subconscious spiritual connection to humans, to spirits, and to gods, and he offers an operational definition of the concept: "Behind each man there is a Self," and "Behind each Self there are lesser and greater Selves / ranging up to that Great Self called Deity" (*Wayward* 428). Marshall (*Praisesong* 238–39), Perry (*Stigmata* 45–47), Brodber (*Louisiana* 58–65), and Wideman (*Cattle Killing* 76–77) dramatize the concept without providing a name for it. Charles Johnson uses a similar concept ("shadow-self"), but its meaning is slightly different from Toomer's (*Middle Passage* 112–13). Morrison's variation on the concept in *Beloved* is a narrative formation in which the respective "shadows" of Sethe, Beloved, and Paul D alternately accompany, follow, and precede the three, and Sethe interprets this as "a good sign. A life" (46–49). To be sure, the diasporan myth contends that conditions attendant to the diaspora separated the diasporan subject from his or her shadow selves/Selves. The result was that most Africans transported to the West and their descendants became what Wideman (*Cattle Killing* 158, 185–97), Toomer (*Wayward* 424; see also Avey in *Cane*), and other writers call and dramatize as spiritual exiles and orphans.[31]

Orphanhood, therefore, is a concept that refers to a subject's spiritual (and sometimes physical) disconnection from other subjects similar to himself or herself.[32] In chapter 3 of his 1789 *Narrative*, Oladuah Equiano in effect provides a narrative model for orphanhood when he describes his psychological and physical experience on first arriving in the United States. Equiano arrived in "Virginia county" where he "saw few or none of [his] native Africans, and not one soul who could talk to [him]" (44). Wideman uses orphanhood to refer not only to a subject's estrangement from other subjects but also to the lack of a harmonious balance between the different parts of a subject's self (158).

Orphanhood names a "condition" (to use Wideman's term) that many Western blacks share (13). Charles Johnson speaks of the same condition. One distinction Johnson makes in *Middle Passage* between the Europeans and the Allmuseri is how each views the self. (Johnson's distinction basically parallels one Senghor makes between white Europeans and black Africans.)[33] Europeans consider the self an individuated entity, while the Allmuseri consider the self an integral part of a collectivity. One consequence of diasporization is that in the West the black self is situated in what Johnson calls "the world of multiplicity, of *me* versus *thee*" (*Middle Passage* 140; Johnson's emphasis). The latter part of Johnson's phrase emphasizes difference rather than similarity, and in the West this difference translates into a racial hierarchy (that is, racism) the white practice of which Wideman calls "the madness" (*Cattle Killing* 113 and elsewhere) and the black response to which Morrison and Perry call "the Misery" (*Beloved* 171, 177; *Stigmata* 50). The diasporan myth's account of the first humans' rebellion against their godhead foregrounds the origin of difference in general and racial difference in particular as salient features of Western social interaction. Johnson's phrase "the madness of multiplicity" (*Middle Passage* 65) generalizes difference in Western thought; Wideman's "the madness" particularizes it to race; Morrison's "the Misery" specifies the effects of and blacks' response to it.

In the context of the diasporan myth, what Setiloane calls "Seriti" or "vital force" is equivalent to the soul, and his phrase "vital force in participation" is equivalent to the active soul (which diasporization renders inactive or dormant in most diasporan subjects). Charles Johnson on occasion uses the term *kra*, which in the context of *Oxherding Tale* is synonymous with "vital force" and soul/spirit. Setiloane points out that a subject's (human's or animal's or plant's) vital force "can be felt by any object with which it makes contact, like electric energy" (14). Everyone who resides in the house at 124 Bluestone Road (*Beloved*) at some point feels the vital force or spirit (often pernicious) of the dead baby, including the dog Here Boy (3, 12, 18). In *Oxherding Tale*, Reb sends forth his *kra* to dwell in other animals and in objects (49). When the itinerant preacher enters "the clearing" in *The Cattle Killing*, it is through the soul that he is able to connect spiritually with other worshippers in this "brush arbor" (72) as well as with "ancestors" and with "generations yet to be born," with those "airy presence[s]" who are made from "the stuff of the invisible ether where angels float" (76). The result, to use Mulago's words (cited above), is the preacher's active participation, through the connection of souls, in the "harmonic unity of the visible and invisible worlds" (Mulago 145). A subject who experiences this harmonic unity with the animate and the inanimate from the past, present, and future is a palimpsestic Self, forms of which are the intersubjective self, the plural Self, and the multiplicity of Being.

When this harmonic unity is fractured, which is a condition for Western blacks that obtains beyond the Middle Passage and slavery into the contemporary world, it creates one form of orphanhood, a fissure in intersubjectivity, and a rupture in the unity of Being. In reference to traditional African societies, Mulago refers to this fracture or rupture as a "decrease" in the vital force (145–50). Setiloane contends that such a condition of rupture or orphanhood is contrary to "African nature," and he notes that numerous Africans who emigrate to Europe and the United States complain of "loneliness" and of the "distance of people in spite of their closeness and numbers" (10)—what Charles Johnson refers to as the West's "world of multiplicity, of *me* versus *thee*" (*Middle Passage* 140; Johnson's emphasis). It is a similar kind of loneliness, an extension of "the Ebo melanchology" (Wideman's term in *Cattle Killing* 103), that defines the mental state of several subjects in diasporan novels.

According to Setiloane, the vital force is linked to and emanates from "the Source of Being, divinity—Modimo" (15). What the traditional African societies Setiloane references call Modimo is what this study calls the Primordial Soul, which means the same as Toomer's term "the Great Self called Deity" and Johnson's term "the Author of All Things" (*Middle Passage* 186). "The interaction of one's 'Seriti' (vital forces) with those of other people in the community does not terminate with death. Even after death 'the vital participation' of the deceased is experienced in the community in general and in the home and clan circle in particular" (Setiloane 17). The idea is relevant to the formation of subjects such as Beloved and to narrative formations such as that of "the clearing" in *The Cattle Killing* (72–78), "the Clearing" in *Beloved* (94–99, for example); "the Big Drum" in *Praisesong for the Widow* (see 236–51); and the ritual dancing in *Salt* (5). *Cattle Killing* and *Praisesong* speak respectively of "the clarity" and "*connaissance*," and the subject centered in each novel undergoes a spiritual conversion and intends to convert others. Understood in African terms, conversion is a kind of possession, and this meaning of the term certainly is dramatized as the preacher's "fits" in *The Cattle Killing* (66–77) and as Ella Townsend's "fits" in *Louisiana* (35, 88).

Integral to the diasporan myth's theory of black Being, then, are the premises that a Western black subject is ontologically one of two or more selves who constitute one Self. Johnson calls this Western black subject "the I," the "Self," and the "perceiving Subject" (*Oxherding Tale* 152). Wideman calls this subject "Eye or I" (*Cattle Killing* 4) and emphasizes the subject's capacity to be simultaneously the perceiver and the perceived. Whether using these or other terms, authors of diasporan novels contend that black Being is not synonymous with the individuated self; black Being is a plural entity. The intersubjective Self, the plural Self, "confraternity" (*Praisesong* 249), and the multiplicity of Being are terms that name closely related concepts different novelists use and that emphasize a subject's spiritual connection to other human subjects. The concepts are predicated upon the diasporan myth's premise of the bisected Self whose component selves may be of the same or of a different race and gender and may or may not exist in the same temporal and spatial zones.

Johnson's term "intersubjective Self" seems most appropriate when speaking generally of a diasporan subject's emotive, intellectual, experiential, spiritual, genetic, or sociogenic bond with or relationship to other diasporan subjects. The plural Self designates this intersubjectivity as gender exclusive (male or female), and the multiplicity of Being designates it as gender inclusive. All of these concepts have anchors in the diasporan myth and are features of subject formation in diasporan novels. For example, one consequence of the original human bisection was that humans' physicality became subject to temporal and spatial boundaries, which in turn effected a fissure in their intersubjective nature. The bisection's creation of a self and an other precipitated further divisions—that is, additional selves and additional others who may or may not share the same time and space.

In more ways than one, *Beloved* exemplifies premises of the plural Self in its formation of Sethe and Beloved. On the one hand, both Sethe and Beloved as selves in the 1870s have other respective twin selves who exist during the Middle Passage and in Africa before the Middle Passage (210–13). On the other hand, the two are halves of the same Self in the novel's present (the 1870s) and in the novel's past (the Middle Passage episode). In fact, mother (Sethe), daughter (Beloved), sister (Denver), and their female progenitors (that is, other selves) are all components of (have been severed from) a primordial Self named Beloved. The repetition of the sentence "I AM BELOVED and she is mine" (210, 214) and a variety of discursive formations in the novel bespeak the desire of these female subjects to reunite with their progenitors and other components as one (female) Self. Desire for the reunion of female progenitor and progeny is the motivation for subject formation and plot structure in *Stigmata*. In this novel the primordial Self's African name is Ayo (her Western name is Bessie Ward), who was captured in Africa and subjected to the Middle Passage and the horrors of slavery. Her controlling desire is for reunion with her Western female progeny—her daughter Joy, her granddaughters Grace, Mary Nell, and Eva, her great-granddaughter Sarah, and her great-great-granddaughters Ruth and Elizabeth (the novel's centered subject). Ayo's desire alters the life and the lifestyle of her Western female progeny, especially of Grace and Elizabeth.

The reunion of male progenitor and progeny (genetic and sociogenic) is at the heart of subject formation as a plurality and plot structure in *The Cattle Killing*, a novel that also foregrounds the partitioning of the Western black self. Consistent with the diasporan myth, a character in this novel asserts that diasporization fractured the intersubjective bond among Africans transported to the West and subsequently partitioned the black self (158). The centered subject in this novel, who is a component of a plural male Self, is "on a mission to save [his and] other [diasporan] souls" (190). His mission forms the novel's narrative foundation, and to accomplish his mission he must negate the effects of diasporization by reforming his self and reconstituting the Self—he must harmoniously balance his self's different parts and reactivate his intersubjective nature. Caryl Phillips utilizes this same premise of the plural Self (female and male) in *Crossing the River*'s formation of its focal black subjects. The three African children (two boys and a girl) sold into slavery in the 1750s are, respectively, the same three black adults who exist in the West in the nineteenth (one male and one female) and twentieth (one male) centuries.

To reconstitute the Self as a plural entity is to reunite the self with his or her other(s). Several novelists dramatize this reunion process, which Toomer (*Wayward* 217), Morrison (*Beloved* 213), Wideman (*Cattle Killing* 207), and Brodber (*Louisiana* 124), among others, call "the join." Complementarity is the conceptual rubric, inclusive of the join, for narrative formations that actually or potentially reunite the self with his or her other(s). Some authors of diasporan texts use "the other," "an other," "the self's other," and "the other self" interchangeably; some make slight but important distinctions between the terms. Among the distinctions, "the other" and "an other" are the terms most general and most inclusive of race, gender, and experience. As critical terms used in and applied to diasporan texts, "the other" and "an other" most often signal sameness rather than difference.[34] "The self's other" generally refers to a genetic kinship or to a sociogenic bond between and among persons of the same gender, while "the other self" generally refers to a conjugal nexus, whether heterosexual or homosexual. More specialized terms include "perfect correspondence" from Toomer's poem "Sing Yes!" and "Objective Complement" from Senghor's critical essay "On Negrohood." Subject complement, a term this study employs throughout, is a synthesis of these options. The two principal forms of complementarity in diasporan novels are conjugal and nonconjugal. Both of these forms often transgress boundaries of race, gender, time, and space, and both have strong anchors in the diasporan myth's component that posits reunion with one's severed half/halves as one of humans' principal desires.

Conjugal complementarity is a narrative formation that actually or potentially reunites subject and subject complement through a conjugal love bond. This reunion or fusion may be of selves of different genders and the same race, such as the fusion of Dessa and Harker in *Dessa Rose* and the potential fusion of the preacher and the patient in *The Cattle Killing*. The reunion also may be of selves of the same gender but of different races, such as the potential fusion of Nash and Edward Williams in *Crossing the River* and the fusion of the slave mistress and her female slave in Ann Shockley's short story "The Mistress and the Slave Girl."

Nonconjugal complementarity is predicated on an emotive and nonsexual nexus between subject and subject complement(s). It is the form of complementarity whose discursive formations are the most expansive and varied in diasporan novels. In female-centered novels such as Octavia Butler's *Kindred* and Gayl Jones's *Corregidora*, this form of complementarity involves a genetic nexus, sacred in *Kindred* and profane in *Corregidora*. In *Kindred* the components of the female Self exist in different times and spaces, and in *Corregidora* they exist in the same time and space. Gloria Naylor's *Linden Hills* inscribes the plural female Self as components whose nexus is experiential and sociogenic, all of whom exist in the same space but some of whom exist in different times.

Nonconjugal complementarity in its various forms is more frequent and more expansive in female-centered texts than in male-centered texts. Nevertheless, male-centered diasporan novels such as Phillips's *Higher Ground*, Johnson's *Oxherding Tale* and *Middle Passage*, and Wideman's *Cattle Killing* typically inscribe the plural male Self by using a series of historical formations that connects the centered subject to the experiential lives of his genetic or his sociogenic (or both) forefathers.

In most diasporan novels the concept of the plural Self, male or female, is a positive aspect of black Being. There are, however, a few instances in which authors use this concept to emphasize negative aspects of black Being, which they attribute to diasporization. In *Corregidora*, Jones uses the concept of the plural female Self to stress the pernicious nexus among generations of genetic female kin. Naylor does essentially the same for male kin in *Linden Hills* when she forms the Luther Nedeeds as a genetic male line in which each succeeding Luther is a physical, psychological, and diabolical "twin" of the first Luther (that is, Lucifer) Nedeed, and the first of these is a psychosexual clone of a white slaveholder.

This form of identical twinness that Naylor inscribes in the Luther line, which includes physical duplication, is rarely concept or praxis in diasporan novels. In addition to the Luthers in *Linden Hills*, the exceptions include Dana Franklin and her matrilineal ancestors in Butler's *Kindred* and David/Dawit in Due's *My Soul to Keep* and *The Living Blood*. Not only are Dana (in 1976) and Alice (in 1819) kindred spirits in that their bodies (along with Alice's mother's body) house the same soul, but also Dana is physically Alice's mother's "twin sister, almost" (41). In *My Soul to Keep* and *The Living Blood*, David's body in different centuries and on different continents is host to the same soul that Dawit's body hosts. When David's adult body is destroyed periodically, his soul regenerates the body as a replica (an identical twin) of his original adult body. Another form of this identical twinness is included in Johnson's *Middle Passage* when the Primordial Soul (inherent in the Allmuseri god) replicates and inhabits (or shape-shifts into) the physical form of Rutherford Calhoun's deceased father (168).

Authors who inscribe the duplication of a subject or a thing as a power endemic to black ontology do so under the rubrics of twinness and shape-shifting. The diasporan myth contends that in the original social organization there were restrictions on the forms humans could assume. The full powers of shape-shifting were privileges reserved for gods and spirits. In diasporan novels shape-shifting includes not only a being's (god's, spirit's, or human's) ability to assume another form but also the ability to occupy simultaneously different spaces and times. Though humans before the first rebellion could not shape-shift into the form of a god, they could assume various animate and inanimate forms and could occupy different spaces and times simultaneously. In his description of Liam's father in *The Cattle Killing*, Wideman inscribes this ontological power as it survived among remnants of the Ur-tribe in Africa and was lost to most diasporan blacks in the West, such as Liam. In Wideman's words, Liam's father "could change his shape or disappear instantly," and he "could be many different places at once" (104). A centered subject's ability to shape-shift is rare among contemporary novels that are grounded in the diasporan myth, but occasionally secondary characters exercise this power.

Beloved is a centered female subject whose formation incorporates this ontological power. One might argue that Beloved assumes the forms of her self (twinness) in different times and spaces (as noted above), and that the dead baby Beloved who reincarnates in the form of the adult Beloved is an instance of shape-shifting. Dana Franklin does not literally assume the form of another, but through time travel she does occupy spaces that are centuries apart in time. David/Dawit reincarnates as an adult several times over a span of more than four centuries and in geographical spaces located on different continents. Typically in contemporary fictional slave narratives, however, shape-shifting refers to a subject who assumes the form of another subject or of some other animate or inanimate entity. Paule Marshall gives the concept rather full exploration in *Praisesong*. During a ritual dance, diasporan subjects summon "the Old Parents." These "kin, visible, metamorphosed and invisible," reappear in shape-shifted forms of small land crabs, hard-back beetles, moths, flies, and mosquitoes (238–39).

In his fictional slave narratives, Charles Johnson provides some of the subgenre's most interesting examples of shape-shifting. The concept is integral to his formation of Horace Bannon, the Soulcatcher in *Oxherding Tale* who assumes the form of other humans and consumes the form of other animate things. Johnson predicates his formation of the Allmuseri god in *Middle Passage*, who shape-shifts into both animate and inanimate forms, on this ontological quality. Through his formations of the Soulcatcher and the Allmuseri god as shape-shifters, Johnson offers an example of a profane and a sacred version, respectively, of the palimpsestic Self.

Both the Soulcatcher (who is alternately black and white, but not biracial) and the Allmuseri god possess extraordinary epistemological power. According to the diasporan myth, this power was endemic to humans before the rebellion, and those whom the Supreme Being exempted from punishment after the rebellion were allowed to retain it. This power inheres as primordial memory in Western black subjects, though it is dormant in most of them. Authors of diasporan novels often incorporate this feature of black Being into the formation of both central and secondary characters and often use different terms to designate it. For example, Wideman uses *the clarity* and Marshall uses *connaissance*, and both define the concept as special ways of seeing and knowing that go well beyond the ordinary powers of vision and knowledge (*Cattle Killing* 76; *Praisesong* 218, 246). Marshall's *connaissance* (or *li gain connaissance*) is a term applicable to the concept that other authors use a different name for or leave unnamed.

As Johnson does for the Allmuseri, most authors of diasporan texts indicate that *connaissance* is innate. Paule Marshall adds that it is genetically transmitted (*Praisesong* 178, 218). One may translate the vernacular phrase *li gain connaissance* to mean to gain, to possess, and to genetically inherit special ways of seeing and knowing (see *Praisesong* 218 and *Stigmata* 34). The origin myth Due constructs in *My Soul to Keep* and *The Living Blood*, therefore, does not, as it appears initially, differ significantly from the feature of *connaissance* in the diasporan myth. In *My Soul to Keep, connaissance* is not innate to Dawit/David and the other Immortals (a group of blacks quite similar in function and meaning to Johnson's Allmuseri); the Immortals gain their extraordinary powers after decades of formal study and training (*My Soul* 264, for instance). At the end of *My Soul* and in *The Living Blood,* this power is transmitted genetically from David to his daughter, just as Lebert Joseph in *Praisesong* genetically transmits this power to his daughter, Rosalie Parvay (218). Thus, Due's origin myth aligns neatly with the diasporan myth.

The diasporan myth posits desire for wholeness (harmonious realignment of the self's parts) and complete wholeness (reunion with the self's other or others) as humans' ruling passion. Whether the desire is conscious or subconscious, for a diasporan subject to regain complete wholeness the subject must first be whole, which Toomer in *Cane* and "Split Men" (*Wayward* 423–26) inscribes as a subject whose various parts (such as body, soul, intellect, emotions) are in harmonious balance. A subject who lacks wholeness is a partitioned self, and this partitionedness (which is a re-invention of the black self) is largely a consequence of diasporization. Using terms and images that signify the black self's partitionedness, Wideman (*Cattle Killing* 185–86, 76–77), Morrison (*Beloved* 212), Johnson (*Middle Passage* 124–25, for instance), and others trace this condition to the Middle Passage as historical event. Though the steps desiring subjects take to reposition themselves in the unity of Being vary from one novel to another, the novels uniformly assert that wholeness is a prerequisite for complete wholeness.

Whether expressed as an estrangement from the unity of Being, a loss of the palimpsestic nature, a lack of complete wholeness, or a separation from the shadow selves/Selves, novelists are uniform in forming their centered subjects as ones who consciously or subconsciously desire to regain what Toomer calls "the ideal state of being" (*Wayward* 423). From the formation of a centered diasporan subject's ontological and epistemological dimensions emanate a given novel's principal formal properties. The major formal properties of a contemporary fictional slave narrative, such as setting, secondary characterization, point of view, and structure, are anchored in the diasporan myth.

Contemporary fictional slave narratives occasionally include a secondary character who possesses the ontological and epistemological characteristics of an African black before diasporization. Such a character is a primordial parent. More often than not, authors include the primordial parent as concept or reference rather than as a participant in a novel's narrative action. Variations on the character archetype include Liam's (and in effect the plural black male's) biological African father who possesses extraordinary ontological and epistemological powers (*Cattle Killing* 104) and the African father in the opening and closing sections of *Crossing the River*. In the latter instance, this biological parent sold his children into Western slavery and thus is consumed with guilt for having been a complicitor in the African diaspora. His ruling desire is to defy Western notions of time, space, and circumstance and to reposition his family in the unity of Being.

Another secondary character with functions similar to the primordial parent is the primal parent, who is a Western black. Though positioned in the West, the primal parent retains more vestiges of the original African Self than most other diasporan subjects. The primal parent's relation to the centered subject usually is spiritual and symbolic rather than biological. Barlo's "visioned African" (*Cane* 39) is an example of a primal parent who exists as concept and image rather than as an active character. In diasporan novels from the United States, the primal parent as a character who participates in a novel's narrative action typically is an older African American, often is a slave or a former slave, and, among other functions, acts as a spiritual guide who helps the focal subject to achieve spiritual wholeness. In a few instances this character was born in Africa (for example, the African man in *Dessa Rose*). The archetypal character retains vestiges of the primordial past and, usually, experiential knowledge of institutional slavery. Quite often in contemporary fictional slave narratives, this character is male, even in female-centered texts.[35] He possesses knowledge of the spiritual world as well as exceptional ontological powers. Father John from Toomer's *Cane*, whom the character Lewis describes "as symbol, flesh, and spirit of the past" (217), is the archetype for this secondary character in contemporary fictional slave narratives. Reb in *Oxherding Tale*, Lebert Joseph in *Praisesong for the Widow*, the "Af'ca man" in *Dessa Rose* (33–34), and Robin in *Flight to Canada* are variations on the archetype.

Though her approach and concerns are in the main different from my concerns here, Karla Holloway in *Moorings and Metaphors* provides a salient discussion of ancestors and ancestry in contemporary African American women's texts, some of which belong to the categories that I call contemporary fictional slave narratives and diasporan novels. Holloway notes the "spiritual presence of the ancestor" (22) in the lives of the women centered in the texts she examines. Her observations provide a useful parallel to some of my concerns about the form and function of the primal parent in the group of novels I examine.

2 The Subject(s) of Diasporan Desire
Jean Toomer as Literary Ancestor

Whether in their fictions or in their nonfiction texts, most authors of contemporary fictional slave narratives acknowledge the slave narrators as their literary ancestors. Many of these authors (and others) also include Jean Toomer among their most influential literary ancestors. Indeed, while the form of the contemporary fictional slave narrative is predicated on the antebellum master text, the philosophical and theoretical architectonics of this contemporary subgenre have strong anchors in the writings of Jean Toomer, especially his novel *Cane*. Originally published in 1923 and not long after basically relegated to oblivion, *Cane* was reissued in 1967 and shortly thereafter caught the admiring attention of scholars, writers, and students. In 1980 Darwin Turner published *The Wayward and the Seeking: A Collection of Writings by Jean Toomer* and thus made readily accessible several of Toomer's out-of-print and previously unpublished works. From praxis in *Cane* and from the philosophy and theory contained in Toomer's writings included in *Wayward*, one can discern the close affinities Toomer's works have with the philosophical underpinnings of contemporary fictional slave narratives and with other contemporary Western black novels.

Cane *and the Figurations of Desire*

An interpretative reading of *Cane* retrospectively through the lens of the diasporan myth and its theory of Being reveals that in the novel's construction of subjects, in its imagistic and symbolic patterns, in many of its narrative formations, and in other aspects of its form and content are several parallels to the myth's principal morphological features. These features combine with sacred geometry to help configure *Cane* thematically and formally as a discourse of diasporan desire.

In a letter to Waldo Frank dated 12 December 1922, Toomer uses the language of geometry to describe *Cane*'s design, and he privileges the circle and the triangle in the description.[1] "From three angles," he writes to Frank, "*Cane*'s design is a circle." He identifies the three angles as aesthetic, regional, and spiritual. Circularity and triangularity operate on different levels of meaning in *Cane* and apply to several aspects of the novel's formal design. In a more general sense, one can say the same about the design of diasporan novels, especially contemporary fictional slave narratives. Innovations in novelistic form mark their "aesthetic" design. Philosophical premises that conjoin geography and ontology, that interconnect physical place and psychological space, and that emphasize spirituality as the true nature of Western black Being are earmarks of these novels' "regional" and "spiritual" design, in which circularity and angularity figure prominently.

Grounded in the circularity and angularity of sacred geometry, *Cane*'s design incorporates interrelations of the Monad, the Dyad, and the Triad.[2] The symbol of the Monad is the circle, and in the diasporan myth the circle is the symbol for the Primordial Soul. It is a sign for the unity of Being in that it signifies the interrelationship of the Primordial Soul, the human soul, and the natural world (the universe). The philosophical meaning of the circle in *Cane* is consistent with its meaning in diasporan novels. One example is Wideman's *The Cattle Killing*, whose narrative design of form and meaning is, to use the novel's language, "circles within circles within circles" (144), "orphan tales" without "beginnings" or "ends" (29). In fact, among contemporary fictional slave narratives included in this study, *The Cattle Killing* best exemplifies, through referentiality and intertextuality, through form and meaning, the influence *Cane* and Toomer's other writings have on the subgenre.

Within the scheme of sacred geometry, the Dyad refers to humans, who are extensions of the Monad. Michael Schneider observes that "the Dyad's fundamental characteristic is the existence of a pair of distinct but equal opposites that seek to unite in an urge to return to unity" (28). This "urge" is desire, and practically all of the subjects in *Cane* (especially in the first two sections) are driven by an instinctual, primeval desire to fuse ("unite") with a subject complement, which is prerequisite for a resumption of complete wholeness and thus for a repositioning in the unity of Being.

From the purview of sacred geometry, the Dyad is a creation of and a separation from the Monad. The Dyad is a consequence of the "Primordial Scission": "One, the Absolute or unity, created multiplicity out of itself. One became Two" (West 44). The Dyad, therefore, represents division and polarity, among other things. The Triad represents transformation and rebirth (Schneider 39). As a sign of the reconciliation of opposition within the Dyad, the Triad signifies a return to the Monad. The Monad, Dyad, and Triad are inextricably bound: "One, in becoming Two, became Three simultaneously" (West 47). Stated in the language of secular geometry, one circle (the Monad) becomes two circles (the Dyad). The intersection of the two circles produces an almond-shaped space called the *vesica piscis*, or mandorla (Schneider 31). Connecting the points in this space where the circles intersect produces the triangle, and the triangle (the Triad) reestablishes the properties of the circle: "The unity of the circle manifests as a trinity: center, radius, and circumference" (Schneider 40). In *Cane*, sacred geometry and the diasporan myth coalesce in the formation of subjects, in the inscription of images and symbols that evolve into motifs and themes, and in the design of the novel's structural and thematic symmetry.

Geometric glyphs, particularly parts of circles, are the signs for thematic and formal figurations of desire in *Cane*. The arcs or partial circles that precede the novel's second and third sections signify a lack of wholeness and of complete wholeness in the subjects whom these respective sections foreground, as do other images of circularity (spiritual and material ones, natural and artificial ones) interspersed throughout the novel—such as the sun, the moon, and wedding bands. The partial circle operates on different levels of signification. When viewed from the context of the novel's construction of its centered subject (Ralph Kabnis) as well as its secondary subjects, the arc's absence as a prefatory symbol from the novel's first section is as important to textual meaning as is its presence preceding the second and third sections.[3]

Section 1 calls attention to female diasporan subjects whose souls are withering and dying because they lack complete wholeness. Though most of them are whole, they lack and therefore desire fusion with a subject complement, which would give them complete wholeness. They all are like "a November cotton flower" (2, 7)—vibrant life existing in a spiritually sterile social landscape. Though most are harmonized with nature, the lack of a subject complement has fractured and thus threatens to dissolve the unity of their Being. Concentrating thematically on the women's desire as exemplary, section 1 indicates that the state of Western society is at a very low spiritual ebb. The absence of a partial circle from this section underscores this premise.

Section 2 shifts thematically to an emphasis on desiring subjects who manifest discernible traces of the Primordial Soul and who individually and collectively embody the potential for spiritually reviving Western society. The partial circle that follows section 1 and precedes section 2 signifies these traces and this potential. Narrative formations in both sections call attention to desiring subjects who are seeking a subject complement and thus who are groping toward complete wholeness. Expressed in the language of scared geometry, these subjects' desire is for Oneness (for the fusion of Twoness and Threeness, of male and female).

The partial circle that is situated between sections 2 and 3 intimates diasporan subjects' potential for reactivating their primordial souls (as in "Calling Jesus"), which is conveyed through the formation of several desiring subjects in section 2 (Dan, Muriel, Dorris, John, and Paul) and is dramatized in the formation of Kabnis's subjectivity in section 3. Viewed through the lens of the Monad-Dyad-Triad nexus, narrative formations in the novel's first two sections involve the subjects' thwarted attempts to fuse with their opposite-gender other in order to reestablish the complete wholeness of their Being.

Throughout the novel, geometric images of circularity combine with images from the natural world (for example, the sun, the moon, pine trees) and with Judeo-Christian motifs (for example, resurrection and salvation) to support the narrative's teleological structure, connecting its end to its beginning and merging physical and metaphysical realities. The novel opens with an image of the sun setting, an indication that, like the Western soul, its life-giving and life-sustaining powers are waning. The novel ends with this source of life rising and sending "a birth-song" (239) across the social and physical landscapes, indicating that the Western soul is being rejuvenated and thus the partial circles (the arcs) of spiritual life are being reconnected to form a complete whole. The narrative closure of several diasporan novels, particularly contemporary fictional slave narratives, is similar to *Cane*'s—*Stigmata, Louisiana, Dessa Rose, Middle Passage, Praisesong for the Widow,* and *The Cattle Killing,* among others. Centered subjects in these novels typically progress from partitioned to whole selves; in many the primordial soul is reactivated; some achieve complete wholeness; and some become harbingers of a renewed spirituality among Western blacks.

Like the sun, the moon is a symbol of life-giving and life-sustaining forces, of fertility and the reproductive cycle of life. But it also is a symbol of misguided and thwarted sexuality, of a rupture in the circle of life. Thus, it is simultaneously a sign of completeness and of partitionedness, simultaneously a symbol of life and of death, of the sacred and the profane. Oppositions such as these that relate man and nature are especially evident in *Cane*'s first two poems, "Reapers" and "November Cotton Flower," and in "Blood-Burning Moon," the sketch that punctuates the novel's second section and one in which motifs and themes associated with the Monad-Dyad-Triad nexus culminate.

Another important image from the natural world in *Cane* is the pine tree of Georgia. Tall and stately, it stretches toward the heavens and whispers to Jesus, signifying both a rupture between the physical and the metaphysical worlds in the West as well as the potential for reuniting these worlds. The pine tree is both a life-negating and a life-affirming force, a symbol of death and of rebirth, as is evident in "Karintha" and in some of the novel's other sketches and poems. The pine trees' whisper to Jesus is a call for the Second Coming, for a renewal of life in a spiritually dying race of humans, for a rejuvenation of the withering soul and the soul's rightful balance with the body and with other aspects of Being. It is a call for self-(re)birth and self-salvation. Combined with what the wedding band symbolizes, it is a call for a renewed "marriage" between the human self/soul and the Primordial Self/Soul.

In its formation of subjects, *Cane* portrays representative selves who are in different stages of incompleteness and who suffer from different degrees of lack. For the most part, those subjects who are whole are women (such as Karintha, Becky, Avey, Fern, Bona, and Carrie Kate) whose souls are active and who are in touch with the primordial and metaphysical forces of life. They possess a proper balance between the female (spiritual) and male (material) principles of Being. Within themselves, they have reconciled the oppositions inherent in the Dyad. Yet their inability to fuse with their spiritual other threatens to diminish their soul's vibrancy.

On the other hand, practically all of the men in the novel lack wholeness. Within themselves the polar forces of the Dyad are unreconciled, and thus they suffer from an imbalance of the female and male principles, for they privilege the material over the spiritual. With Father John and Lewis as the notable exceptions, the men of *Cane* are the same kind of split men that Toomer describes in his poem "Split Men." The components of their individual selves are in discord. Among the men (and again excepting Lewis and Father John), Kabnis eventually is the subject who most fully harmonizes the components of his self and thus achieves wholeness. Very few of the men have knowledge or understanding of their desire for complete wholeness and none achieves it. The most likely candidate is Paul ("Bona and Paul"), but at the last minute Paul loses the opportunity to fuse with his other (Bona).

Desire to reunite with their other self is the ruling passion for the subjects in *Cane*, even for those who lack knowledge of this object of desire. Only Becky ("Becky") "meets" (Toomer's term from "Sing Yes!") and fuses with her opposite-gender subject complement, but her acquisition of complete wholeness exacts a great price. It is a similar price that Liam and Mrs. Stubbs, an interracial couple, pay in *The Cattle Killing* and that Willa Nedeed pays for reunion with her same-gender subject complements in *Linden Hills*. With its inclusion of Becky, a white, the novel indicates that its governing themes are not exclusive to blacks, but that through a portrayal of blacks the novel speaks about and to Americans in general. Becky's (as well as Bona's and Art's) inclusion in *Cane* is similar to the philosophical and thematic function of Mrs. Stubbs in *The Cattle Killing*, Joyce Kitson in *Crossing the River*, Irene in *Higher Ground*, Amy Denver in *Beloved*, Rufel in *Dessa Rose*, and Tommy O'Toole in *Middle Passage*. The inclusion of these nonblack subjects argues against the West's social construction of race and posits that, from the purview of the diasporan myth, they share a spiritual nexus with Western blacks and thus with the Primordial Soul.

Prominent images and motifs of decay and death in *Cane*'s section 1, of confinement and repression in section 2, and of sterility and partitionedness in section 3 interface with the narrative's imagistic, structural, and thematic geometry and with its biblical allusions to forecast the potential rejuvenation of the diasporan soul and a return to an ideal state of Being. In this regard, Toomer's ideas align neatly with the diasporan myth in that America's social organization has the potential to become like humankind's first social organization in Africa. In America, the Eden of the West, the tribes (specifically blacks and whites) severed long ago from the original human social organization have the potential to reunite into one human race, to reestablish the intersubjectivity and unity of Being indicative of humankind before the rebellion against the godhead.

Toomer's idea of an American race, of "the universal Human Being" in America, is one that he explores in his poem "The Blue Meridian" and in other of his writings (*Wayward* 232; 17–18). In *Cane*, Toomer conveys this idea in part through his formation of the white characters Becky and Bona. In this sacred space (the United States) there is the possibility of reconciling socially constructed oppositions of East and West, of South and North, of black and white, of male and female, of the physical and the metaphysical. Black subjects in the novel, particularly women, exemplify how the human race can survive in this alien land. But the point is not gender-exclusive, for the novel's formation of its centered subject, the participating and observing male I/eye, provides perhaps the best blueprint for how a diasporan subject can reverse his or her diasporization. The same is true for the male I/Eye in *The Cattle Killing*. In *Cane*, this blueprint is contained in both the production and the meaning of the I/eye's poem "Song of the Son."

"Song of the Son," then, functions as a version of the novel in miniature. It is the manifestation of its diasporan speaker's (Kabnis's) ability to sing the Lord's song though in a strange land, as *Cane* is a manifestation of Toomer's ability to do the same. The singer functions as a primal parent in the West, an extension (son) and a messenger of the Primordial Soul. He is a spiritual guide for the spiritually weak, and his task is to teach the others how to re-member the self/Self and to re-turn to primordiality (much like the preacher's "mission" in *The Cattle Killing* and Avey's in *Praisesong for the Widow*). Both the poem and the novel are creative outpourings of desire as well as vehicles for attaining that desire. The diasporan singer's creation of song is also a means for reestablishing the intersubjectivity of his own Being, which he accomplishes in part through mystifying and mythologizing African diasporan subjects. The same process and purpose apply to John Edgar Wideman's creation of his novel *The Cattle Killing* (see 7, 13). And, like *The Cattle Killing*, *Cane* also may be defined as "metafiction" (R. B. Jones 60).[4]

The drama of desire centers Kabnis in the novel's third section, whose opening scene draws his dilemma as person and as poet to the discursive fore: he is a partitioned self, is estranged from nature and from his fellow man, and therefore lacks/desires the unity of Being. In this regard Kabnis and the itinerant preacher in *The Cattle Killing* are very similar diasporan subjects. As the discursive and dramatic formation of Kabnis's subjectivity unfolds in this section, Toomer draws attention to Kabnis's body, mind, and soul as disparate components of his self. The narrative movement in the section is toward harmonizing these disintegral parts, a movement from the stage of the Dyad to the stage of the Triad. Kabnis's repeated admonition to himself—"pull yourself together" (162)—reveals not only that he knows he is partitioned but also that he desires wholeness.

The section's thematic structure makes it a drama of self-regeneration. Each of the drama's six scenes functions as a demarcation point along Kabnis's geospiritual journey from partitionedness to wholeness. Each of the "stories" in the itinerant preacher's narrative (*Cattle Killing*) functions as a demarcation point along his geospiritual journey toward wholeness. What began for Kabnis as a physical sojourn in the South (Georgia) inadvertently evolves into his spiritual quest for primordial Being. It is from being situated on the soil of his ancestors that Kabnis eventually is able to reconnect with the primordial past, that as person and as poet he is able to gain the powers to rejuvenate himself and thus to reverse his diasporization. As the novel's narrating I/eye declares, "When one is on the soil of one's ancestors, most anything can come to one" (31). In this regard Georgia is a magical landscape where "things unseen to men [are] tangibly immediate" (31). In *Louisiana*, Ella Townsend takes a similar "journey into knowing" (38), and Louisiana is the magical landscape where her mystical experiences occur. The I/Eye of *The Cattle Killing* experiences and recounts a mystical experience when, through what he calls a "trick of the mind" (143), he is transported to the soil of his African ancestors (see 143–48). An inadvertent journey to Africa and contact with his primordial ancestry cause Rutherford Calhoun (*Middle Passage*) to undergo a spiritual transformation similar to those of Kabnis, Ella Townsend, and *The Cattle Killing*'s preacher. Inscribed in a variety of ways, the fusion of (sacred) geography and ontology is indeed evident in several other contemporary fictional slave narratives, Due's *My Soul to Keep* and *The Living Blood*, Perry's *Stigmata*, and Condé's *I, Tituba* among them.

In section 3 Kabnis arrives in Georgia an incomplete self, and his body is a text that inscribes this incompleteness. He is likened to an "artificial man" (163) and a "scarecrow" (181). With his soul disengaged from his body and mind, he is form without substance. Suffering from the spiritually drained condition of Western man, Kabnis is unable to distinguish between love as an emotion and (making) love as a gesture, a condition from which Rutherford Calhoun (*Middle Passage*) also suffers. For Kabnis, the physical gesture has replaced the emotion and he has privileged his body over his soul. His spiritual debility and his lack of sexual potency are reflexive, an indication that the bond that would connect him to other diasporan souls has been breached. In the first scene's opening section he is masturbating. This nonprocreative act with an object ("pillow" 158) rather than with a subject is a symbolic action intimating not only that he is a partitioned self but also that he lacks a female subject complement. Though Gayl Jones reverses the gender, the closing scene of *Corregidora* repeats this same premise of nonprocreation.

The turning point in Kabnis's movement toward wholeness comes when he embraces Father John, in whom the Primordial Soul actively inheres. Father John is the primal parent who is "symbol, flesh, and spirit of the past" (217). Revisions of this kind of symbolic subject formation appear in *Praisesong for the Widow, Louisiana, Oxherding Tale,* and *Kindred,* among other diasporan novels. Father John is also primordiality and diaspority, ancestor and progeny—ideas that are operative in the formation of centered and secondary subjects in *The Cattle Killing, Stigmata,* and *Oxherding Tale.* Somewhat like Lebert Joseph (*Praisesong*), diasporization has deformed the physicality but not the spirituality of his Being.

Indeed, once Kabnis achieves wholeness, he (like Jean Toomer) gains epistemic and artistic agency and thus the inspiration and capacity to write *Cane.* Seen from this perspective, *Cane* is a novel written, and thus one that must be read, beyond its narrative ending. It is similar to Johnson's *Autobiography of an Ex-Coloured Man* (1912) and Ellison's *Invisible Man,* as well as to contemporary diasporan novels and fictional slave narratives such as *Louisiana, Kindred,* and *The Cattle Killing,* novels whose retrospective narrative structure simultaneously inscribes the centered subject's Being and Becoming, novels that reveal not only who the subject is but also how he or she came to be. From this purview, author and centered subject merge as artistic agent; as the centered subject is writing self into Being, he/she simultaneously is being written into Being. In praxis, *Dessa Rose, Stigmata, Louisiana,* and *The Cattle Killing* are among the novels that present discursive variations on this premise.

Given the teleological structure of its narrative, *Cane*'s end is indeed its beginning, and the narrating I/eye progresses from unnamed (sections 1 and 2) to named (Kabnis) and acquires epistemic and artistic agency. In the opening of section 3, Kabnis as poet states his dilemma: he writes from the head (intellect) rather than from the soul (e-motion). He has become so Westernized that he privileges white over black, the material over the spiritual, and thus as poet he has muted the source of his artistic inspiration. Beyond the narrative's end (or in the space—the *vesica piscis*—that joins its end to its beginning), Kabnis solves the problem he has with artistic inspiration and production: he achieves wholeness, and thus his relationship with his subjects (both beings and subject matter) emanates from a balance between the e-motion and the intellect rather than exclusively from the intellect. It is this kind of balance that allows authors of womanist novels (Morrison and Condé, for instance) and particularly of textually androgynous novels (Phillips and Brodber, for instance) access to the interior lives of their subjects and their subjects' worlds.

Cane's form is a compilation of parts ("songs") that yields a whole and is inextricably bound to its meaning. On the surface, its form appears to be a compilation of disparate parts, of loosely connected fragments inscribed in the forms of prose, poetry, and drama. Yet diaspority as central theme unifies the parts and produces a hybrid but whole and complete text. Indeed, hybridity defines *Cane*'s form and its diasporan subjects, just as it defines the form of and subjects in *The Cattle Killing* (see *Cattle Killing* 8).

Toomer includes dance (rhythmic motion) as narrative formations in *Cane* ("Karintha" and "Theatre," for example). It is dance as concept, however, that is integral to the production and interpretation of *Cane*. Toomer's poem "The Lost Dancer" (*Wayward* 209), which on one interpretative level is about an artist's desire for the unity of Being, for continual fusion with his art form, seems an appropriate gloss on the formation of Kabnis's subjectivity as person and as poet.[5] The poem's speaker laments the mortality of a dancer's physical self and his inability to sustain an ideal state in which the dancer and the dance are bound perpetually in the unity of Being. The dancer's ruling desire is for a

> . . . source
> Of magic adequate to bind
> The sand upon his feet, his feet
> Upon his dance, his dance upon
> The diamond body of his being.

In *Cane,* Kabnis as artist eventually finds the "source / Of magic adequate" to bind him (the poet) and his poetry in a bond of Being. This source is the Primordial Soul, and reestablishing his lifeline with this transcendent force gives him the emotive (ontological, epistemological, and teleological) powers to dance the other(s) and thus to dance the self. This bond does not, however, confer immortality on the physical self. As poet, Kabnis's situation is like the dancer's (and like Toomer's). The "Spatial depths of [his] being survive" his mortal body, and "Vibrations of the dance survive / The sand; the sand, elect, survives / The dancer." Mortal being is ephemeral; spirituality is not. The art, which is an expression of the soul, will survive the artist.

As a theoretical concept, to dance is to enter into the complexity of the other's Being, which allows one to enter into the complexity of one's own Being.[6] To accomplish one is to accomplish the other. It is after Kabnis has (re)constructed the intersubjectivity of his own Being (has activated the resources of his soul) that he can narrativize the process of his Becoming, can inscribe his Being, and can write (that is, dance) the other, male and female, into Being. Léopold Senghor, one of the formulators of Négritude and a literary writer and theorist strongly influenced by Toomer's writings, succinctly explains dance as a theoretical concept and the concept's relationship to Being. Senghor posits that to *be* is to dance the other. It is to know the other as intimately as one knows the self, to enter into that other self's complexity so thoroughly that the perceiving subject can reconstruct the world in which the perceived subject lives.[7] As the ostensible "author" of *Cane,* Kabnis dances and sings (synonymous terms in this instance) his subjects as other(s). In dancing the other, self and other become one Being.[8] This fusion of self (often an author) and subject(s) through the concept of dancing the other is at the foundation of form and meaning in diasporan novels such as *Louisiana* and in contemporary fictional slave narratives such as *Dessa Rose, Beloved, Stigmata,* and *The Cattle Killing.*

Theorizing Desiring Subjects: Toomer's Poems, Maxims, and Aphorisms

One might say that *Cane* is praxis and that many of Toomer's other writings, particularly poems, maxims, and aphorisms, are "theory," what he refers to as his "views and ideas" "about human life" (*Wayward* 413). Much of Toomer's theory is contained in a manuscript of poems entitled "The

Wayward and the Seeking" and in a 400-page manuscript entitled "Remember and Return." Darwin Turner published large segments of the two manuscripts in the collection *The Wayward and the Seeking*. In Turner's publication the poems have titles, but most of the maxims and aphorisms are untitled. As Toomer explains in the preface to the manuscript "Remember and Return," his intent is to "produce a certain inner revolving of ideas, meaning, and effects" by arranging "the statements in such a way that the mind of the reader [is] able to catch hold of the central themes and follow them through" (*Wayward* 414). The central theme in the two manuscripts, as Toomer states in the final version of "The Blue Meridian," is for humans to "spiritualize" (215). Supporting themes in the different poems, maxims, and aphorisms relate to this central theme. For humans in the West to spiritualize is for them to abandon their false nature, to embrace their true nature, and thus to "become *whole* men aiming to become *complete* whole men" (226). Re-membering the self, re-turning home, abandoning one's false nature, and assuming one's true nature are the controlling "views and ideas" in Toomer's theoretical and philosophical writings (as published in *Wayward*).[9] Though still referencing *Cane*, the following section of this chapter concentrates on affinities between Toomer's central and supporting themes (his theory) and praxis in contemporary diasporan novels.

Thematic structure in diasporan novels organizes narrative action that monitors the centered subject's desire to re-member the self/Self and to re-turn home. To re-member and to re-turn are respective terms that Toomer uses to name the processes a desiring subject must undergo in the conscious or subconscious pursuit of wholeness and complete wholeness (compare to "Split Men"). In this regard, home is a primordial state of Being, and the process of re-turning home is what Toomer calls a "psychospiritual movement" to a psychospiritual space rather than to a geophysical one. To re-turn home is, according to Toomer, to

> detach ourselves from the harmful
> properties of our false natures, [to] attach ourselves to
> the creative functions of our true natures, and [to] enter
> purely into those cosmic processes which are particularized
> in human beings. (*Wayward* 430)

To re-member and to re-turn are internal processes, and memory, both historical and primordial, is the principal vehicle that effects the diasporan subject's internal transformation (actual or potential) from a false nature to a true nature. As concepts, to re-member and to re-turn are the foundations of narrative architectonics in the contemporary fictional slave narrative and in other kinds of diasporan novels.

The structure of narrative action in diasporan novels often leads to and follows from a diasporan subject's memory of the historical and the primordial pasts. For example, a subject in the present (such as Lizzie in *Stigmata* or the itinerant preacher in *Cattle Killing*) can recall incidents from the personal history of a person who died before this subject was born. This journey into historical memory often activates extraordinary ontological and epistemological powers that are lodged in the subject's primordial soul. From an indelible trace of the historical past, a diasporan subject (whether author or character) is able to reconstruct the self/Self and the World; according to Charles Johnson, the self/Self and the World are synonymous (*Oxherding Tale* 153).[10] Morrison refers to this reconstruction process metaphorically as an archaeological excavation during which an author discovers a trace of an authentic self ("Site of Memory" 112, 115). From this trace the author is able to reconstruct the diasporan subject's authentic self/Self and the Self's World (historical and primordial). This is the process Morrison uses to reconstruct Sethe and Sethe's World in *Beloved* (see "Site of Memory" 114–20). Williams uses this same process to reconstruct Dessa's authentic Self and Dessa's World (*Dessa Rose* ix–x). The same is true for Wideman's reconstruction of the itinerant preacher and his World in *The Cattle Killing*. Variations on this construct can be found in *Stigmata*, *Louisiana*, *I, Tituba*, and *Linden Hills*, among other novels. In these instances memory (primordial, genetic, or common/racial) is the nexus that effects the merging of the selves into a Self.

According to the diasporan myth, most Africans transported to the West and their descendants became victims of a subject transformation in which a false nature supplanted their true nature and rendered the soul dormant. As Toomer maintains in "White Arrow" and "Honey of Being," this "experience" can be reversed through a reactivation of the soul. The speaker in "White Arrow" assures the reader/listener that "Your force [the soul] is greater than your use of it," and instructs him/her to "awake and be" (*Wayward* 202). The speaker in "Honey of Being" concurs and states that one can reverse the diasporan "experience [and return] / To essence [where] source / and end [are] identical" (*Wayward* 204). Typically, a diasporan novel explores the differences between a centered subject's true and false natures and monitors the subject's hunger (conscious or subconscious desire) for complete wholeness. That diasporization could not efface a subject's soul accounts for diasporan subjects' capacity to negate their false nature and to reassume their true nature. This capacity is integral to narrative action, thematic structure, and subject formation in diasporan novels, and especially in contemporary fictional slave narratives.

In "Peers" (*Wayward* 211) and in other of his writings, Toomer asserts the spiritual connectivity of the inanimate and the animate. From *Middle Passage, The Cattle Killing, Beloved,* and other diasporan novels comes the contention that the Primordial Soul can inhabit the animate and the inanimate or can exist independently of either. Though the human soul is either dormant or not fully activated in most diasporan subjects, it is, like the Primordial Soul, indestructible. In this regard the soul is primordial memory, which encompasses historical memory. A diasporan subject's dormant soul usually is reactivated by contact with a twin soul that is housed in an inanimate object (such as the "rock" in "Peers"), in an artifact (such as the pendant in *Louisiana* [131]), or in another human host.[11] In the first instance one also might say that a subject who comes into contact with an inanimate object (such as an artifact) that houses memory has his or her own memory reactivated. This is the case with authors Morrison (*Beloved*) and Williams (*Dessa Rose*) and with characters Lizzie DuBose (*Stigmata*), Willa Nedeed (*Linden Hills*), and Ella Townsend/Louisiana (*Louisiana*). When a subject comes into contact with his or her twin soul that inhabits another human host, a form of racial memory prevails and is akin to what Phillips calls "the common memory" (*Crossing the River* 235) and what Marshall characterizes as memory passed down in the blood (*Praisesong* 178). One example of this latter instance is the author of—and most black male characters in—*The Cattle Killing*. Indeed, the soul as memory is passed from one host to another, from one generation to another, and it survives well beyond a host or a generation. When a diasporan subject whose soul is dormant spiritually connects with a subject whose soul is active, his or her own soul is reactivated. For example, spiritually connecting with the itinerant preacher, whose soul is active, allows Liam to reactivate ("thaw" is Wideman's term for this) his dormant soul (*Cattle Killing* 101).

According to Johnson's *Middle Passage*, an Allmuseri who has not come under Western influence is a true African Self whose soul is active. The novel also states that the mutation of the African Self's soul begins immediately when the African Self first comes into contact with members of the European tribe. This initial contact begins the transformation from an

African Self to a Western black self, from a true nature to a false nature. The "horrors" the Allmuseri experience during their middle-passage ordeal on the *Republic* begin the subtle "reshaping [of] their souls" (125). Phillips concurs in his novel *Higher Ground*. The unnamed native African in this novel, who eventually acquiesces in the reshaping of his soul, calls it "murdering the memory" (24). Johnson's Allmuseri on the *Republic* and Phillips's unnamed African are prospective primal parents whose progeny will suffer a more intense form of diasporization than these primal parents suffer. Marshall certifies the latter point when Avey Johnson notes that "lacking memory" defines the diasporized condition of countless diasporan blacks in the state of New York (*Praisesong* 255). The same principle obtains generally for Western black subjects in other diasporan novels.

Johnson, Phillips, Marshall, and other authors of diasporan novels agree with Toomer ("Split Men") that diasporization is a reversible condition. Having been subjected to numerous horrors while a captive of slavers and having survived the Middle Passage on "the trading ship, *Young Saint Paul*," the unnamed African in *Higher Ground*, now "an old man," laments that his "present has finally fractured; the past has fled over the horizon and out of sight."[12] Nevertheless, he speaks for himself and for other diasporan subjects of the present and future when he says that "we are all promising to one day return, irrespective of what might happen to us in whatever land or lands we eventually travel to. . . . And the promise comes from deep inside of our souls" (60). It is essentially this same sentiment that the speaker in "Song of the Son" expresses in *Cane*. Speaking for and about the descendants of those who survived the Middle Passage, he notes that "though the sun is setting on / A song-lit race of slaves, it has not set." He offers himself as an exemplar: "Thy son, in time, I have returned to thee" (that is, to the sacred "land and soil" of his ancestral African origin).

In the passage quoted above, Phillips's diasporized African in *Higher Ground* intimates the significant relationship between geography and ontology that is contained in several diasporan novels. In a broad sense, the diasporan myth's cultural geography recounts the distribution of human life on earth and the effects this distribution had on human activity and subjectivity. Johnson weaves several details of this distribution into *Middle Passage* as part of his invention of the Allmuseri nation. More particularly, the diasporan myth's cultural geography recounts the transportation of African blacks to and their distribution within the West, the principal effect of which was an alteration of the true nature of black Being. Once (re)-

constructed as an object of the West whose corporeal, psychic, and spiritual components are in a state of continual rupture, the diasporan subject, consequently, is defined almost totally by lack and therefore exists in a perpetual state of desire (conscious or subconscious) to harmoniously balance the self's disintegral parts and to be repositioned in the unity of Being. According to diasporan novels, rejuvenating the soul's original power is the first major step toward regaining the unity of Being, and there are two principal routes a diasporan subject can take. One is by embracing fully the spiritual forces of primordial Africa through either a physical or a "*psychological*" (Toomer's term, *Wayward* 426) pilgrimage to this sacred land of origin.[13] Such a geospiritual re-turn to the Fatherland/Motherland is a mechanism for the subject to reassume his or her true nature. But the return home is difficult because, as Phillips writes in *Crossing the River,* "There are no paths in water. No signposts" (1–2). In other words, a physical journey to Africa is not by itself sufficient to reactivate a dormant soul.

Phillips calls it a signpost, Morrison calls it "remains" ("Site of Memory" 112), Toomer calls it a "seed" ("Song of the Son" from *Cane*), and both Marshall and Toomer call it "threads" (*Praisesong* 249; "Split Men," in *Wayward* 423). Whatever the name, this indelible remnant of the primordial past is lodged in memory, and it is the vehicle that can effect a diasporan subject's re-turn home. The re-turn home as concept is built upon a component of the diasporan myth that is located in historical time. Within this component is a legend that narrates how a group of diasporan Africans in the West, the Ibos, exercised their extraordinary epistemological and ontological powers and literally walked across the Atlantic back to Africa. From extended versions, such as those in Marshall's *Praisesong for the Widow* (37–40) and Julie Dash's *Daughters of the Dust* ([1997] 100–105), to abbreviated ones or references, such as in Reed's *Flight to Canada* (123, 131–32) and Wideman's *The Cattle Killing* (103), several texts install or reference the story of the walking Ibos. Another legend in this component contends that some New World blacks flew back to their native land, and uses of this legend can be found in *The Cattle Killing* (205) and Morrison's *Song of Solomon* (3, 6) as reference or motif, in *Flight to Canada* and Julius Lester's "When People Could Fly" as a central trope, and in other works that install or reference the story of the flying Africans.[14]

This memory of and longing for home is what Wideman calls "homesickness, the Ibo melancholy" (*Cattle Killing* 103), and as concept it is basically equivalent to Morrison's "rememory" and to what Toomer characterizes as Kabnis's "impotent nostalgia" (*Cane* 163). Rememory and Ibo melancholy are terms that can be used to distinguish generally between how the conjunction of the concepts to re-member and to re-turn as forms of desire are inscribed, respectively, in female-centered and male-centered diasporan novels. However, the pairing is not exclusive. For example, in *Praisesong for the Widow*, "Ibo melancholy" is the rubric Marshall privileges to inscribe her centered subject's desire to re-turn home. In *The Cattle Killing*, Wideman uses Ibo melancholy to describe the male centered subject's desire to (re)acquire a primordial state of Being, but rememory is a more apt description of this subject's reunion with his other selves. Rememory and Ibo melancholy can be conscious or subconscious in the diasporan subject. In most instances, the emergence of this desire from the subject's subconscious to his or her conscious structures narrative action in a diasporan novel.

The re-turn home is a more arduous task for the Western descendants of African blacks than it was for the walking Ibos and the flying Africans. This is true primarily because Western blacks became diasporized: they became salt eaters.[15] Earl Lovelace opens his novel *Salt* (1996) with a variant of the legend of the flying Africans that explains the inability of some Western blacks to fly back home: "They had eaten salt and made themselves too heavy to fly" (3). For New World Africans and their descendants, eating salt was/is both a literal and a figural form of diasporization. It was literal in that some (but not all) Africans in the New World came from cultures that did not include salt in the diet. Eating salt as part of the New World's diet was a signification that these New World Africans were undergoing cultural transformations.

Being a salt eater is figural in that it signifies both cultural and ontological transformations. As the New World's conditions of slavery forced Africans and their descendants progressively to lose their culture and consequently to alter the nature of their Being, they became, figuratively, increasingly salt eaters. As Lovelace explains, these salt eaters began "to curse their elders . . . [and] to curse their gods" (*Salt* 3); and as Reed, among others, contends, they lost their language and thus the power to communicate with their gods (see *Flight* 9 and *Higher Ground* 24). In effect, they also lost or were forced to lose primordial memory and other epistemological and ontological powers endemic to their true nature (*Salt* 3;

Middle Passage 124–25, for instance; and *Praisesong* 255, for example; see also *Higher Ground* 24). They became too heavy with European culture to fly or to walk on water in order to re-turn home.

However, for these descendants, home is rarely synonymous with geographic Africa. The farther diasporan subjects are removed temporally from home (Africa or some Western spiritual space), the farther they are removed from their true nature and the more difficult the re-turn. Diasporan novels indicate that through the generations Western blacks' ontological powers become more and more diluted and their re-turn home becomes more an interior journey than an exterior one. Nevertheless, the re-turn is not impossible. As Toomer contends, "There are di- / rections as to how to do it formulated by those / who have done it" (*Wayward* 429). "Those who have done it" include not only the walking Ibos and the flying Africans but also diasporan subjects who reversed their diasporization and regained their true nature.

This is the lesson Ishmael Reed teaches in *Flight to Canada* through his updated and unconventional revision of the legend of the flying Africans. Among its various meanings in the novel, Canada means home and "liberation" (88), and the vehicle for this re-turn home is flight, albeit a contemporary, literal, and technological version of it. It is indeed a re-turn in the example of those predecessors (the flying Africans) who formulated and taught how it could be done, which the novel suggests by pointing out the proliferation of "avian imagery in the poetry of slaves" and by its statement "each man to his own Canada" (88). Raven Quickskill learns this lesson from experience, and through his poem he teaches the lesson to others.

That a diasporan subject can re-turn home is the lesson Rutherford Calhoun (*Middle Passage*) learns and that his narrative teaches. For Calhoun and most other diasporan subjects, geographic Africa is less a destination than it is a way station en route home. In fact, in contemporary diasporan novels relatively few subjects physically return (either journey, which is permanent, or sojourn, which is temporary) to geographic Africa; the majority re-turn to metaphorical or symbolic Africa. Subjects in Phillips's *Cambridge* (Cambridge) and *Crossing the River* (Nash Williams) are among the exceptions. These subjects travel to Africa (Nash's journey; Cambridge's sojourn), but their soul's power is so diluted that they cannot reposition themselves in the unity of Being. In instances such as these the journey/sojourn is exterior rather than interior and does not accomplish the goal of regaining complete wholeness.

In several diasporan novels narrative structure is closely related to the time and space of setting. Rutherford Calhoun's geospiritual re-turn home begins as a physical sojourn through space to Africa the Fatherland. In *Beloved*, the plural centered subject takes a mental geospiritual journey through time to Africa the Motherland. Each novel uses this geospiritual journey as the scaffolding for its narrative structure. Other novels, such as *Crossing the River* (Nash Williams's story), *Cambridge*, and Tananarive Due's companion novels *My Soul to Keep* and *The Living Blood*, are variations on this geospiritual re-turn home. Through her formation of David/Dawit as the subject centered in her companion novels, Due provides an unusual exploration of the true nature–false nature construct. David/Dawit's geophysical journey back to his ancestral origin, Africa, is also a geospiritual one back to his true self.

Because in most diasporan novels Africa (that is, home) refers to a psychospiritual rather than a geophysical space, authors use memory as the vehicle that transports the subjects home. Memory allows the subjects to traverse Western (Eurocentric) notions of time and space, and at the same time it allows the authors' texts to remain within Western notions of literary time and space. For example, it is through primordial memory that Minty (*Oxherding Tale* 167) and Martha Randolph (*Crossing the River* 73, 89, 94) re-turn to Africa and to a primordial state of Being. In both instances Africa is "a place of reunion" where the diasporan subject can "be reunited" with her other selves/Selves and repositioned in the unity of Being (*Crossing* 89; *Oxherding* 167). The same general principle obtains for the itinerant preacher in *The Cattle Killing*, which he effects through the power of story (a form of memory) and the conjunction of story and being. As he explains it, "memory," "return," and "stories" are inextricably bound into one (55), and through this fusion he is transported to Africa where he is reunited with (metamorphoses into) one of his other selves (Liam) and briefly is repositioned in the unity of Being (143–44).

In some diasporan novels (though seldom in contemporary fictional slave narratives) the American South and other Western locales serve the same symbolic function as geographic Africa. There are a few variations on this standard formation. For example, Nash Williams considers the American South home (*Crossing the River* 35), but for him home is the material white South rather than the spiritual black South. For many another diasporan subject, in the example of Toomer/Kabnis, the American South is the symbolic Africa in the West, and the subject's re-turn home is to this spiritual Western landscape. In the majority of these formations, a primal parent who is symbol, flesh, or spirit of the primordial African past (for example, Father John in *Cane* 217) facilitates the subject's journey toward complete wholeness, to a resumption of his or her true nature. The narrative formation turns on the subject's geospiritual journey to what in *Cane* Toomer calls "the soil of one's [American] ancestors"—that is, the South (31). The "soil of [one's] homeland" (*Cane* 85) has restorative powers for the subject, part of which includes the restoration of *connaissance.* In such formations the southern "soil" is literal and figural, simultaneously a physical, psychological, and spiritual landscape. In some novels, such as *Cane,* the spiritual space that helps restore a diasporan subject's true nature is designated as Georgia; in others it is specified as the entire geographic South or as a region of it (though rarely Mississippi or Alabama). Whatever the southern space (often that of a subject's origin) in a given novel, it represents his or her spiritual home. One of the most innovative diasporan novels to conflate the literal and the figural, the physical and the spiritual, and to fuse geography with epistemology and ontology is *Louisiana.*

The geospiritual re-turn home as a ritual for regeneration is also a standard formation in novels by and about blacks whose Western home is not in the United States. Marshall's *Praisesong for the Widow* is illustrative of the meaning embodied in the configuration this formation assumes in African Caribbean and African British literature texts. *Praisesong*'s Avey Johnson does not re-turn to the physical place of her most immediate Western ancestral origin (Tatem Island, South Carolina) but to the Caribbean, a mediating cultural and spiritual space between Africa and the United States. In African Caribbean culture, particularly in language (Patois), Avey Johnson finds common spiritual ground between coastal South Carolina and the Caribbean. As she expresses it, "These [Caribbean] strangers . . . become one and the same with people in Tatem" (250). The same kind of spiritual nexus across cultural spaces is conveyed through the dancing of nations in the novel that links the Caribbean (Carriacou, in this instance) to Africa. Dancing the nations is part of the Big Drum, a ritual in the novel that reaffirms the interconnectedness of African nations under the larger cultural banner of African (or black) tribe, that rekindles the spiritual unity of diasporan subjects descended from different African nations, and that rejuvenates one's intersubjectivity. Earl Lovelace includes a similar ritual of nation dancing in *Salt* (5).

Western materialism was the most immediate catalyst for Avey's partitioning. Her disavowal of this materialism and her ritual "remembrance" (Marshall's term, 166) of her primordial origin begin her movement from partitionedness to wholeness. An androgynous primal parent named Lebert Joseph becomes her ritual guide and facilitates her inadvertent sojourn that evolves into her spiritual quest for complete wholeness. Joseph is an exemplar of primal parentage. He is "the oldest one still living from that part of the island" (Carriacou), and the islanders call him "father or uncle or grandfather, granduncle or great-grand father or cousin or something" (163) out of reverence for his age, wisdom, and special powers. Indeed, like *Cane*'s Father John, Joseph "possess[es] *connaissance*" (218, 246), which for Joseph includes "memories that had come down to him in the blood" (178). His epistemological and ontological features are primordial. The essence of the primordial and the primal parents (whom Joseph calls the "Old Parents" and the "Long-time People") inhere in Joseph, and he passes this essence on to his daughter Rosalie Parvay (218). Part of this essence is androgyny, and Rosalie, who also possesses *connaissance,* appears to "have sprung whole from his head, a head-birth without benefit or need of a mother; an idea made flesh" (216).

One of the elderly women who participates in the dancing of nations, "Bercita Edwards of Smooth Water Bay, Carriacou," is also an androgynous primal parent, "an old woman who was at once an old man" (251). She, too, is an idea made flesh. The brief exchange between her and "Avey, short for Avatara" (251), reveals that Avey also is an idea made flesh—an incarnation, as her name indicates. *Avatara* derives from *avatar,* which refers to the incarnation of a Hindu deity, especially Vishnu, in human or animal form. Avey's name links her spiritually to the islanders at the Big Drum as well as to the "Old Parents" and the "Long-time People," who are avatars in that the Primordial Soul is housed in the human form of the islanders and in the animal forms into which the "Old Parents" and the "Long-time People" have shape-shifted (238–39). As her name indicates, Avey is a human host for the Primordial Soul as well as an archetype for diasporan subjects who consciously or subconsciously desire to re-turn home.

Another part of the essence of Western black Being is that those who possess the "special powers of seeing and knowing" (218) can assist diasporan subjects who are seeking rebirth, which is what Lebert Joseph and his daughter do for Avey Johnson. For example, recognizing her movement toward wholeness, Avey explains that Rosalie Parvay's role "has been putting me back together again" (229). Once she regains wholeness, Avey is positioned to acquire complete wholeness.

In several African Caribbean and African British novels, the subject's re-turn is to his or her physical place of origin in the Caribbean. In most instances the re-turn is not as regenerative as it is for Avey Johnson, for the subject's diasporization has been so thorough that regeneration is difficult if not almost impossible. Prominent examples include the female centered subject in Joan Riley's *The Unbelonging* (1985) and Moses Aloetta in the third novel, *Moses Migrating* (1983), of Samuel Selvon's trilogy. Together, the novels in this trilogy, which include *The Lonely Londoners* (1956) and *Moses Ascending* (1975), treat several facets of Western blacks' diasporization through the formation of the centered subject and several secondary subjects.

A diasporan subject's (re)acquisition of complete wholeness is a rebirth. The subject's reunification with the essence or source of his or her Being effects this rebirth, what Toomer explains as "a birth *above / the body,* and hence a birth *above* Nature, into / spheres which are characteristically *human* and / at the same time *universal*" (*Wayward* 430; Toomer's emphasis). For this rebirth to occur, the subject must have regained the proper balance between body (materiality) and soul (spirituality). Kabnis (*Cane*) and Avey Johnson are examples of subjects who regain this balance and thus ones who are reborn. In these two novels a primal parent, who is both a spiritual guide and a representative of the source of black Being, facilitates the respective subject's rebirth.

In *Cane,* the character Lewis, a southern migrant who re-turns home, "merges with his source [Father John] and lets the pain and beauty of the South meet him there" (214). It is a wedding of geography and ontology. Following Lewis's example, Kabnis embraces Father John and thus is reborn. Avey Johnson's rebirth is in a similar fashion. Her sojourn in Carriacou is in effect a re-turn to the sacred soil of her ancestors, which begins the restoration of her true nature. In *Cane* and *Praisesong,* as in *Flight to Canada, Middle Passage, Louisiana,* and some other diasporan novels, the diasporan subject evolves from pupil to teacher, from pilgrim to spiritual guide. For example, following their rebirths, Kabnis, Avey, and Louisiana become spiritual messengers who attempt to show other diasporan subjects the route home (note Kabnis's function in *Cane* and the story that follows the narrative's end; *Praisesong* 254–56; and *Louisiana* 124–25, 136).

The biocultural nexus between Lebert Joseph and his daughter Rosalie Parvay reveals that the essence of primordial Being is a transmissible sociogenetic feature. Yet as the generations of diasporan subjects come and go and they become increasingly Westernized, their capacity for the rebirth of self is diminished. Nevertheless, as the formation of both Ralph Kabnis and Avey Johnson indicates, there is hope. There is a "seed" (*Cane*'s "Song of the Son") from which this essence can germinate. There are "threads" (*Wayward* 423; *Praisesong* 249) from which the fabric of primordial black Being can be rewoven; in *Stigmata,* these "threads" are both literal and figural. As the "author" of *Cane,* Kabnis becomes the embodiment of the Primordial Soul and the son who sings the others into authentic Being. The same is true for Avatara Johnson, who vows that on her return to New York she will become a guide for other diasporan blacks who have lost their way, those who rush "blindly in and out of the glacier buildings, unaware, unprotected, lacking memory and a necessary distance of the mind" (255). Indeed, part of the dilemma for some diasporan subjects in diasporan novels is that time and circumstance have all but erased their capacity for rebirth, which results in these subjects undergoing a never-ending quest for complete wholeness. The erasure is incomplete, however. A trace, a seed, or a thread remains, and thus it is a condition of *sous rature* in that what ostensibly has been erased is still discernible, if only barely.[16] This means that a trace of primordial black Being remains in each diasporan subject, that a "signpost" (Phillips's term) directing the diasporan subject back to his or her true nature is visible if the subject is willing and able to see. (For Wideman in *The Cattle Killing,* this trace manifests as "story," if one is willing to listen.)

Several subjects in post-1975 diasporan novels who begin the rebirthing process never bring it to closure within the novel's time frame. Many of those who do achieve wholeness never achieve the ultimate object of their desire, complete wholeness. Authors often inscribe complete wholeness as the fusion of a self and an other, and they use it as a signal that the subject is repositioned in the unity of Being. Though the fusion of the self and the self's other is part of Aristophanes's explanation of the birth of love and desire (*Symposium* 87–89), Toomer's explanation of this fusion more nearly fits praxis in diasporan novels' inscription of mythopoeic reality.

In section 3 ("Split Men") of the 400-page manuscript appropriately entitled "Remember and Return," Toomer foregrounds the idea of generic man as a bisected and partitioned being: "We are split men, disconnected from our own resources, / almost severed from our *Selves,* / and therefore out of contact with reality." He asserts that though man is bisected and partitioned, there are traces ("threads") of wholeness and complete wholeness, however fragile and slight they may be, that still connect the parts of generic man's partitioned self and the components of man's original whole Self. Otherwise, according to Toomer, there would be "no contradictions between our actual behavior and / the ideal state of being." In other words, the condition of *sous rature* obtains. As long as these threads (which include instinct, knowledge, and memory, among other qualities) obtain, there is possibility for regaining wholeness and complete wholeness, for with these threads we can "bridge the gap" between our disparate parts "and re-member ourselves" (*Wayward* 413–14, 423–30).

The formation of Ralph Kabnis and Avey Johnson as subjects exemplifies the premise that the bisection of the Self and the consequent partitioning of the self created a division between body and soul, with the self's body being "the lesser divorced part." According to Toomer, because we locate our essence in this lesser (or material) part rather than in the greater (or spiritual) part, we are, therefore, "out of life." The African diasporan subject, therefore, is "an exile, an orphan, out of touch with 'something' [the soul/Soul] he ought to be in touch with." Moreover, "because of this split," the subject is ruled by "deep drives [desires] . . . to get in touch, to enter into life [the unity of Being]." Yet often this hunger for complete wholeness—those "deep drives" for re-membering and re-turning—is so compelling that the subjects misdirect their pursuit of the ultimate object of desire. In the example of Avey Johnson before she is widowed, they confuse the material with the spiritual, the body with the soul; they turn outward in pursuit of what is internal, falsely "believing that [they] can / enter *into* life by driving *outward.*" Though the movement of this pursuit is "logical," it is, nevertheless, fatal for diasporan subjects to believe "that what [they] desire is to be gained by going *out* / after it."

According to Toomer, one way for diasporan subjects to achieve complete wholeness is by "re-turning our drives so that instead of seeking / out we seek *in* for contact with the Greater Part [Soul], which now is and always has been *within* life, awaiting our union with it, even while conscious—we exist in exile." We must reunite with the primordial African

Soul: "Thus and thus only will we re-member ourselves and / become *whole* men aiming to become *complete* whole / men" (*Wayward* 423–30).

Toomer's ideas about balance (an equilibrium of a self's physical and spiritual sides) and fusion (the sexual and spiritual integration of two selves—conjugal complementarity) provide a gloss for narrative formations in diasporan novels that treat romantic relationships between males and females as well as between subjects of the same gender. Detailed treatments of these relationships more often are in female-centered than in male-centered novels. Most of these treatments depict two subjects, at least one of whom suffers from a fissure between body and soul, between materiality and spirituality, which hampers her or his fusion with another subject. The typical case is that the male subject is grounded in a material existence and the female subject either is balanced or is anchored in a spiritual reality to the neglect of her physical side. Because an unbalanced subject cannot fuse harmoniously with another unbalanced subject or with a balanced one, each subject's desire for complete wholeness remains unfulfilled.

Among Western black writers, Toomer provides probably the most detailed explanation of this aspect of black Being, particularly in writings that were not published during his life. One such work is the prose-like poem "Sing Yes!" which states the concept of complete wholeness so explicitly that its first two stanzas bear quoting in their entirety:

> Each being, each life may find his or her perfect correspondence, the other self. Each man may meet the woman who answers him. To meet without is to meet within. Each woman may meet the man who answers her. To meet within is to meet without. The eyes open, the heart trembles and is stilled. Incredulous recognition! With his whole being each feels the authentic shock of the other. The spirit is raised and humbled. We want to weep, we want to sing. What beauty! What unutterable beauty!
>
> No one else has ever seen us, no one else has ever known us, no one else has ever claimed us. Now we are seen and known and claimed. This person comes to liberate us, to energize the deepest unimagined reaches of our soul. And he or she becomes a sacred presence. When being meets being, a cosmic note is struck. When man meets woman, a being note is struck. It is then we love. (*Wayward* 205)

This theory of fully regenerating the self through fusion with the self's subject complement is one of the narrative anchors of *Cane.* It is also a major thematic and structural formation in several contemporary fictional slave narratives, especially in female-centered ones. Female-centered novels in the subgenre that use sexual fusion to explore the concept of complete wholeness are not instances of the negative adage that a woman needs a man to be complete, an adage ostensibly disparaged in some interpretations of works by Terry McMillan, Alice Walker, Toni Morrison, Gloria Naylor, and several other womanist writers. The negativity of this adage places emphasis on the man rather than on the woman. The positive reading of the adage centers the woman, as does Morrison in *Sula* and in *Beloved* and Naylor in *The Women of Brewster Place. Beloved* inscribes the relationship Sethe has with two men in her life, Hally and Paul D. It is Sethe's relationship with Paul D that helps move her closer to realizing that she (not a man or any other beloved) is her own "best thing" (273). The problem articulated in several unsuccessful migrations of the heart in female-centered diasporan novels is the female subject's view of man as the direct object rather than the mediation of her desire. Ursa Corregidora, the centered subject in Gayl Jones's *Corregidora,* is a prime example of the destructive and lasting effects of this misplaced desire.

Though male authors of contemporary fictional slave narratives treat love relationships in a similar way, fusion is seldom a key component of plot structure in a male-centered novel. Charles Johnson's *Oxherding Tale* and *Middle Passage* include romantic relationships. Yet Andrew Hawkins's marriage to Peggy Underwood is not an instance of the fusion between the male self and his female other, and at the end of his journey toward an authentic identity, Hawkins remains a subject who lacks complete wholeness. So, too, does complete wholeness elude Raven Quickskill in *Flight to Canada.* And though in *Middle Passage* Rutherford Calhoun achieves wholeness of self, the novel's concluding paragraphs are ambiguous about whether his relationship with Isadora Bailey is an instance of the fusion between subject and subject complement. These and several other diasporan male subjects in masculinist novels regain wholeness, but the vast majority never seek nor have conscious knowledge of a desire (given the respective novel's content) for complete wholeness. Among the few exceptions is *The Cattle Killing.*

Feeding the Gods

A fully diasporized Western black subject is one who is unpositioned in the unity of Being, a partitioned self whose intersubjective bond with other beings in the visible and invisible worlds and with the Supreme Being has been fractured. To mend this fracture the diasporized subject must reactivate his or her dormant soul in a manner that will lead to wholeness, complete wholeness, and a repositioning in the unity of Being. The reactivation requires a subject to feed the gods. In this sense, *gods* is a comprehensive term that is inclusive of the soul that dwells in humans, in spirits, and in the Supreme Being. Some African societies and some contemporary slave narratives and diasporan novels use the terms *soul* and *spirit* interchangeably and posit that this spirit-soul dwells within and without the subject. As a concept, feeding the gods can be traced to traditional African societies. Narrative formations of this concept appear in *Cane* and in several contemporary fictional slave narratives and other diasporan novels.

Stephen Ezeanya explains that in African societies the "Supreme God, a multitude of lesser divinities and spirits, the ancestral spirits, and evil spirits" constitute "the world of spirits" ("Gods, Spirits and the Spirit World" 35). He also points out that "the world of men and the world of spirits are not two independent worlds" but "complementary" ones. Ezeanya notes that "man has need of the spirit-world, while the minor spirits have need of men to gladden their hearts, to *feed* them with fat things" (36; emphasis added). It is the soul that links humans to entities in the spirit world. For humans to maintain this link, they must feed the gods, and to feed the gods is to feed the self, for indeed this interdependent relationship requires mutual sustenance.

In contemporary fictional slave narratives and other diasporan novels, images and formations of feeding, eating, ingestion, and regurgitation are part of the tropology of feeding the gods. In such texts the concept generally means that for diasporan subjects to maintain their true spiritual nature, they must feed these "spiritual beings" (Ezeanya's term, 35), who in turn protect the diasporan subjects by helping sustain their true nature. Toomer includes the formation in *Cane* by having Carrie Kate (206, 233), Lewis, and eventually Kabnis feed Father John, who, in Toomer's words, is flesh, symbol, and spirit of the past (217). In articulating his own dilemma, Kabnis notes that it is his "soul that needs the risin'" (234), that he needs and "want[s] t feed th soul," "got t feed it" (224). Kabnis feeds Father John and

Father John in turn feeds Kabnis's soul, what Kabnis refers to as "that ornery thing thats livin on my insides" (231). The mutual feeding is a rejuvenating experience for Kabnis. The feeding of Father John in *Cane* is both literal and figural and is one of the foundations for literal and figural formations of feeding the gods in contemporary fictional slave narratives and other diasporan novels.

Reed's *Flight to Canada* incorporates a figural form of this conceptual formation. Reed notes that the African gods abandon those diasporan subjects who out of "stupidity" embrace diasporization; they lose recognition of and thus fail to feed the gods. The gods, in turn, become "mean and demanding. They want to be fed. But before you can feed you have to recognize" (8). Johnson's *Middle Passage* also contains a figural form of this concept. Having also captured an Allmuseri god and housed the god below deck, the slave traders on the *Republic* direct that "no one is to feed the new cargo" (67). Once the Allmuseri mutiny and take over the ship, each goes "below to feed their god" (155). Before Rutherford Calhoun's (the narrator's) diasporization is significantly reversed, he ponders, "But on what did it feed? . . . None had taken food" (166). Calhoun points out that the feeding of the Allmuseri god is not of "food" but is an affirmation of the concept of the unity of Being, similar to what Mulago calls "vital participation" and defines in part as "that concentric and harmonic unity of the visible and invisible worlds" (145). Feeding the Allmuseri god is a symbolic action that recalls subjects in *Cane* descending into "The Hole" that is Father John's "home" (195) in order to feed him. For the Allmuseri, this ritual feeding of the god is an apparent effort to reverse their own diasporization. It is a ritual in which the white Tommy O'Toole also engages.

In *Praisesong*, Marshall associates this ritual of feeding the gods with a Ghanaian practice of feeding the ancestors (188), and in this novel the ancestors (the "Old Parents"), some of whom are "visible" in shape-shifted form and some of whom are "invisible," are inhabitants of the spiritual world (238–39). In the novel's opening chapters it is clear that Avey Johnson has lost a spiritual connection with her African past, her ancestral nation, and has become diasporized through her embracing of Western materialism. Her vomiting episode later in the novel is one signification that she can reverse her diasporization. Purging herself of food that she has ingested is figurally a purging of her false nature in preparation for assuming her true nature (204–9). The formation suggests an inverse of one in

Cane in which Kabnis was offered but then "vomited" a reflection (or twin) of his true self, embodied in Lewis (200).

Morrison's variation of this concept in *Beloved* is a blending of figural and literal feeding/eating. The interdependent relationship between Sethe and Beloved (when viewed as a spirit inhabiting an adult human host) is one of mutual protection. When the "evil" side of Beloved emerges, she becomes selfish, eating (literally) voraciously while Sethe is denied and denies herself food. Literal and figural images of hunger, desire, food, and eating abound in this novel, as they do in *Cane*. Sethe's lack of food is a signification of her diminishing and unbalanced spiritual connection with Beloved. "The flesh between her . . . forefinger and thumb [becomes as] thin as China silk" (239). Her withering body is a reflection of her withering soul, a formation that recalls one in *Cane* in which Kabnis's withering body reflects his withering soul (for instance, 180–81).

Part of the character Beloved's hunger/desire is for "the join," which would fuse her with Sethe as a primordial Self. One means of satiating her hunger/desire is through knowledge of the past, through storytelling. "Sethe learned the profound satisfaction Beloved got from storytelling," and thus storytelling "became a way to feed her" (58). This metaphor in *Beloved* expands into a trope in Wideman's *The Cattle Killing*, a novel in which storytelling is the chief mechanism to effect the join. *The Cattle Killing* succinctly expresses the meaning of this concept of feeding the gods as contemporary fictional slave narratives incorporate it: to feed the spirit without is to feed the spirit within, and vice versa. Wideman uses "the light" within/without as synonymous with the spirit within/without, and he asserts that the light within must be fed in order to be sustained (20). In this regard gods, spirits, and ancestors who become spirits all belong to what Wideman calls "the world of special seeing" (76). A variation of this formation is in Brodber's *Louisiana*. The title character's change of diet is concomitant with her being (re)positioned within the unity of Being through her fusion with the spirits of Anna and Louise. For example, after she becomes a vegetarian she travels to a nearby market to shop for these foods, and on these "vegetable days" she has especially meaningful conversations with Anna's spirit (115). Louisiana's "vegetable days" are ones of ritual storytelling; Anna is the teller and she is the listener.

Storytelling as a means of feeding the gods, of nurturing the spirit-soul within and without, is one of the tropological functions of contemporary fictional slave narratives and other diasporan novels. Again, Toomer/Kabnis, *Cane*'s eye/I, is a foundational exemplar. Having rejuvenated his soul, this eye/I engages in storytelling, the result of which is the novel *Cane*. This process of writing the self's others, of feeding the gods, is the process of writing the self. It is a premise that Wideman states in the opening section of *The Cattle Killing* and one that Johnson dramatizes through Rutherford Calhoun's writing of his manuscript in *Middle Passage*. As Morrison explains (particularly in reference to her writing of *Beloved*), storytelling, this form of feeding the gods within and without, gives her "access" to her own interior life as well as to the interior lives of her subjects ("Site of Memory" 115–17). Brodber states the premise as well as dramatizes it in *Louisiana*. The manuscript Ella writes (and perhaps the novel Brodber writes) is her "story too. It is the story of the conduit, the scribe as much as that of the actors" (165).

3 Modalities of Rememory
The Womanist Project

Attempting to bring some psychological and spiritual stability to her life, Elizabeth Joyce ("Lizzie") DuBose, the subject centered in Phyllis Alesia Perry's *Stigmata*, begins an appliqué quilting project in 1995 that will narrativize segments of her grandmother's, Grace Lancaster's, life. Attempting to escape the psychological and physical pains of remembering the diasporized experiences of her own grandmother, Ayo (Bessie Ward), Grace leaves her husband, children, siblings, and other relatives in Alabama in 1940, moves to the North, and is "never seen alive by her family again" (9). Literally and figuratively, Lizzie's "quilt project" (93), like her painting project at the novel's end (235), is a symbolic action to effect healing and wholeness for her foremothers and for herself. Lizzie's sewing of the appliqué quilt parallels the suturing of her wounded body and soul. Ultimately, Lizzie's narrative quilting project seeks to reunite as one Self several generations of the female bloodline to which she belongs, a bloodline that in this novel goes back to Ayo's mother and grandmother in Africa before Ayo became a victim of the Middle Passage, probably in the middle to late 1830s (50). This narrative quilting project is one that Lizzie shares with her mother in the novel, with the author of this novel, and with several other black female subjects and authors.

The womanist project in most diasporan novels intends to liberate the black female self from deforming Western discourses and to initiate the process of restoring her to her primordial state of Being. Rememory is the discursive device many of the novelists use for this rescue and restoration. For the purposes of this discussion, rememory as a conceptual framework is a conjunction of memory and re-membering, and it is integral to the narrative strategy of several female-centered diasporan novels. In such novels the power of memory—author's, narrator's, or centered subject's—situates the centered subject's story within the historical plight of her gender and race and reveals the principal sources of her self's partitioning. Memory engenders a healing process whose goals are the harmonious re-alignment (re-membering) of the subject's disparate parts and the subject's spiritual reconnection to her genetic and her sociogenic female kin, to her primal (Western) and her primordial (African) parents, and to the Primordial Soul. However, not all the female subjects centered in diasporan novels achieve these goals. Nevertheless, the conjunction of memory and re-membering reveals desire (conscious or subconscious) as the subject's ruling passion. Rememory, then, forms the foundation for narrative scaffolding in the production of several womanist novels that are diasporan.

Especially in post-1975 fictional slave narratives, rememory is a narrative process that proffers a psychohistorical relationship between the female author and her centered female subject. This mental, empathetic nexus between the two is so intimate that the author *knows* the black centered subject she (re)creates.[1] Consequently, through her creative imagination the author is able to evoke, to reproduce, and to convey her subject's thoughts, feelings, motives, and actions truthfully, despite any temporal and spatial distances between the two. It is, therefore, a novelistic praxis that emanates from the e-motion rather than from the intellect, and it manifests as a fictive discourse that flows subjectively rather than from self-conscious intellectual effort. Thus, it is grounded in an oral rather than in a written literary tradition.

By no means is this to suggest that the womanist author effects her project without a high degree of intellectual acumen and novelistic skill. It is to note, however, that content in the womanist novel seldom prominently displays through referentiality or any other fictive device the workings of the author's intellect in the production (conception and execution) of the text. Among the diasporan novels this study discusses, only Erna Brodber (*Louisiana*) and Octavia Butler (*Kindred*) construct a female centered subject whose intellect approximates the author's. In both novels the respective centered subject is a college-educated writer (not a slave, as in Reed's *Flight* or Johnson's novels),[2] and the respective novel's limited use of referentiality and intertextuality is confined primarily to the twentieth-century period in which it is set. This is especially the case in *Louisiana*.

Jean-Paul Sartre states that "emotion is a certain way of apprehending the world" (*Emotions* 52), and he uses the concept to distinguish between how Africans and Europeans apprehend the world.[3] In his essay "On Negrohood: Psychology of the African Negro," Léopold Senghor defines e-motion as "*the rise of consciousness to a higher state of knowledge*" (15; Senghor's emphasis). It emanates from an epistemology and an ontology anchored in the mystical, a situation in which, according to Sartre, "the affected subject and the affective object are bound in an indissoluble synthesis" (*Emotions* 52). As Senghor explains, "The attitude towards the *object*—towards the external world, the *Other*—[is what] characterizes a people, and thereby their culture" (2; Senghor's emphasis). Senghor and Sartre agree that Europeans and Africans differ in their attitudes toward the external world and thus they differ culturally. Germane to this difference is that European subjectivity is marked by what Senghor calls an "*objective intelligence*" (2; Senghor's emphasis) that creates and maintains temporal and spatial distances between the perceiver (subject) and the perceived (object). The European perceiver's relationship to the perceived is analytical and factual ("On Negrohood" 2); it is historical. The African perceiver's relationship to the perceived is "*intuitive*," "primordial" (8, 3; Senghor's emphasis). Temporal and spatial distances between the perceiver and the perceived—"tree or pebble, man or animal, fact of nature or society" (3)—are not a factor because perceiver and perceived are intertwined in the unity of Being. Thus, Senghor and Sartre conclude that the intellect characterizes European subjectivity and the e-motion characterizes African subjectivity. These differences manifest in how the European and the African perceive and represent the external world in literary discourse.

Sartre and Senghor's e-motion/intellect paradigm, with slight modifications, is useful for distinguishing between ways black female and black male authors perceive, understand, and fictively represent the world—more specifically, for distinguishing between different forms of gendered discourse in the contemporary diasporan novel (especially the contemporary fictional slave narrative) without asserting that one form is superior to the other. To be sure, e-motion and intellect are features in the production of both womanist and masculinist texts; the differences between these gendered discourses hinge on whether the text's production foregrounds the e-motion or the intellect. As Jean Toomer indicates, the intellect and the e-motions—the "brilliance" and the "glow," respectively—are complementary aspects in his literary consciousness and thus in his literary productions (Kerman, *Lives* 126). Brilliance and glow are related terms yet ones distinct in meaning. Adapting Toomer's statement for a characterization of gendered discourse in the contemporary fictional slave narrative, one might say that masculinist discourse glows from the manner in which the author foregrounds the intellect, and womanist discourse's brilliance emanates from the manner in which it privileges the e-motion. Thus, the presence of one does not mean the absence of the other.

Sartre's statement (quoted above) about the emotive relationship between the perceiver and the perceived, which binds them in an indissoluble synthesis, is a salient description of the relationship between several womanist novelists and their female centered subjects, a relationship not typical of black masculinist novelists and their male centered subjects. This indissoluble synthesis is the heart of plot structure, subject formations, and themes in Brodber's *Louisiana*. The emotive bond between Brodber and her novel's title character is duplicated and expanded in the one that develops between Louisiana and the principal subject (Sue Anna King Grant) of the text Louisiana writes. Within the novel the power of memory defies Western notions of temporal and spatial boundaries, engenders a re-membering of the novel's centered subject and some of its secondary subjects, establishes an emotive bond between the centered subject and the subjects (female and male) of her text, and thus foregrounds rememory as the discursive device that rescues and repositions the novel's diasporan subjects within the unity of Being.

The emotive nexus between author and centered subject in a diasporan novel often is an instance of dancing the other. In "On Negrohood," Senghor provides an operational definition of the concept: "To dance is to discover and to *re-create*, to identify oneself with the forces of life, to lead a fuller life, and in short, to *be*. It is, at any rate, the highest form of knowledge" (6; Senghor's emphasis). Through a trace of the other's existence, the author (re)discovers and (re)creates both the other and herself or himself; it is a ritual merging (through the act of writing) of epistemology and ontology.[4] Senghor's revision of a well-known Cartesian premise ("I think, therefore I am") in the distinction he makes between a Eurocentric and an

Afrocentric subjectivity is particularly applicable to the epistemological and ontological relationship between the womanist author and her female subject. It is dancing the other, not thinking, that allows the author to know "I am" (see "On Negrohood" 6).

An author dancing her other effects a reciprocal relationship between author and subject. The construct is, therefore, simultaneously an action and a state of being. Through writing as a creative process, the author (re)-discovers and (re)creates the authenticity not only of her subject's Being but also of her own Being.[5] It is an act of creativity and of creation in which both author and subject transform from partitioned selves to whole and intersubjective selves. From the purview of the diasporan myth, author and subject are extensions of the severed halves of a primordial female Self who was bisected during primordial Time. Most female-centered diasporan novels include the concept of serial bisectioning, and thus they proffer not only an emotive nexus the author has with the novel's centered subject but also an emotive nexus these two share with other female selves who are extensions from a primordial Self (*Beloved, Linden Hills, Stigmata,* and *Louisiana* are examples). The author, centered subject, and the other selves share a consciousness (twin souls) and a similarity in experiential reality. One knows the other(s); they are subject complements. As Toomer explains, when they (re)discover each other, "each feels the authentic . . . other" and "Being *knows* being" (*Wayward* 205; emphasis added). Rememory as an epistemological and ontological process is initiated. Having been partitioned during historical time, the selves begin to be re-membered, the component selves are reunited and thus move toward complete wholeness. From this purview, rememory is both a mental and a discursive process of reconstituting the partitioned female self as a whole and authentic (primordial) Being.

The initial contact—or (re)meeting—between Sherley Anne Williams and a slave woman named Dinah (the fictional Dessa Rose) and that between Toni Morrison and Margaret Garner (the fictional Sethe Garner) was between emoved subjects (perceiving authors) and emoving objects (perceived subjects).[6] In both instances the (re)meetings were effected through textual representations (traces or remains) of the perceived subjects. Through the author's e-motion this seminal contact transformed both the perceiver and the perceived and melded them into one Self. Drawing upon Sartre's definition of Négritude (Negrohood) as "a certain affective attitude towards the world" (10), Senghor's explanation of the black African's (male and female) "*emotive attitude* towards the world" (15; Senghor's emphasis), and particularly toward another self, is especially applicable to these two authors' emotive relationship to their respective subject as well as to the emotive relationship between author and subject in womanist novels and textually androgynous novels in general.

Such a (re)meeting stimulates the author's creative imagination. Senghor's explanation of the emotive bond between perceiver and perceived appropriately describes the creative process that reunites the womanist author with her centered subject: "Here, then, is the subject who leaves his I to *sym-pathize* with the *Thou,* and to identify himself with it. He dies to himself to be reborn in the Other. He does not assimilate it, but himself. He does not take the Other's life, but strengthens his own with its life. For he lives a communal life with the Other, and in *sym-biosis* with it: He knows [and is thus born with] it. Subject and object are dialectically confronted in the very act of knowledge [and thus of common birth]" ("On Negrohood" 6; Senghor's emphasis and translator's brackets). In other words, Williams and Morrison, respectively, found a subject complement in the historical slave woman that allowed author and subject "to realize [her] *being*" (6; Senghor's emphasis).

Toomer's explanation of what occurs when the subject (re)meets his or her "perfect correspondence" (subject complement) provides a useful gloss on what happens in the womanist project when author and subject (re)-discover each other: "With [her] whole being each feels the authentic shock of the other"; each "comes to liberate [the other], to energize the deepest unimagined reaches of [her] soul. . . . Skin knows skin. Touch knows touch. Taste knows taste. The lines, the curves, the faintest tracings and bold designs of each are known. Body knows body. Being knows being. Acceptance is complete and joyous" ("Sing Yes!"; *Wayward* 205). The author (perceiving subject) then feels, knows, dances, sings (Toomer's equivalent term for Senghor's dances), and therefore writes her other and consequently her self into authentic Being.

A diasporan novel in which dancing the other and rememory are not only conceptual frames but also narrative content is *Louisiana*. In fact, *Louisiana*'s narrative content, a melding of theory and praxis, illustrates as well as any diasporan novel the theoretical concepts of dancing the other and rememory. The novel's title is key. It signifies the conjunction of epistemology, geography, ontology, and narratology as the internal author (Ella) and her subjects (Anna and Louise), through a shared consciousness and experiential reality, (re)discover and (re)create the authenticity of self and other. They are twin selves, extensions of a bisected primordial whole female Self, and their (re)meeting facilitates each woman's acquisition of wholeness and of complete wholeness.

Because diasporization could not destroy every trace or remain of the primordial Self, a trace is all one needs to reconstruct one's other and one's self. As I stated above, Williams and Morrison (re)met their respective subject complement through a trace or a remain of her. This trace, in whatever form (and its form differs from one novelistic project to another), often is what reactivates the sociogenic nexus between an author and her female centered subject. Morrison refers to the process of using a trace of the other to reconstruct the other (and the self) as an archaeological dig ("Site of Memory" 112). Wideman calls a similar part of his writing process an excavation (L. Baker 265). Williams provides an explanation (applicable to other authors and subjects and novels) of this process and nexus in the author's note that prefaces the narrative of *Dessa Rose* (discussed more fully below). The process appropriately can be called dancing the other.

In the cultures African people forged in the West, song and dance (music and rhythmic motion) are manifestations of the soul. The ritual of singing among the diasporan subjects in *Louisiana* stimulates and reactivates the subjects' souls, signifies a shared spiritual affinity among diasporan subjects who occupy different geographic spaces in the West, and reconnects them to their Western and to their primordial home. Marshall illustrates these same principles well in the ritual of the Big Drum (specifically the ritual of nation dancing) in *Praisesong for the Widow* (165–68, 175–80, 235–51). Song and dance, therefore, are creative acts and acts of creation that (re)establish and (re)affirm the bond between the diasporan subject and the Primordial Soul. So, too, is imaginative writing, which is closely linked to singing. Reed certifies this point in *Flight to Canada* when the narrator points out that the centered subject's (Raven's) "typewriter was his drum he danced to" (89). Imaginative writing in African diasporan societies is a correlative of orature in traditional black African societies. The diasporan writer often shares some of the functions of the griot in traditional black African society in that both inscribe the bond between present and past realities and define the subject as a communal rather than an individuated self.[7]

But whether grounded in a written or an oral tradition, the narrative of diasporan subjectivity is a discourse of rememory and of desire. In both indigenous and diasporan black African cultures, singing and dancing often are ritualized discourses of desire. They are ontological constructs in which the creator and the creation are (or become) indistinguishable. Western black writers use a variety of terms to express this fusion: the singer and the song (Toomer, Ellison, Wideman, Reed); the dancer and the dance (Toomer); the worker and the work (Wideman); the teller and the listener (Wideman); the laugher and the laugh (Morrison).[8] Dancing as ritual reaffirms a spiritual bloodline not only between two (or more) selves but also between the dancer and the culture from which the dancer originally sprang. It is the melding of epistemology and ontology that Paule Marshall dramatizes in the nation dance episode of *Praisesong*. In this novel the ritual melding endows the dancer with special powers of knowing (epistemology) and being (ontology)—powers that Marshall calls "*connaissance*" and that Wideman and Brodber call "the clarity."[9]

Dancing the Other: The Examples of Williams and Morrison

The relationship between Sherley Anne Williams and her title character in *Dessa Rose* and between Toni Morrison and her centered subject in *Beloved* aptly illustrate the emotive production of the contemporary fictional slave narrative that is female centered. In the author's note to *Dessa Rose*, Williams succinctly expresses the conjunction of epistemology and ontology as it defines her emotive relation to her centered subject. For this prefatory statement she adapts a convention (an authenticating device) from the slave narrative genre and uses it to inscribe her (re)meeting with her subject complement. She first (re)met Dinah/Dessa in other texts (one by Angela Davis and one by Herbert Aptheker).[10] Through these mediating texts, Williams came to *know* and to *be* her novel's centered subject, if only metaphorically (as she indicates in the last paragraph of the author's note). This (re)contact proved to be transformative (liberating) for both. For Dinah/Dessa, it initiated the process of her transformation from historicized "object" to historical subject to authentic self, a rememory process duplicated in the novel's discursive praxis, thus allowing the novel's form and meaning to coalesce.

Among contemporary fictional slave narratives, both womanist and masculinist novels revise through refutation specific and generic texts that have deformed (partitioned) the black self. This dialogic and intertextual stance obtains regardless of the race or gender of the authors of such deforming texts. Principally through intertextual dialogics and the power of memory (author's and centered subject's), *Dessa Rose* chronicles Dessa's partitioning, her re-membering, and her (re)acquisition of wholeness and complete wholeness.

Speaking in her own voice in the author's note, Williams posits a distinction between fact and truth. She decries "a certain, critically acclaimed novel of the early seventies that travesties the as-told-to memoir of slave revolt leader Nat Turner." Her reference is to William Styron's *The Confessions of Nat Turner* (1967), which within the context of this discussion is an example of whitemale discourse. As this study employs the term, *whitemale discourse* is a race- and gender-biased hegemonic discourse. It aggrandizes ideas, actions, and qualities that through the agency of white males have come to be associated with white males, and it deprecates ideas, actions, and qualities that through the same agency have come to be associated with blacks and with women. Assuming an authoritative stance, whitemale discourse positions the white male as controller of the word and the white male perspective on reality as definitive. It advances the contentions that definitions belong to the definers, not to the defined (compare *Beloved* 190), and that a whitemale reality is the defining criterion for all other realities. Through *Dessa Rose*'s form and content, Williams refutes such contentions.

Williams installs the character Adam Nehemiah as a perpetrator and perpetuator of whitemale discourse, and her juxtaposition of Nehemiah's text and Dessa's text (a dialectic of discourse and counterdiscourse) as part of the novel's narrative strategy makes the reader aware that Nehemiah's reconstruction of the details of Dessa's life does not accurately reconstruct the truth of Dessa's experiences. Williams rhetorically and dramatically uses textual space—Nehemiah's discourse and Dessa's counterdiscourse—to indicate that historical facts and historical truths are not necessarily the same. As a white male who presumes authority over the word, Nehemiah attempts to record the facts and, from his perspective, the truth of Dessa's personal history. Dessa's story is her essence, her Being,[11] and the text Nehemiah writes and the text Dessa speaks of her personal history are at odds. By contrasting these two versions of Dessa's history, Williams indicates that Nehemiah might have recorded facts but that he did not—indeed, could not—record truth. Nehemiah's race, sociohistorical experience, gender, class, and other facets of his socially constructed self prevent him from apprehending and thus from recording the truth of Dessa's life, just as, Williams suggests, these same limitations prevented Styron from recording the truth of Nat Turner's life. Nehemiah cannot know and thus cannot dance Dessa as other.

Through the novel's intertextual dialogics, Williams emphasizes that novelists such as Styron and sociohistorical writers such as Nehemiah use facts to distort truth, and thus they construct deformed and inauthentic portraits of black subjects. She concludes her author's note by pointing out that *Dessa Rose* is a fiction, and that, while based on fact, the novel's contents are inventions. Yet in a statement that signifies the fusion of author and subject through rememory, she states that "what is [in this novel] is as true as if I myself had lived it" (x). From the author's note to *Dessa Rose*'s narrative closure, there is a steady progression from the author feeling and living to dancing (and writing) her other. Beginning with the novel's last section, author and subject speak as one voice.

The dialogic use of textual space, the thematization of point of view, the insertion of parodic intertexts, narrative formations and interpolations, and the function of a variety of discursive markers work in tandem in *Dessa Rose* along with other fictive devices not only to descry whitemale discourse's penchant for deforming black female selves but also to posit that the black woman can tell her own story more truthfully than anyone else. Among the novel's discursive markers are the respective titles and epigraphs of its three sections. These markers signal the discursive deformation and reformation of Dessa as a self, a definition of her Being that is borne out in the content of the respective sections.

The novel's first section, "The Darky," foregrounds whitemale discourse's deformation of Dessa from subject to object, from human to animal, from Being to thing—from true nature to false nature. The section thus reinscribes and negates one of the most pernicious portraits of black Being to emerge out of antebellum and early postbellum discourses on race.[12] The text that Nehemiah is writing positions Dessa at its center and defines her as darky. The title of his previous book, *The Masters' Complete Guide to Dealing with Slaves and Other Dependents* (17), suggests that essentializing blacks and women is endemic to his mental structure. His actions and a particularly revealing statement—"womanhood . . . All alike. Sluts" (255)—during the episode in which he last appears in the novel reveal Nehemiah's peculiar form of racism and misogyny (241–56).

The novel's first section thematizes point of view in a manner that establishes a dialectic of discourse and counterdiscourse. It contains four voices—Dessa's, the author's (who identifies with Dessa's point of view), Adam Nehemiah's, and the narrator's (who supports Nehemiah's point of view)—that seek to reconstruct the events of Dessa's history and from these events to construct the facts of Dessa's life and the essence of her Being. The paired voices stand in binary relation, and the merged voice of subject and subject complement constitute a discourse in opposition to whitemale discourse.

Counterpoising Dessa's text with Nehemiah's, Williams uses textual space to reveal the deformative nature of whitemale discourse. For example, after Dessa narrates an event from her experience, Nehemiah deciphers and reconstructs (10) that event to fit his preconceived notion of reality, and from these reconstructed events Nehemiah manufactures what he proffers as "the facts of the darky's history" (34). In this instance of thematized point of view conveyed through the use of textual space, Williams affirms Hayden White's premise that facts are constructed from events (43). Through the novel's thematized point of view and other of its fictive devices Williams echoes Sartre's premise (which affirmatively acknowledges Husserl) that "essences and facts are incommensurable, and one who begins his inquiry with facts will never arrive at essences" (*Emotions* 9).

It is not the case that all discourses on race and slavery by white males are deformative discourses, as Williams suggests by corroborating Herbert Aptheker's text about Dinah and by installing Herman Melville's *Benito Cereno* as an intertext in her construction of Wilson, the slave trader (14–15). Nor is it the case that all whitemale discourse is written by a white male, as Williams indicates through her interpolation of an event that she uses in part to signify upon Stowe's *Uncle Tom's Cabin* (20–21) and other romantic novels about slavery (35) as well as in her installation of Douglass's 1845 *Narrative* as a parodic intertext.[13]

The thematization of point of view in the novel's first section asserts that males, whether white or black, have not danced, perhaps cannot dance, the black slave woman as other.[14] While race, gender, and other facets of their socially constructed selves make virtually all white males incapable of this task, difference in gender (and therefore perspective) places limitations on black males' ability to dance a black female as the other.[15] For example, the novel's construction of Dessa Rose's subjectivity is an implicit refutation of David Walker's inscription of the slave woman, Dinah, on whom Williams bases the character Dessa, and Williams uses Douglass's 1845 *Narrative* in this novel's content to underscore this point.[16]

Signifying on an important discursive marker from Douglass's *Narrative*—"You have seen how a man was made a slave" (77)—the epigraph for *Dessa Rose*'s first section suggests that the reader of this novel will see how a *woman* was made a slave (a human deformity). Indeed, the majority of book-length extant slave narratives are by and about males, and thus the classic slave narrative is black masculinist discourse, of which Douglass's *Narrative* is a prime example. Douglass discursively reinvents himself in the mold of the mythic American white male. To underscore his defiance, rugged independence, and other qualities of socially constructed maleness, he concomitantly veils his portraits of slave women and diminishes the roles they and others played in effecting his transformation from property to person, from slavery to freedom.[17] Though in *Dessa Rose* the male slaves who tell Dessa's story give her full credit for helping effect her and their freedom from the slave coffle, they, and other blacks, fail to provide an accurate portrait of her Being because they romanticize her (52 and 158, for instance). The harrowing diasporization process has altered Dessa's subjectivity to the point that, in her words, she has "become a self she scarcely [knows]" (56). Williams's point is that regardless of intent (to deform or to romanticize), a male discourse is insufficient to write or to speak—that is, to dance—the slave woman into authentic Being.

The epigraph that begins the novel's second section, a quotation from Sojourner Truth's *Narrative*, provides further commentary on the black woman's role in the community of slaves and stands in dialogic opposition to the epigraph of the novel's first section.[18] This section draws into focus the re-membering of her partitioned self and her gradual movement toward wholeness. Entitled "The Wench," an appellation that Dessa and Rufel (mistress of Sutton's Glen plantation) use for each other, this section foregrounds and invalidates a male-defined womanhood. Though both women eventually reject a male definition of their gender (of self and of an other) and by the end of the novel transcend differences in class to form a close and lasting friendship, the novel's second and third sections demonstrate that gender alone is insufficient for a self to dance the other. Dessa and Rufel come to understand but not to *know* each other. The power of race as a social construct prevents them from bonding hermetically as selves of the same Being, and thus one is not the other's true subject complement. Though their meeting as a liberating act for both women goes beyond the level of the literal, it does not reach the level of the transcendental. Neither can dance the other.

Like other womanist novelists, Williams gives her own signature to the concept and discursive technique of rememory, which includes gender bonding as a liberating act. While *Dessa Rose* is a novel primarily about the self-emancipation and thus self-actualization of the slave as woman, it is secondarily about the self-emancipation of the plantation mistress, and the two emancipations are intertwined. To convey this, Williams uses prison as a trope, and she proceeds to liberate both Dessa Rose and Rufel from physical, psychological, and textual prisons. The physical structures in which Dessa is incarcerated near the novel's beginning and near its end provide a frame for the narrative of her movement from "that prison house" of slavery (220–21) to the open space of freedom (the symbolic American West). These physical structures also reflect Dessa's psychological imprisonment, which causes her to linger behind the bars of race and class that separate her from another of her gender.

As a plantation mistress who initially accepts a male-generated definition of her womanhood (a southern belle), Rufel, too, is psychologically and socially incarcerated. Yet she is not as hesitant as Dessa in recognizing the affinity the two share in the social and textual construction of their gender (see 98–101), a construction perpetrated and perpetuated largely through the plantation romance, of which, in the instance of the southern belle as a character type, John Pendleton Kennedy's *Swallow Barn* (1832) is the novelistic progenitor. In effect, Rufel's residence on Sutton's Glen—simultaneously a physical, symbolic, and psychological space in which her husband placed her—has separated her from meaningful interaction with members of her race and class. It is clear from the novel's opening and closing sections that women in the slave South have been incarcerated by whitemale discourses of history and of literature, whether those discourses have been written by women or men, by blacks or whites.

To liberate these women, black ones and white ones, ones of the past and ones of the present, Williams engages in an intertextual dialogue with and revisions of such texts as Margaret Mitchell's *Gone with the Wind* (1936) and other types of plantation romances. She revises the textual images of the antebellum woman (white and black) and redefines them. More important, perhaps, Williams creates situations in the novel that allow Dessa and Rufel to collaborate in liberating themselves from physical, psychological, and textual prisons. What these women discover is that the gender that binds them is much stronger than the social constructions of race and class that separate them. For Rufel it is the Mammy incident (119–27) and for Dessa it is the Mr. Oscar incident (214–20) that allows her to feel the life of the other by realizing the extent to which each has been subjected to male definitions of Being. Though both incidents are respective liberating moments, they do not effect the fusion of the two women.

Both *Dessa Rose* and *Beloved* include narrative formations that allow for the bonding (though not the fusion) of black women and white women in the slave South, yet the focus of both novels is on the regeneration of the black slave woman. As part of the narrative process of rememory, these authors and their black female protagonists become both the definers and the defined, the signifiers and the signified, and language gives them this power to move from sign to signified to transcendental signified. They tell their own stories. When Dessa assumes control of her own story in section 3, her language is markedly different from the language she uses in the novel's first two sections. While on the surface this might appear to be an authorial slip, it is not. Nor is it merely an indication that time and improved circumstances have brought Dessa's language closer to standard usage.

In the novel's first section Dessa is well aware of the word-definer-defined nexus. In this section Nehemiah is the controller and the definer, and Dessa, aware of her powerlessness, consciously manipulates her language as a way of diminishing Nehemiah's power over her (36–37). In the novel's second section she begins to reverse the diasporization process, however, and in the novel's third section she speaks herself into authentic Being, having traveled the narrative and experiential route from slavery to freedom. In the third section, as she progressively frees herself from textual prisons, she progressively renders Nehemiah's control of the word and of definitions null and void. Consistent with its use of prison as a trope, the novel's culminating scene is set appropriately in a jail and places in binary opposition the literal and metaphorical word of women (slave and free, black and white) against men (Nehemiah). Condé installs a similar narrative formation in *I, Tituba* by placing Tituba and Hester Prynne in the same Puritan New England jail cell. She uses the formation (setting and trope) to raise issues of race, class, and gender, and in doing so she revises both *Dessa Rose* and Nathaniel Hawthorne's *The Scarlet Letter* (*Tituba* 95–103).

In *Dessa Rose*'s third section the author fuses with her subject complement. Viewed through the lens of the diasporan myth, Williams and Dessa are now one Being, one voice; Dessa's story is Williams's story, and Dessa's voice is Williams's voice. From the purview of textual interpretation, Williams relinquishes control of Dessa's story to Dessa and thus allows Dessa to speak herself into authentic Being. From the purview of textual production, Williams is controller of the word and thus is Dessa's liberator. The relationship of Williams as author to the novel's focal female subjects exemplifies Toomer's characterization of the (re)meeting of subject and subject complements as a liberating act. Indeed, Williams dances and thus liberates her female others (including Rufel).

The quotation from Taj Mahal's "The Cajun Waltz" that prefaces the novel's third section contains a reference to dance. When placed in the context of the diasporan myth, this reference expands Williams's formation of Dessa and signals Dessa's progression from wholeness to complete wholeness, which is this section's structural design. In the womanist novel, complete wholeness typically occurs when subject and subject complement of opposite genders fuse spiritually. It is, as Toomer illustrates, a state of being that the principal characters in *Cane* desire but very few achieve. Dessa Rose, however, achieves this state twice, once in her relationship with Kaine and again in her relationship with Harker. Williams inscribes Dessa's fusion with her subject complements by using singing (music) and dancing (rhythmic motion) as controlling metaphors: "Kaine was like sunshine, like song; Harker was thunder and lightning" (209).

For Dessa the diasporization process reaches its most destructive state when it severs the bond between her and Kaine—between the lover and the beloved, between the subject and subject complement. Exponents of the peculiar institution having first destroyed Kaine's symbolic link to his primordial past (the banjo, a musical instrument that signifies the African soul), they then take Kaine's life and in doing so sever Dessa from her subject complement, rendering her even more partitioned than previously. She compares this increased state of her fragmentation to the physical deformity that signifies it: "I felt as crippled as Dante" (207–8), a young male slave whose congenital physical deformities reflect the deformative impact of the system of slavery into which he was born. The cruelties of slavery having reduced her to a state in which she feels "like an animal" (207), she initially hesitates to embrace Harker as her soul mate. But when Harker reads the deforming scars of her body not as a sign of her debasement but as a sign of her innate value (208), Dessa, in Toomer's words, sings yes.

Fusing with Harker restores that complete wholeness Dessa had known with Kaine. This fusion also brings closure to her journey from a spiritually deformed self to a spiritually reformed self. She restores the intersubjectivity of her Being. Part of this intersubjectivity lies in the intergenerational bonds between Dessa and members of her family, and it is nurtured through rituals of memory and story. Williams repeats in the novel's epilogue the emotive nexus between author and centered subject that she inscribes in the novel's prefatory author's note. Like Sherley Anne Williams, Mony (Dessa's son) tells Dessa's story "like the memories was his, stead of things he heard when he was coming up" (259). The statement intimates a kind of genetic memory, what Marshall speaks of as "memories that had come down to him in the blood" (*Praisesong* 178). More important, though, Dessa ritually passes on her own story to the subsequent generations (females and males) who through memory and re-membering will come to own themselves.

Explaining why and how she wrote her fictional slave narrative, *I, Tituba, Black Witch of Salem*, Maryse Condé describes a situation similar to Williams's production of *Dessa Rose* and Morrison's production of *Beloved*.[19] Condé (re)met the historical Tituba of Puritan New England in a text and realized that the "eclipse" of this slave woman's story/self in history texts, archives, and literature texts "was completely unjust."[20] "I decided I was going to write her story out of my own dreams," Condé explains. She felt "compelled" to use her "imagination" and "intuition" to fill in the gaps and silences about Tituba's life in "existing versions of history" texts and literature texts, to give "her a childhood, an adolescence, an old age" (199, 201). "I wanted to offer her her revenge by inventing a life such as she might perhaps have wished it to be told," Condé explains. The numerous "conversations" Condé had with Tituba while writing the novel allowed her to complete the project (200). Thus, *I, Tituba* is not, Condé maintains, a historical novel, but "just the opposite" (201–2). It is a diasporan novel about a historical subject, time, and place. *I, Tituba* "is not history for the sake of history. It is searching for one's self, searching for one's identity, searching for one's origin in order to better understand oneself" (203–4). The novel's production is exemplary of the black womanist project.

Like Williams and Condé, Toni Morrison reconnected with a female soul mate, the historical Margaret Garner, while reading a textualized and abbreviated account of this fugitive slave's ordeal.[21] From this "trace" Morrison constructed a mystical novel in which she dances Garner as her other. Her conception of Beloved the character and narrative formations within the novel bespeak the mythic view of the Western black woman as a serially bisected African Self whose component selves historical time, geographic space, deformative texts, and other circumstances partitioned and whose ruling desire is to regain complete wholeness. The emotive bond Morrison effected on (re)meeting her subject was so intimate that she, from a Senghorian perspective, *knew* and therefore reproduced the truth, rather than the facts, of Margaret Garner's thoughts, feelings, motives, and actions. She (re)discovered and (re)created Garner's Being in the form of story, filling in spaces left empty in the historical record about Garner and giving voice to Garner's silence.[22] Morrison, like Williams for Dessa Rose and Condé for Tituba, dances Margaret Garner as her other.

Dancing the other as concept, however, is not confined to *Beloved*'s author-centered subject nexus. The concept also helps elucidate salient features of subject formation, plot structure, and other of the novel's formal and thematic contours. On its most basic level of story (what is told), the novel appears to be a ghost story about a dead female child whose restless spirit (often benign, but sometimes not) or "soul" (5) haunts the house at 124 Bluestone Road for almost twenty years (3–19) before incarnating "in the flesh" of an adult (200) and attempting to reintegrate herself into the life of her genetic female kin. Beloved is this child-now-adult, spirit-now-flesh, and her closest genetic female kin are Sethe (her mother) and Denver (her sister).[23]

But *Beloved* is much more than a conventional (or even unconventional) Western ghost story. It is, indeed, a story of diasporan desire. On one of its complex levels of discourse (how the story is told), the novel is a powerful rendering of myth and history, blending fact and fabulation into mythopoeic reality. The skeleton of its mythopoeic plot structure combines the mystical and the realistic in narrating a situation in which a soul, once housed in the body of a female child who became a victim of infanticide and now housed in the body of a character referred to as Beloved, desires reunion with its twin soul, which is currently housed in the body of the character named Sethe. Beloved lacks and therefore desires "vital participation" in the life of her others.[24]

Certain African origin myths, especially ones concerning twinness, provide a gloss on the character Beloved's form and function in the novel as well as a gloss on some of the novel's formal features. The novel's textual and grammatical ambiguity, or double entendre, indicates that Beloved is not the "given name" of Sethe's dead baby (208), but a name assumed for the dead baby and for the nineteen-year-old woman referred to as Beloved and, as Denver says, for "more" (266). As Sethe points out to the adult Beloved, "I got out of jail and bought, so to speak, your name" (204). She also explains to her that the inscription on the baby Beloved's gravestone is partial: "Dearly Beloved, which is what you are to me and I don't have to be sorry about getting only one word" (184). As the narrator points out, "Everybody knew what she was called, but nobody anywhere knew her name" (274).

"Beloved," therefore, is also a descriptive quality, the state of being the beloved. As noun and adjective, the term applies not just to Sethe's dead baby and the nineteen-year-old woman but also to Sethe, Denver, and other components of the plural female Self, all of whom are (the) Beloved. When applied to the adult character referred to as Beloved, the term, as in the case of Rosalie Parvay, also names "an idea made flesh" (*Praisesong* 216).[25] The idea is that a soul inhabits different human hosts at different times and in different geographic spaces. Viewed from the lens of African mythologies, such as the Yoruba belief in Abiku and the Ibo belief in Ogbanje, this particular soul inhabits (is born in) the human form of Sethe's baby and later inhabits (is born again in) the human form of the adult character referred to as Beloved.[26] As the novel's ending suggests, this soul will inhabit yet another human host (will be born yet again in human form) at some time and in some space in the future. Indeed, Morrison suggests that the character Wild from her novel *Jazz* (1992) is in effect a human host that subsequently houses the soul that the character Beloved once housed (Carabi 43).[27]

African concepts of Being and time provide a gloss on essential features of the novel's plot structure. From a Western purview on Being and time, a dead child from the past (Beloved) remanifests (first as spirit and then as flesh) in the present and gives shape to the novel's narrative action. From an African (and diasporan) purview, Beloved as character (the living-dead) exists on the threshold between what John Mbiti in *African Religions and Philosophy* calls Sasa and Zamani time, and the novel's narrative action is situated between these two time dimensions. "Sasa is the time region in which people are conscious of their existence, and within which they project themselves both into the short future and mainly into the past (Zamani). Sasa is in itself a complete or full time dimension, with its own short future, a dynamic present, and an experienced past" (28). Mbiti states further that "Sasa generally binds individuals and their immediate environment together. It is the period of conscious living. On the other hand, Zamani is the period of the myth, giving a sense of foundation or 'security' to the Sasa period; and binding all created things" (29). The novel's narrative action, therefore, occurs in the space between Sasa and Zamani time ("the period of the myth"), and the character referred to as Beloved, in one of her novelistic functions, represents a vehicular force of memory and re-membering that facilitates the self's re-turn to the primordial "home" in order to restore the self's intersubjective nature and, thus, complete wholeness.

Though he is speaking about the common gender (gay subjects), Aristophanes's comments (in Plato's *Symposium*) about the beloved provide an interpretative gloss on Beloved's function as a force of memory and remembering in this novel. According to Aristophanes, "A beloved . . . always welcomes what is akin" (88). And indeed Sethe, Denver, and Beloved embrace one another as spiritual and genetic kin. Sethe and Denver welcome Beloved's (re)appearance (at least initially) and Beloved welcomes them. This rather mystical and potential reunion of female kin also portends the reunification of a primordial female Self's severed components. The (re)-meeting kindles the three women's flames of desire ("a hot thing"; see *Beloved* 210–13), and, in the words of Aristophanes, this desire of each is "to be united and melted together with [her] beloved, and to become one." Aristophanes states further that the reason for this desire "is that this was [their] ancient natural shape, when [they] were one whole; and so the desire for the whole and the pursuit of it is named Love." Love's function is to bring "us home to our own," to "restore us to our ancient nature and [to] heal us and make us blessed and happy" (88, 89).

In *Beloved*, the love of the twin souls, whose hosts are Beloved and Sethe, is "too thick" (203). It is "a hot thing," so powerful, demanding, and consuming that the two women "are locked in a love that wore everybody out" (243). Thus, this love has the potential both to heal and to make happy as well as to destroy and to cause dejection. Emanating from the character called Beloved, whose spirit is both benign and malign, this love initially makes both Sethe and Denver happy by healing their psychic wounds. Later, however, it almost destroys Sethe and plunges Denver into dejection (see part 3 of the novel).

In his dialogue with Agathon (*Symposium*), Socrates points out that a person "desires what is not in his possession and not there, what he has not, and what he is not himself and what he lacks." He concludes that "love is, first of all, of something; next, of those things which one lacks" (96). As the interpolated section (*Beloved* 210–17) specifically and the novel generally indicate, what Beloved and Sethe (and other women in the novel) lack/desire is "the join" (213), or reunion with their other(s), in order to achieve complete wholeness, to return to the pre-diasporan state of the African female Self. With this ruling desire being pivotal in the novel's plot structure, Morrison, therefore, envelops the formation of the novel's focal female subjects (Sethe, Beloved, and Denver) within the diasporan myth.

Morrison installs a mystical section in the novel's last quarter (210–17) in which the centered subject (who is the character Beloved and "more" than the character Beloved[28]) recounts the history of her diasporization. The section's narration is situated in a linguistic space between European and African phenomenology, and it uses Western language to describe what is essentially African epistemology and ontology. This section, which is an integral feature of the novel's production and interpretation, moves the narrative outside the boundaries of a Eurocentric ghost story and situates it within the parameters of an Afrocentric discourse of diasporan desire.

The interpolated section begins with the statement "I AM BELOVED and she is mine" (210), which functions on different levels of meaning. Though the principal speaker (the "I" in the section) is the character Beloved in a form that transcends Western concepts of time and space and Being, it is a statement that bespeaks the emotive relationship any one of the focal female characters could and does have with one another. The subject spoken about is the character Sethe and more than the character Sethe. The section narrates the severing of a primordial female Self into a self and others. On one level the speaker is a female self (a beloved) who has been severed from the whole Self. More specifically, she is a daughter who has been separated from her mother and whose ruling desire is for reunion with her mother in order to reconstitute herself as a complete whole self.

The opening paragraph depicts a scene indicative of the unity of Being. The scene is set in the Zamani period, which binds "together all created things" (Mbiti 29). The entire interpolation is an abbreviated narrative of the black African diaspora, and the speaker uses a series of images (the "things that are pictures") to describe the historical ordeal. The speaker (the "I") describes a woman in her native Africa who is filling a basket with flowers she is picking. The woman is in harmony with her surroundings and the speaker is one with the woman ("I am not separate from her"; "her face is my own") and with the environment. This bucolic state of unity is fractured by the gunfire of white outsiders ("I would help her [pick the flowers] but the clouds are in the way").

The remainder of the section principally describes conditions on a slave ship during the Middle Passage and ends with a brief section about life following the Atlantic crossing. It establishes the continuity and perpetuity of diaspority ("All of it is now——it is always now") as part of the Zamani time dimension, and it uses the term "crouching" to signify the further bisectioning of the primordial female Self and the partitioning of these other selves, and to extend the meaning of the Middle Passage beyond a singular historical event ("there will never be a time when I am not crouching and watching others who are crouching too").

Packed tightly in the ship's hull, the captives lie in their own waste ("some who eat nasty themselves") and are plagued by rats. Denied water, they are forced to drink the white slavers' urine. The horrific conditions of the Atlantic crossing prompt the captives' desire to sever their bodies from their souls ("we are all trying to leave our bodies behind"), to abandon their corporeal hosts and to return to the spirit world. Some succeed, such as the man with filed teeth. Apparently this man, who dies on top of the speaker, is from an ethnic group different from the speaker's.

The fifth paragraph describes the captives having been brought from the hull to the deck to be fed and, apparently, forced to exercise. The speaker is too hungry to eat the molded bread and too weary to exercise. The slavers bring "the little hill of dead people" from below and throw them overboard ("the men without skin push them through with poles"). The speaker's subject complement or twin self ("the woman . . . with . . . the face that is mine") is also among the captives and is shackled with a neck iron, which the speaker would bite away if she had the filed teeth of the man who died upon her. The "men without skin" (whites) and their "clouds" (gunfire) prevent her from helping the woman. The woman with the neck shackle is dejected. She longs for her earrings (which the slavers have taken) and for her basket, which signifies her longing for the pre-diasporan unity of Being. Bereft, the woman fails to smile at the speaker and commits suicide (212) by plunging into the sea.

The slave ship tosses and turns, mixing the men and the women. The speaker is thrown onto the back of a captive man who sings of home ("of the place where a woman takes flowers from their leaves and puts them in a round basket") before the whites came ("before the clouds"). The man's song indelibly imprints in the speaker's mind a memory that will become rememory.

The white slavers begin to rape the captive women. Eventually, one of the men takes the speaker (apparently) to his cabin, where he eats, gives her food, and then rapes her. The rape exacerbates her partitioning ("he hurts where I sleep"; "I drop the food and break into pieces"). Countless days and nights pass, on the sea and on the land. The Middle Passage evolves into slavery in the Americas and then into emancipation ("no iron circle around my neck"; "no boats go on in this water"; "no men without skin"), and still the speaker, a bisected and partitioned self, longs for "the join" with the woman who committed suicide. Fusion with the woman would complete her: "she is the laugh"; "I am the laugher."

During a mystical encounter with the woman's soul, the speaker learns from her subject complement how and where they can be reunited ("a place to be"). The woman whispers to the speaker that the place where she/they can *be* "is a house," which ostensibly is located at 124 Bluestone Road in Cincinnati. The section's first part ends by identifying the woman as Sethe, and the beginning of the next section affirms this identification. The speaker, therefore, as the beginning of each of the sections' two parts states, is (on one interpretative level) the character Beloved and more. The section's second part also establishes the hermetic nexus among the women—mother, sister, daughter—in which each is the other's beloved. It is an intergenerational, genetic nexus in which the Beloved is great-grandmother, grandmother, mother, daughter, and sister—all of whom once were part of one female Self.

Employing a narrative technique such as the one Herman Melville uses in *Benito Cereno* and Richard Wright uses in *Native Son,* Morrison installs this interpolated section to explain the preceding actions as well as to advance the overall narrative toward closure. The section is integral to the novel's form and its meaning as a diasporan text. Indeed, reading *Beloved* as a discourse of diasporan desire helps resolve conflicting opinions about the novel's meaning.

Critics have disagreed about who Beloved the character actually is: the reincarnation of Sethe's dead baby; a stray woman in the neighborhood; Sethe's mother reincarnated; some other original "cargo" from the Middle Passage, among other speculations.[29] In many instances, one critic negates another on this point by attempting to situate the novel's narrative action and the character Beloved within historical realism or even within a "rational" fantasy world. When viewed from the perspective of the diasporan myth, Beloved is all and everyone that most critical opinions have identified—and more than these.[30] That is, Beloved is a plural Self whose Being defies the West's temporal and spatial boundaries as well as its concept of individuation. Not only are Sethe and Denver also Beloved the Being, but so too are other members of this kinship group referenced in the novel. In effect, Morrison speaks to the plurality of Beloved's Being when she comments on "the levels on which [she] wanted Beloved to function" (Darling 247).

Along with Charles Johnson (*Oxherding Tale,* discussed in chapter 4) and John Edgar Wideman (*The Cattle Killing,* discussed in chapter 5), Morrison in *Beloved* creates one of the most engaging intersubjective and plural Selves in all of African American literature. Beloved as character is the plural Self in female form. She is "we" and "me" (215), I and Thou, self and other, daughter and mother and grandmother. Johnson's and Wideman's central characters in *Oxherding Tale* and *The Cattle Killing,* respectively, are simultaneously son and father and grandfather (among other selves). As Johnson's Andrew Hawkins states the premise, "I was my father's father, and he my child" (176). *The Cattle Killing* is more demonstrative than *Oxherding Tale* in its expression of this premise.

Similarly, when placed in the context of dancing the other, not only is Beloved her mother's mother (grandmother), and Sethe is Beloved's child, but Beloved also is some of the female characters the narrative of her experience inscribes. From the purview of the novel's post-emancipation setting, Beloved's soul in spiritual and corporeal forms exists in the past, the present, and the future. She is born in Africa before the end of the transatlantic slave trade, she is born again into slavery in Kentucky in the early 1850s, she is born again in the 1870s, and she is born again at different junctures in the twentieth century as the character Wild (in *Jazz,* whose principal setting is the 1920s and whose publication is the 1990s). The novel's ending suggests that her soul will incarnate again at some points in the future as story and as Being.

The intersecting physiological, biological, historical, and psychological relationships that bind Sethe, Denver, and Beloved constitute much of the novel's narrative action. After the departed baby reincarnates as the young woman Beloved, all three women begin the process of dancing the other and move toward (but only Denver actually achieves) wholeness. The primary focus is on Beloved as character. As the novel's narrative action that centers Beloved unfolds and moves toward closure, Beloved is the catalytic agent that initiates Sethe's and Denver's re-membering and movement toward wholeness. And Morrison uses rememory as a narrative strategy to make the realistic and mythic qualities of the novel cohere.

Manifesting some of the same shape-shifting powers and qualities as the Allmuseri god in Johnson's *Middle Passage*, the character Beloved is a conglomeration of dialectics and binaries: flesh and spirit, alive and dead, human and nonhuman, sister and daughter and mother. As her presence becomes more dominant in the household, Beloved begins to assume not only the social role but also the physiological and psychological forms of mother, while Sethe concomitantly begins to assume the role and the psychological form of child (241 and 250, for example). As Beloved begins to metamorphose into the sister, the sister begins to metamorphose into Beloved. Mother, daughter, and sister begin to meld into one Self: "Beloved / You are my sister / You are my daughter / You are my face; you are me" (216). This melding is "the join" (the dance as concept) that begins not long after Sethe and Denver (re)meet Beloved. In other words, Beloved as character is both self and other in the vast variety and complexity of this complementarity. Rememory is the emotive process the characters themselves use to turn binary opposition into complementarity. And rememory is the artistic device Morrison employs to negate the literary and historical deformation of the black woman, to begin harmoniously re-assembling her partitioned parts, effecting her regeneration and wholeness, and reclaiming her authentic self.

During this process of subject (re)formation, all three women move toward the restoration of the primordial female Self, the beloved, which is signified in part through the refrain that begins each of the interpolated section's two parts: "I AM BELOVED" (210, 214). Though the three move toward complete wholeness, within the novel's time frame neither Beloved the character nor Sethe achieves complete wholeness, because neither regains the prerequisite of wholeness. At the novel's end, Beloved the character remains in the state of the living-dead, which means that she (as character and as concept) has the capacity to effect regeneration, to turn lack into fulfillment, and to effect the attainment of desire. Her absence at the novel's end is Sethe's lack, Sethe's "loneliness." But it "is a loneliness that can be rocked," "a loneliness that roams," and one that "smooths and contains the rocker." "It [Beloved as concept] is alive, on its own" (274).

The community attempts to forget Beloved as character ("Remembering seemed unwise"), but it cannot forget her as concept. "Disremembered and unaccounted for, she cannot be lost because no one is looking for her" (274). To be sure, diasporan subjects then and now are looking for her, though perhaps subconsciously, because Beloved is diasporan desire, and what Beloved is lives, as the production of the novel verifies. Beloved as story is Beloved as Being. And while "it [Beloved] was not a story to pass on" (274, 275), it is passed on. It lives, remanifesting in the 1870s, in the 1920s, and in the 1990s,[31] and moving those diasporan subjects it encounters toward wholeness and complete wholeness, turning (re)memory into re-membering and allowing a diasporan self to dance her or his other(s).

Kindred Spirits: Deformations and Reformations of the Female Self

Wideman dedicates *The Cattle Killing* to his daughter, Jamila, "who arrived with one of those / tough, beautiful old souls / that's been here / before." One interpretation of the dedication is that Jamila is a human host for a benign soul that has inhabited other human hosts. The novel's epigraph speaks of "African spirits" whose "serial inhabitation of mortal bodies" is not benign. Wideman's dedication and epigraph easily could apply to Beloved, whose mortal body (from one perspective) is inhabited by a tough and beautiful soul who has been here before and (from another perspective) by a malignant spirit. In the hierarchy of Being, a spirit is an entity situated between gods and humans and often is considered synonymous with the soul. When distinctions are made between the soul and the spirit, the soul carries a positive connotation and the spirit may carry a negative or positive connotation. Indeed, as Wideman and others assert, not all spirits are benign.[32]

Several authors of post-1975 diasporan novels, including fictional slave narratives, incorporate referential elements, subject formations, and narrative formations that align closely with features of traditional Ibo and Yoruba belief in what Westerners would consider reincarnation. In part, Morrison's formation of Beloved strongly suggests the traditional Ibo concept of Ogbanje (Anglicized spellings vary). As Cosmas Obiego explains, "The Ogbanje are a set of children . . . [whose] sole purpose is to be born on earth in order to torment parents by their premature and early death." These children "are born out of the influence of malignant spirits . . . [,] are generally considered very beautiful and endowed with many natural gifts which endear them quickly both to their parents and others; their sudden death is in consequence most painful" (191). These and other characteristics of the Ogbanje are discernible in *Beloved*'s title character and in a variety of the novel's narrative formations.[33]

As a benign spirit, Beloved's character also aligns with the traditional Ibo concept of Ino uwa (Anglicized spellings vary). This concept of reincarnated benign spirits overarches narrative and subject formations in Wideman's *The Cattle Killing,* Perry's *Stigmata,* and Brodber's *Louisiana,* even though *The Cattle Killing*'s epigraph speaks of the Ogbanje's malignant influence. In all three novels the benign spirit of deceased persons reincarnates in the respective novel's centered subject and helps configure that subject as a plural Self.

Subject formation in Perry's *Stigmata* aligns in specific ways with features of Ino uwa. One feature of this concept is the belief that the deceased returns to earth (reincarnates) in a genetic line one generation removed—in a grandchild and a great-great-grandchild, for example (Obiego 192). Ayo, the primal parent in *Stigmata,* reincarnates in her granddaughter Grace and in her great-great-granddaughter Lizzie. Grace reincarnates in her granddaughter Lizzie and, as the novel's ending suggests, this reincarnation will continue in the genetic line one generation removed. Ino uwa also holds that this reincarnation of the deceased ancestor can reincarnate in different persons simultaneously as well as in other genetic kin—"brothers, sisters, cousins, aunts and nephews, uncles and nieces, ad infinitum" (Obiego 192).

Brodber's formation of her title character in *Louisiana* demonstrates what Obiego describes as "a vital relationship" between a living subject and the "principle" that subject shares with a deceased "namesake" (192). In this instance, the namesakes are the deceased Louise and Anna, who are Ella/Louisiana's sociogenic rather than her genetic ancestors. In these and in other contemporary diasporan novels, and in these and other ways, the kindred concepts of Ogbanje and Ino uwa from traditional Ibo religious mythology dovetail well with salient features of the diasporan myth.

For the focal women in *Beloved,* Beloved the character is rather literally a kindred spirit whose presence is both positive and negative and thus exemplifies characteristics of both Ogbanje and Ino uwa. Certainly in the diasporan novel, not all spirits are benign, nor are all the relationships between female characters who are kindred spirits inscribed or interpreted as benign ones. However, as a characterization of spiritual affinities between and among women in diasporan novels, the term *kindred spirit* typically connotes a positive nexus that emanates from genetic, sociogenic, or experiential affinities between or among women. The nexus is emotive.

The emotive bond between subject and subject complement assumes a variety of discursive formations in the womanist novel. At times this bond is between the author and her centered subject, as in *Dessa Rose* and *Beloved*. At other times, of which Gloria Naylor's *Linden Hills* is an example, it is between characters. On occasion in such character-to-character bonds, one of the characters is herself an author, as in Octavia Butler's *Kindred*, Perry's *Stigmata* (Lizzie DuBose authors a visual narrative), and Brodber's *Louisiana*. These and other womanist novels that construct black female subjects as either genetic (as in *Kindred*) or sociogenic (as in *Louisiana*) kindred spirits narrate the deformation and subsequent reformation of the centered subjects' ontology.

In *Kindred*, a novel whose title connotes the biological, historical, and discursive aspects of rememory, Butler's formation of Edana (Dana) Franklin, the novel's centered subject, hinges on the emotive bond between Dana and her genetic foremother, Alice. Dana is a writer, and in *Kindred* (as in *Louisiana*) the term signifies sensitivity, sensibility, spiritual kinship, and intuition—that is, e-motion—more than it does publications. Williams's and Morrison's emotive bond with their respective centered subject allows them as authors figuratively or metaphorically to re-live their respective subjects' experiential life. For Dana, living the experiential life of her other is literal. In the novel's plot structure, the two share what Wideman calls the same "condition"—that is, a lived-world predicated on the sameness of race, gender, and social experience (*Cattle Killing* 13). Thus, Dana's story, which the novel foregrounds, is inseparable from Alice's story and her Being is inseparable from Alice's Being.

A subject's story, as Ishmael Reed contends in *Flight to Canada*, is his or her "gris-gris," his or her "Etheric Double" (8). Like a gris-gris, story has healing and restorative powers, as Morrison suggests in *Beloved* and as Wideman dramatizes in *The Cattle Killing* and Perry in *Stigmata*. To narrativize the experiential substance of a subject's Being, as Sherley Anne Williams explains and demonstrates in *Dessa Rose*, is to tell a truer truth about that subject's experiential ontology than stories contained in other discourses about her; it is to rescue the subject from deformative discourses and thus to restore the subject's true nature. For Dana to narrativize a truer truth about Alice's experience is for Dana to rescue both Alice and herself from deformative discourses and to begin to reclaim their authentic subjectivity. Indeed, without Alice, Dana biologically and historically could not be. Without Dana, Alice probably would have been erased from historical memory. Without Butler, both Alice and Dana as well as others in this kinship group would have been lost to (re)memory. Another member of this black female kinship group is Hagar, a child born to Alice and Rufus (a fusion of the African and the European) and who thus establishes the direct line of Dana as a Western black diasporan subject (234).

Dana is a resident of California in the 1970s, but her time/space travel literally repositions her in the slave past of the early 1800s. She learns that her mission on what becomes a series of sojourns is to save the life of one of her progenitors in order to assure that she can be (born). When she learns that this ancestor is a slaveholder, not a slave, she, like Kabnis in Toomer's *Cane* (217–18), has trouble reconciling and balancing the biological and cultural components of her Being. One does not have to read beyond the ending of *Kindred* to discern its thematic and formal affinities with *Cane*. Dana's sojourns through historical time and space toward her ancestral home (the Western origin of her Being) are eventually artistically and spiritually rejuvenating for her, as is Kabnis's sojourn in Georgia. She reconnects with her primal parents, the African (Alice) and the European (Rufus), who together constitute the biological, historical, and cultural sources of her Western Being. From one perspective, both Alice and Rufus are Dana's kindred spirits, though one is benign (Alice) and the other malign (Rufus).

From her rejuvenative and transformative sojourns, Dana gains the experiential knowledge to write a truer truth about blacks and whites during the slavocracy's diasporization than that contained in most white-authored literature and history texts that represent this past (116–17) as well as that contained in the institutionalized authority of archival records (262–64). Yet the narrative she writes of the slavocracy's black victims (such as Alice, Luke, Sarah, Nigel, and Carrie) and its white victimizers (such as Rufus Weylin and his parents, Margaret and Thomas Weylin) is not absolute truth; it is a "kind of truth" (Morrison's term, "Site of Memory" 115).

As the novel's epilogue indicates, one cannot definitively know the facts of the past; knowledge of the past is always textualized. According to Dominick LaCapra, "The past arrives in the form of texts and textualized remainders—memories, reports, published writings, archives, monuments, and so forth" (128). In the formation of Dana, Butler demonstrates that the cultural and psychological baggage Dana brings to the past from her twentieth-century lived-world textualizes her perspective on the past. Nevertheless, guided by her intuitive (which becomes experiential) knowledge of the past, Dana writes both the others (blacks) and the Others (whites) into Being, and thus she takes the first major step toward writing herself into authentic Being. The process of (re)discovering her true self is significantly facilitated through her interaction with a female ancestor, Alice. As Morrison contends in "Rootedness," such "ancestors are not just parents, they are sort of timeless people whose relationships to the characters are benevolent, instructive, and protective, and they provide a certain kind of wisdom" (343).

Emphasizing the significance of an ancestor's presence in the life of a contemporary character, Morrison contends that "when you kill the ancestor you kill yourself ("Rootedness" 344). Butler's rather literal inversion and corroboration of this maxim in *Kindred* is that when you save the ancestor (Rufus and Alice), you save yourself. Butler constructs Dana and Alice as subject complements, as components of the same Self. Dana (re)-discovers and (re)creates her subject complement. From the purview of the diasporan myth, she and Alice are "One woman. Two halves of a whole" (257; see also 228, 229), "twin sister[s], almost" (41). Though Dana dances Alice as her other, the emotive bond between the two does not succeed in fully restoring Dana's authentic subjectivity. Because she never fully achieves wholeness of self, she is not prepared to acquire complete wholeness; she never fuses with her white husband, Kevin Franklin, as a subject complement. This lack of fusion is not because Kevin is white but because he is a false complement.

Through her formation of Dana Franklin, Butler demonstrates that not every residual effect of diasporization can be erased, and that while excursions into the past can be positively transformative, they also can have lasting negative effects if the sojourner is not psychologically prepared to confront the past. Thus, within the narrative Dana never completely reverses her deformation, and therefore the novel is more about Becoming than about Being. Like Kabnis, she is an aspiring writer who journeys toward primordiality. Yet, unlike Kabnis, she does not reach the spiritual source of her Being as artist and as person. She never fully achieves wholeness or complete wholeness because, unlike Kabnis, she never merges with the Primordial Soul.

The novel's closure emphasizes that she continues to be a partitioned self. It is debatable whether her partitioning is less or more severe than before her time travel. Her sojourns into the historical past leave her body scarred. The slave master Tom Weylin leaves her with a permanent facial scar from a kick and she loses her left arm when attempting to extricate herself temporally, spatially, and physically from the slave past. These are corporeal deformations, but as *Dessa Rose* and *Beloved* indicate, a scarred body does not mean an indelibly scarred soul. Yet in Dana's case her deformed body signifies not only the deformative effects of slavery's legacy but also that her parts of self have not been brought as yet into harmonious balance.

Given the manner in which the novel conjoins past and present realities (the subject's traversal of time and space), some critics have defined *Kindred* as science fiction, a definition Butler rejects because, she says, there is no science in this novel.[34] Though *Kindred* is a fictional narrative of slavery in which the centered subject's time travels take her into but not beyond historical time and space (63) to primordial Time, it is, nevertheless, a mystical rendering of the nexus between subject and subject complement that is characteristic of womanist novels in this subgenre.

Naylor's *Linden Hills* joins womanist novels such as *Beloved* and *Dessa Rose* in using a text as the site on which subject and subject complement (re)meet, liberate each other, and eventually fuse into a plural Self. *Linden Hills*'s variation on this epistemological and ontological formation is that the perceiving subject, Willa Prescott Nedeed, is not the novel's author but a character in the text. Willa's (re)meeting with her subject complements is effected through written and visual remains of these women, whose experiential lives (including Willa's life) are repetitions of historical formations from slavery to the novel's present. All of these women are literal and figural victims of a socially constructed ontology and thus they all share the same condition. The master-husband of each deforms her by reducing her subjectivity to the skeletal social forms of wife and mother and consequently almost erasing the integrity of her Being. Yet each woman's true nature remains *sous rature*,[35] for each leaves a written or visual trace of her authentic self. From these traces Willa re-creates each previous Mrs. Nedeed's true self, and she learns in the process that "she [can] rebuild" (268) her self and reclaim her true nature.

Rememory is the mechanism Willa uses to re-member her others and her self, which is effected through a kind of gendered collective memory that facilitates her journey back in time. Her first stop is the slave past, where she (re)meets and subsequently reinscribes salient aspects of the experiential life of a surrogate primal parent, Luwana Packersville Nedeed. Luwana was the first Nedeed wife-mother, and she and Willa (re)meet on a psychohistorical and textual site that extends to a point "where memory mingles with desire"—memory of "the miracle some called divine creation" and the desire to reclaim that original state of Being (288). The site is Luwana's narrative, "the diary of a slave" scrawled "onto the gold-edged tissue paper that separated one book of the Bible from another" (117). Lacking signs of chronology, the "fragments" of Luwana's "mind"/story appear random (117). Yet Luwana's careful placement of these fragments between specific books of the Bible gives each fragment meaning and allows Willa to reconstruct Luwana's story from the fragments and thus to reconstruct Luwana's self. The reconstruction process melds story and Being.

Traveling beyond the psychohistorical site where she (re)meets Luwana, Willa moves toward primordiality. It is "an unconscious journey in toward the power of will that had crept alone in primordial muck eons before being clothed with fins, scales, wings, or flesh" (288); it is a journey toward the true Western black female self/Self and toward the primordial soul/Soul. The journey's conclusion will connect the end (Willa) to the beginning (the Primordial Soul) and will reveal to Willa knowledge not only of who she is (her Being) but also of how she came to be (her Becoming) (278–79). It is a journey whose end will reunite components of the bisected primordial female Self.

The first Luther Nedeed treats and considers Luwana as his property, as a necessary part of his design to establish a patrifocal dynasty that will assure his immortality. Naylor's construction of Luther and her inscription of his pernicious design and its consequences echo Faulkner's *Absalom, Absalom!* (1936) and Baldwin's *Go Tell It on the Mountain* (1953).[36] According to rumor, the first Luther sells "his octoroon wife and six children" into slavery and uses the money to begin his design (2). Also according to rumor, he buys her back (4), marries her, and assigns her a surname (Mrs. Nedeed) that connotes her continued status as the Other's property. Luther (and later his and her son) claims ownership of her Being (119), and thus they reduce Luwana's subjectivity to the form of wife and mother without the substance of these roles. Her primary function is as a vehicle for Luther to replicate himself (which he does) in order to effect his design. Existing as merely a vessel for male replication becomes the primary function of the succeeding Mrs. Nedeeds.

Having reached the border between historical time and primordial Time, Willa then moves forward in historical time where she (re)meets successively two of her other subject complements, Evelyn Creton Nedeed and Priscilla McGuire Nedeed, and realizes fully that she and the Nedeed wife-mothers who preceded her share a male-defined and therefore a deformed ontology. Begun by a white male, the social formation of a man (white or black) holding the "deed" (or ownership) to a woman's subjectivity is repeated in the lives of the succeeding Mrs. Luther Nedeeds. Willa's temporal and spatial journey is thus into the history (story) of the women whose social place and historicized space she now occupies. To borrow a concept from Wideman, black woman "is the name of the space they occupy" in the material and lived-world of the West (*Cattle Killing* 13).

Evelyn Creton Nedeed's text is a compilation of meticulously inscribed recipes. Willa's interpretative reading of these recipes allows her to re-create Evelyn's story and thus discern Evelyn's true self. As is the case for Luwana's text and Priscilla's text, insight into Evelyn's story/Being gives Willa insight into her self. As the novel demonstrates and as Willa comes to realize, the story of each Nedeed wife-mother is the same story, regardless of the discursive format in which it is recorded. Thus, as a self, each of these Nedeed wife-mothers is the same self/Self.

Willa's reading and reconstruction of her predecessors' true selves is concomitant with her erasure of the collective Luther Nedeed's power to deform black female selves. In reading the history/herstory of and thus re-creating one of these women, Priscilla, Willa uses a technique of visual representation (inverted in this instance) that is central to Jamaica Kincaid's *The Autobiography of My Mother* (1996). "History is a written photograph" (*Linden Hills* 266). From a series of photographs, Willa re-forms Priscilla McGuire Nedeed's story and Priscilla's self. The chronologically successive fragments of Priscilla's visual text chronicle the process of her erasure: "The only thing growing in these pictures was her absence" (209). Through the succession of photographs, Priscilla gradually disappears. In the last one Willa views, Priscilla's "entire face, the size of a large thumbprint, had been removed," and "scrawled across the empty hole . . . was the word me" (249). Priscilla is under erasure (*sous rature*) but not erased.[37] As Willa deciphers the narrative these visual fragments contain, she gives voice to Priscilla's silence and reconstructs Priscilla's true nature. Through her text Priscilla "speaks" to Willa and identifies her as a subject complement: "I knew you would come, and I'm so pleased to meet you" (205, 249). Their (re)meeting on this textual site will effect mutual liberation.

The (re)meeting between Willa and her soul mates becomes simultaneously an act of creation (of the others) and an act of destruction (of the Others). It is a liberating act for all of the women. From the written and visual remains of their authentic selves, Willa literally and metaphorically reinscribes these sociogenic selves who are *sous rature*, gives voice to their forced silence, and dances them as her others. She liberates these wife-mothers from their socially constructed prisons of a male-defined womanhood,[38] and in turn they liberate Willa from the psychological prison and the physical prison (the basement) in which her husband has incarcerated her. Because Willa has given birth to a son who does not physically and mentally replicate Luther—is not Luther's twin—she has failed to perpetuate the Luther Nedeed dynasty and thus, from Luther's perspective, has lost her only reason for existing. Incarcerating her in the basement is part of Luther's plan to destroy her, but the spiritually liberating voices of the collective Mrs. Nedeeds give Willa the strength to foil his plan.

After her spiritual liberation, Willa rejects her husband's definition of her as wife-mother and redefines the roles for herself and affirms this new "identity without any reservations" (279). This self-definition moves her closer to her primordial self, closer to the fragile but "singular germ of truth" (280) about her Being. "Willa now marveled at the beauty and simplicity of something so small it had lived unrecognized within her for most of her life. She gained strength and a sense of power from its possession" (280). The power Willa gains—what Marshall calls "*connaissance*"—transports her to her primordial origin, where "the amber germ of truth [the trace of her true nature] . . . conceived and reconceived itself, splitting and multiplying to take over ever atom attached to her being" (289). Her "unconscious journey" to "the beginning of time" reconnects her to primordial origins and repositions her in the universe. Her journey effects "a birth"—more specifically, a (re)birth—of her authentic self (288–89).

As Dessa states in *Dessa Rose* (260) and as Morrison states (15) and demonstrates in *Beloved* (particularly in her formation of Stamp Paid and

Sethe as subjects), African Americans (those enslaved and those emancipated) paid a high price to own themselves. Dessa's victory over the perpetrator and perpetuator (Adam Nehemiah) of a whitemale-defined black womanhood is complete. Sethe's inability to totally beat back the past (which Schoolteacher signifies) means that she does not totally liberate herself from a whitemale-defined black womanhood. In *Linden Hills*, the price of Willa's liberation, of self-ownership, is extremely high. Willa's victory, her liberation, is pyrrhic. She destroys the perpetrator but also destroys her physical self.

Broken Lives, Spoken Lives

From one perspective Gayl Jones's *Corregidora* is a womanist novel about broken lives that are "always spoken, and only spoken" (103). That is, it is a novel about black women whose obsession to speak the unspeakables of their diasporization is an end within itself, the result of which is a self-perpetuating deformation. In this novel, speaking one's story does not progress to dancing the self by dancing one's other(s). Unlike the function of story in *Dessa Rose* or *Beloved*, in *Corregidora*, speaking one's life does not effect the re-membering of one's fractured self, nor does it function as a curative for the fractured self and the fractured others, as it does in *The Cattle Killing*. Instead, the story of the Corregidora women's diasporization that is "only spoken" perpetuates rather than mends the fractured self of the novel's centered subject and her maternal progenitors and engenders a pernicious psychological bond among them.

Corregidora incorporates several of the thematic and formal features of the contemporary fictional slave narrative, yet it revises (often through inversion and negation) these features to such an extent that it basically shatters the paradigm of rememory germane to novels such as *Dessa Rose* and *Beloved*. In *Corregidora*, memory's function is more incarcerating than it is liberating for the centered subject, Ursa Corregidora, and her genetic kin. Unlike many other female-centered diasporan novels, *Corregidora*'s narrative progression centers the process of subject deformation rather than reformation by emphasizing the permanent effects of spiritual crippling.

The novel's title (which is operative on different levels of meaning) is a key to its revision and inversion of the womanist paradigm and project. The titles of *Beloved*, *Kindred*, and even *Dessa Rose* emphasize matrifocality as the bond of otherness among women. *Corregidora*'s title foregrounds a patrifocal entity and intimates a pernicious bond of Otherness as the dominant force in the Corregidora women's identity formation.[39] The title draws attention to whitemaleness (Otherness) as the defining criterion in the subjectivity of the novel's four generations of black women. And though Ursa Corregidora eventually recognizes that her biological and experiential kinship to her foremothers is a tie that breaks rather than binds the self's parts, she is never able to extricate herself fully from this psychobiological incarceration. She never liberates herself or her genetic others from a whitemale-defined black female subjectivity and from a male-defined deformative discourse.

Corregidora proffers a nexus between story and Being that is a rather perverse variant of how most diasporan novels (womanist or masculinist) interface narratology, ontology, and epistemology. In this novel, story (meaning narrative as well as a subject's being) hinges on miscegenetic incest, which is one of those unspeakables of slavery usually left unspoken (or at least muted) in the official records of the past. The perpetrators of this erasure and subsequently their collaborators (which include authors of history and literature texts) "tear the pages out of the book and they ain't no record of it. They probably burned the pages" (78). To counter this murdering of memory,[40] the first three generations of Corregidora women offer their bodies and their memories as counterdiscursive texts. But the price of reinventing themselves as corporeal epistemic agents of the past is that they render their souls dormant.

Typically, the womanist project has among its aims to correct the text (story) of the past that has been distorted or to restore the truthful text that has been expunged, the intended results of which are a truer version of the past and the restoration of an authentic black female subjectivity. *Corregidora*'s title (from the Portuguese and Spanish verbs meaning "to correct") suggests that this novel shares these objectives. Yet corrections in the stories of the first three generations of Corregidora women do not lead to a reformation of their selves.

To correct the record of the past, the centered subject's female progenitors are determined to bear witness against the slavocracy's atrocities. This bearing witness replicates an objective of most contemporary fictional slave narratives, which typically accomplish it through a conjunction of epistemology, ontology, and narratology. Aligning the subject's intuited knowledge of his or her true nature with aspects of a respective novel's form, authors of contemporary fictional slave narratives typically replace the West's invention of a false black self with a true black self. In general, the structural pattern echoes Douglass's 1845 *Narrative,* in which he narrates the slavocracy's invention of his false self and his reinvention of his true self. Like other contemporary fictional slave narratives, *Corregidora* adheres to this pattern, but it redefines and realigns the paradigm's components. For example, in the epistemology-ontology-narratology paradigm, *Kindred*'s Dana Franklin literally witnesses slavery (epistemology), is permanently scarred in the process of gaining this firsthand knowledge (ontology), but becomes a witness against the slavocracy and its deformative texts in the story she tells of her experiences (narratology).

Corregidora, however, privileges the paradigm's ontological component, and for the Corregidora women (perhaps excepting Ursa), bearing witness is less a narratological than a biological function. Ursa's foremothers are monomaniacally driven to produce generations whose selves will be witnesses against the slavocracy and will challenge the official record of the past. They intend their female progeny as living memory, and thus memory in this novel is connected to (pro)creation (that is, story to Being) in a way unorthodox for the womanist project. For example, the scars on Sethe's, Dessa's, and Dana's bodies are texts that bear witness against the slavocracy. The Corregidora women (at least the first three generations) intend that the entire black female self (body, mind, emotions, and soul) be a text that witnesses against the atrocities of slavery.

At one point in their lives, the first two Corregidora women were the objects of their master's (Corregidora's) and other white males' sexual desire. Like Mutt's reduction of Ursa, these men's objectification reduced these women's Being to a deformed and vernacular version of the female sexual organ—a "pussy" (45–46). Though this is not the direct experience of the third-generation Corregidora woman, her mother and grandmother imprint their experiential memory so strongly in her mind that the experience in effect becomes hers, too. This male objectification is, however, the direct experience of the fourth-generation Corregidora woman, Ursa. Ursa succumbs to a male-defined subjectivity so readily that it is as though she has been preconditioned for this through her matrilineal bloodline (45). As is the case in *Linden Hills,* it is the original male deformer's role rather than his race (white) that is important in *Corregidora.*

The psychobiological nexus among the four Corregidora women, then, is one in which hate supersedes diasporan desire as the ruling passion in the formation of their subjectivity. They are partitioned selves who never bring the parts of their selves into harmonious balance. As partitioned selves, they are self-perpetuating and therefore are never able to fuse with a subject complement (male or female), which would give them wholeness and potentially complete wholeness. In fact, Ursa's grandmother and great-grandmother reject the idea of a male complement for anything except procreation (in one sense, they are female versions of Luther Nedeed). For them procreation (making generations) facilitates their obsession to keep their hate alive. They have lost the primal parent's function of giving (re)-birth to the self and thus can reproduce only facsimile selves. Making generations as a form of counterdiscourse binds the first three generations of Corregidora women together in an indissoluble bond, and it is this legacy that Ursa inherits and struggles unsuccessfully to negate. The damage to Ursa's womb is one signifier of her indissoluble bond to her foremothers and of her inability ever to give (re)birth to self or to (re)produce an authentic self (an other).

The emotive bond between Ursa and her foremothers is indeed the antithesis of the emotive bond one usually finds in womanist novels within this subgenre, such as *Dessa Rose, Beloved, Kindred, Louisiana, Stigmata,* or *Praisesong.* In *Corregidora,* the trace that inheres in this matrilineal bloodline from Great Gram to Ursa is not an intimation of primordiality but the indelible stain of "another's [Corregidora's] past as well as [their] own" (45). Having accepted that "their past [is] in [her] blood" (45) and that this is an indelible part of her Being, Ursa, then, becomes a duplicate of the experiential life of her foremothers, for a man shifts the center of her Being from her soul to her genitalia (46) and thus claims ownership of her Being. Like her foremothers (and unlike Dessa Rose or Willa Nedeed), she never regains ownership of her self in the course of the novel. This is evident in the novel's closing scene in which Ursa and Mutt are engaged in a sexual act that in effect negates Being. This is not an act of love that signifies Ursa's fusion with a subject complement and thus an intimation of her acquisition of complete wholeness; rather, this is a physical act of mating that negates procreation and thus signifies that Ursa is a permanently partitioned and deformed self.

The novel's closing scene thematically recalls the opening scene of the "Kabnis" section in Jean Toomer's *Cane.* Both subjects are artists whose attempts (for different reasons) to murder memory adversely affect the performance of their art forms. In both scenes sexual intercourse is a simulated act and therefore negates procreation. Kabnis masturbates while fantasizing about a conjugal subject complement. The fellatio Ursa performs on Mutt is a form of masturbation that negates procreation, signifies her lack of wholeness, and indicates her inability to attain conjugal complementarity.

4 The Reading, the Writing, and the Arithmetic of the Black Masculinist Project

In the last paragraph of the epilogue to *Dessa Rose*, Dessa remembers and laments Nehemiah's attempts "to read" her and regrets the inadvertent assistance she gave him for this reading (260). Speaking/writing her self in her own voice in the novel's third section, Dessa negates Nehemiah's assumptions about slaves and women, renders his manuscript, his "scribbling[s]," null and void, and in effect turns the tables in the novel's last dramatic scene by reading Adam Nehemiah (255).

Williams's explicit use of the term "to read" names a discursive praxis in post-1975 fictional slave narratives that precede and follow *Dessa Rose*. Reading is the first component in a primer paradigm of novelistic discourse—reading, writing, arithmetic—that is germane to aspects of form and particularly to the formation of white male subjects in this subgenre. On one level, to read a person is to penetrate below the person's exteriority to ascertain the person's essence or true nature. On another level, to read a person is to signify upon that person by revealing that the person's interiority (or true nature) is debased and is not accurately reflected in his or her exteriority. In contemporary male-centered fictional slave narratives, the first instance usually involves whites' assertion that blacks have not evolved fully on the scale of social evolution and therefore are inferior (particularly in intellect) to whites. The second instance usually involves blacks' assertion of superiority (moral, ethical, intellectual) over whites. (In the context of sexual preference, a portion of chapter 6 discusses "reading" as praxis in contemporary fictional slave narratives.)

Using white males' behaviors and beliefs as the foundation for negative portraiture and offering these characters as representative of the group (such as *Dessa Rose*'s Adam Nehemiah and *Beloved*'s Schoolteacher) is the most direct way post-1975 female-centered fictional slave narratives and textually androgynous ones read the white male as Other. The most direct way post-1975 masculinist fictional slave narratives read the white male as Other is to engage him in intellectual warfare through a novelistic discourse that is highly intertextual and referential. Representative novels in this group install a plethora of written, oral, and visual texts from a variety of subject areas as well as allude to persons and events in the world's (especially the West's) social, intellectual, and literary histories. These novels typically establish a dialogic relationship (explicit or implicit) to male-authored American and European texts, particularly to ones that through their form and content display the Western white male's intellect.

Intertextual dialogism in the masculinist novels challenges history and literature texts, archival records and documents, and other forms of white-male discourse that deform black male subjectivity. It reads the authors of these discourses (men and women, past and present) as perpetrators of and collaborators in the ongoing diasporization of blacks. Singling out the white males, these novels typically disavow the males' self-proclaimed intellectual superiority, revise through negation historical and official images of them, and portray representative ones (actual or fictional) as aberrations in the human family.

In addition to intertextual dialogism, referentiality, and male subject formation (white and black), a typical black masculinist novel conducts this reading through its use of language, parody, satire, and humor. A principal feature of this reading is the novelists' parodic revision of white intertexts, which they install to rival the white male intellect that produced the texts and to challenge the white male intellect that interprets them. Hermetically bonded through the intellect, author, centered subject, and narrator (when other than the author or a character) join in this offensive. In the title to a collection of his essays, Ishmael Reed in effect states black male writers' battle cry: *Writin' Is Fightin'*. In the preface to this collection

("Boxing on Paper") he explains: "A black boxer's career is the perfect metaphor for the career of a black male" (6).

This black male alliance is most evident in those novels that employ first-person narration. This point of view merges the author and his centered subject and therefore foregrounds the intellectual acumen of both. The typical novel accomplishes this merging largely through intertextual layering, a discursive technique in which the narrative uses one intertext to revise another intertext or other intertexts. The revisions usually are to negate, occasionally to corroborate, but almost always to invite the novel's readers to reassess standard interpretations of (white) Western texts. Whatever the discursive reason, the overall intent is to prominently display the speaking subject's superior intellect.

The act of writing and its function in the self-formation (or reformation) of the black male subject often are explicit subject matter within this group of masculinist novels. One example is that an integral part of *Flight to Canada*'s plot is that Raven Quickskill's writing of his poem is simultaneously an act of rebellion and one of self-emancipation/formation. Another example is Rutherford Calhoun's text (Johnson's *Middle Passage*), which is literally a palimpsest. He writes his text on the pages of Captain Falcon's logbook, and his text contains discernible traces of what Falcon previously had written (27, 175). Calhoun simultaneously writes his own text and edits Captain Falcon's text, and thus the two texts merge to form the novel. As part of this discursive process, Calhoun also uses referentiality and intertextuality to revise (alternately through negation, affirmation, and reinterpretation) several white male texts. For both Raven and Rutherford, the act of writing the black Self is inextricably tied to the purpose of reading the white Other (though more for Rutherford than for Raven). A statement Rutherford attributes to another character bespeaks his (and thus Charles Johnson's) purpose and method in this instance: "'Tis scandalous how some writers such as Amasa Delano have slandered black rebels in their tales" (173). This dialogic response to *Benito Cereno* affirms Melville's positive inscription of black subjects and joins Melville in negating Delano's deformation of them.[1] Occasionally, novels in this subgenre offer positive readings of white males (for example, Tommy O'Toole in *Middle Passage*) and negative readings of black males (such as ones in *Flight to Canada*).

Writing is the second component in the primer paradigm. In the masculinist novels the writing or reformation of the black male self is predicated on the premise that the Western black male is already a deformation (that is, a reinvention) of the authentic African male Self.[2] Narrative structure in womanist novels follows a rather standard pattern of negating the deformed self and reconstituting an authentic self based on the African female Self as model. Narrative structure that inscribes the reformation of self varies widely among masculinist novels, primarily because the process of affirming the black male self is so tightly bound to negating (or even affirming) the white male Other. In most masculinist fictional slave narratives the centered subjects cannot fully negate the Western white male as a model of Being, and thus to varying degrees they reinvent themselves using the Western white male as a mold. Andrew Hawkins's (*Oxherding Tale*) social and racial status, Cambridge's (Phillips's *Cambridge*) mastery and use of European language, Nash Williams's (*Crossing the River*) assertion of authority and presumed superiority over African blacks, and Raven Quickskill's challenge to white males' intellect are among the ways that indicate that these subjects' reinvented selves are modeled on white males. Andrew Hawkins is the exemplar.

Unlike Andrew Hawkins, most male centered subjects in contemporary fictional slave narratives are not physiological replicas of white males. (In fact, in post-1950 novels of the United States, white mulattoes are rare as focal characters.) Instead, these physiologically black subjects recast themselves largely from the psychological and intellectual molds of the Western white male. One result of this reinvention is that they are (or become) ontological aberrations in that their (black) bodies do not synchronize with other parts of their selves. A very few (such as Andrew) manifest characteristics of what Du Bois calls double-consciousness; most, however, exemplify Jean Toomer's concept of split men—black males whose components of self are not in harmonious balance.

The following paradigm overarches the formation of the black male as centered subject in the masculinist novels, though each subject in some way(s) deviates from the paradigm. He is not an active communal self, and thus he lacks the spiritual stability that comes from a meaningful interaction with a black family/community, from a nurturing contact with his primal (Western) parent or his primordial (African) parent, and from contact with the Primordial Soul. Rarely does he sustain a spiritual sexual relationship with a black woman, which precludes a fusion that would advance him toward complete wholeness. The consequence of these (and other) lacks is that his soul withers and he becomes a kind of cultural and spiritual orphan. Though he makes significant progress toward regaining his authentic identity, he seldom achieves wholeness, primarily because he privileges his intellect over other parts of his self rather than seeking a harmonious balance of his self's parts. Because wholeness is a prerequisite for complete wholeness, the latter eludes him. Reduced (often a self-induced condition) to a state of orphanhood, the nonpasser becomes a cultural and social liminal in his human environment (for example, Rutherford Calhoun and Cambridge) while the passer exists in a state of racial (and often social) liminality (for example, Andrew Hawkins). Despite a narrative structure that takes the male subject on a journey-quest for an authentic identity, his failure to abandon the false model for his Being (whitemaleness in whatever form) prevents him from repositioning himself in the unity of Being by his narrative's end.

The third component in this primer paradigm, the arithmetic (sacred mathematics), is a more constant and pervasive component than the reading but less than the writing. Indeed, it is an inextricable part of the diasporan myth's theory of Being. Briefly stated, the myth's arithmetic concerns the bisectioning of the primordial African Self (subtraction and division) and the re-membering of the primordial Self's components (addition and multiplication). While in theory post-1975 female-centered and male-centered fictional slave narratives are similar in their incorporation of this arithmetic under the rubric of the plural black Self, in praxis they are quite different. One difference is that most womanist and textually androgynous novels in the subgenre presuppose that the centered subject is one of several components of a primordial Self. In most masculinist novels in the subgenre, either the subject's experiences teach him that he is a component of a plural male Self or he never acquires this understanding of the nature of his Being. Another difference is how the three groups of novels typically utilize the concept of complete wholeness. The subject in a female-centered and a textually androgynous text usually acquires complete wholeness through a fusion with a true subject complement. The subject centered in the masculinist text rarely fuses with a true female complement and therefore rarely achieves complete wholeness. Wideman's formation of Bishop Allen in *The Cattle Killing* is of a black male who for part of his life embraces whitemaleness as his model for Being. Using the language of arithmetic, the narrator's depiction of Allen bespeaks the condition of the typical black male centered in a masculinist text: "Divided first from others, then from himself" (158). Several of the males in their texts fail to reverse completely this state of diasporization, and they remain "orphaned" (divided from others) and partitioned selves at their narrative's end.

Reading the Other(s): Reed's Flight to Canada

A product of the eighteenth and nineteenth centuries, the standard nonfiction male-centered slave narrative is an auto-biographical act, a first-person writing (or reinvention) of a centered black male self and by extension a writing of generic black personhood. In a revised form, this narrative convention (along with others) anchors the formal and thematic contours of Reed's *Flight to Canada*. But as an experimental, futuristic novel, *Flight to Canada* is hardly traditional or conventional in most aspects of its form and content. Neither the novel nor Raven Quickskill's poem "Flight to Canada" is "autobiographical" (63). But each is indeed an auto-biographical act in that the centered subject, Raven Quickskill, purports to write his self into authentic Being in his poem and in the opening pages of the novel, and the novel's multivocal narrator (a fusion of author, third-person narrator, and centered subject) purports "to read" (and thus write) the true nature of others and Others—blacks, Native Americans, and especially whites. Given the amount of narrative space Reed devotes to inscribing the supposedly true subjectivity of these subjects, his novel (as Quickskill says of his poem "Flight to Canada") is indeed "more of a reading than a writing" (7). Consistent with its emphasis on reading the white Other rather than writing the black Self, the novel's use of the diasporan myth applies more to whites than to blacks.

The novel's early chapters situate its focal subjects—whites, blacks, and Natives—within the African diasporan myth. Chapter 2 interfaces this myth with features from the Arthurian legend, and it uses this interfacing as a scaffolding for its reading of white ethnics and their society, inclusive of class, gender, and region. In tracing the genealogy of the Swille family, the Southern white patriarchy the novel foregrounds, Reed establishes this family as direct descendants of the legendary King Arthur. Largely through parody and inversion, he connects King Arthur as well as Arthur's progenitor and progeny to the diasporan myth. Citing Tennyson as its source, the novel briefly describes Uther, King Arthur's father, as a "dark" man, "well-nigh black" (16), and thus indirectly connects this European tribesman to the group of humans who originated in Africa. Later in the novel Reed inverts and parodies the legend of the walking Ibos and applies it to Arthur Swille III (131–32) and to his sister, Vivian (133). Certain other details about the Virginia Swilles' descent from King Arthur are consistent with components of the diasporan myth. For example, King Arthur, one of the historical luminaries of the European tribe, "made war against the Saxons and the old Druid gods . . . [and his] descendants came to his America and made war against the gods of 'Indians' and Africans" (16). The present generation of Swilles is perpetuating this "war" to capture the souls of Native Americans and African Americans and to negate their gods.

Bearing the ancestral name is not the only signifier of the Virginia Swilles' Arthurian descent. Descent is what Werner Sollors identifies as one of the two (the other is consent) contrastive components of ethnicity. Descent refers to "hereditary qualities, liabilities, and entitlements" (6), and descent is a major rubric under which Reed parodically inscribes Southern white ethnicity and subjectivity, especially that of the Swilles. Like Waters Turpin does for the Delaney dynasty in his fictional slave narrative *The Rootless*, Reed uses disease as a trope to construct the members of the Swille dynasty (and by extension white males in general) as deformed subjects.[3] He installs and proceeds to invert and subvert a prevailing notion in the nineteenth and early twentieth centuries that blacks were congenitally diseased. More specifically, he parodically installs Dr. Samuel Cartwright's assertion that those slaves who defied the slavocracy by escaping or attempting to escape from it suffered from a mental disease that Cartwright named *Drapetomania*.[4] As part of his deformative reading of the Swilles, the first of whom "was 'indescribably deformed'" (15), Reed includes congenital mental disease as one of their "hereditary qualities" (their descent).

The "inexplicable malady" (16) that afflicts the second generation of the Virginia Swilles is passed down to succeeding generations, affecting both their minds and bodies. The symptoms of "Swille's malady" (16) as they manifest in the current generation include an alienation from reality so intense that for those who are afflicted, fantasy is reality. Indeed, in their function as representative white Southerners, the Swilles are absorbed in fantasy. The males in particular are locked in time (the past) and in texts, principally in Tennyson's *Idylls of the King* and the arabesque or supernatural texts of Edgar Allan Poe. For the last of the Arthur Swilles, the present is but an extension of the past and the future he envisions will be a repetition of the present. The novel depicts him as the standard-bearer of Southern white ethnicity.

The novel's reading of Southern white ethnics condemns their society's political, social, moral, ethical, religious, aesthetic, and other cultural values and practices. It asserts that Southern white ethnics adhere to a civil religion in which sociopolitical tenets supersede and consume those of church religion.[5] Speaking of the first American Arthur, Reed points out that "Camelot became Swille's bible," that this "fairy tale . . . became for him an Anglican Grand Design" (16). The last Arthur Swille struggles to perpetuate this Grand Design, which in his mind is synonymous with the slavocracy. Within this design some Southern white ethnics envision the Second Coming of Christ as the second coming of Arthur, the once and future king, who in his (Arthur's) second coming probably has reincarnated as Jefferson Davis (16). In the narrative's Civil War time frame, Davis is the savior who will protect what "traces" are left of this "fairest civilization the sun ever shown upon" (10) from outside and inside agitators (the Union and the blacks, respectively) and who will restore it to its once glorious state. Davis is the military and spiritual leader of what the Southern white ethnics consider a holy war.

The white South's tenets of civil religion are closely aligned with their aesthetic values in that they privilege form over substance. Poe is their contemporary literary hero and is the current Arthur Swille's role model (109–10, for example). Poe's works, as the novel asserts, are far removed from social reality, so much so that Poe should be "recognized as the principal biographer of that strange war" (10) and the principal historian of a society so steeped in fantasy that it would wage war to keep its illusion intact. The novel's narrator maintains that "Poe says more [about Southern white subjectivity and ethnicity] in a few stories than all of the volumes by historians" (10). In depicting Poe as depraved and devolved, the novel also posits him as exemplary of Southern white character.

In its construction and scathing reading of white subjects, the novel posits that Southern white ethnics' moral and ethical values are on the lowest rung of the civilized world's social ladder. The men and women are hedonistic, which leads them to indulge in necrophilia, incest, homosexuality, sadomasochism, and other sexual acts that so-called civilized society considers deviant (discussed in chapter 6 of this study). They also are alcoholics, drug addicts, adulterers, and confidence men. Even when measured by their own moral and ethical principles, they are "depraved" (153).

African Americans, Native Americans, and non-Southern whites do not escape the novel's reading of American character/s. Mammy Barracuda, Bangalang, Stray Leechfield, 40s, and some of the other blacks exhibit extreme degrees of diasporization, and thus the novel assigns them to the category of Other. Reed uses the diasporan myth to explain (not to excuse) what is lacking in these diasporan blacks' character. The novel argues that they are victims of a subject deformation so thorough that it has altered their true nature and turned them into "stupid" and "mean-minded" people (9–10). Consequently, they have lost contact with the African gods, who either have deserted the mean-minded or are concealing themselves from them (9). Indeed, given their shape-shifting powers, many of the African gods in the West have assumed "new forms" (9), chief among which are writing (particularly parodic and oppositional discourse) and Hoodoo (whose other appellations include "roots" and "conjure"). However, as a consequence of extreme diasporization, the stupid and mean-minded are "too unimaginative" to recognize the gods in their "new forms" (9). Moreover, many of the gods themselves also have been victims of diasporization and require feeding to sustain their powers over the natural and the supernatural worlds (over writing and Hoodoo, respectively).

Christianization was one of the major ideological vehicles slaveholders used to deform (that is, to partition) the African Self. There are a few blacks in this novel, however, who have resisted the power structure's attempts to convert them to "the Jesus cult" and thus who still pray to the African gods (74, 53). Raven Quickskill, Uncle Robin, and Aunt Judy are among this group of resistors. Part of Quickskill's resistance is his control over the word, over language. From one perspective, his power is Calibanic in that he appropriates and transforms the word of the (white) Other—he "put[s] witchery on the word" (13) that has been used to subjugate him—and then he proceeds to use the transformed word as a weapon to liberate himself (and potentially others) from oppressive discourses.

What this novel and other black texts (from Douglass's 1845 *Narrative* to Wideman's *Cattle Killing*) suggest is that members of the Jesus cult have used their word to profane the sacred and primordial Word as part of their oppression of blacks and Native Americans. In the construction of a character named Rev. J. B. B. Tosamah (who in several ways recalls Ellison's Rev. B. P. Rinehart from *Invisible Man*) and through the use of speech patterns that seem aligned with both African American and Native American vernacular, N. Scott Momaday in his novel *House Made of Dawn* (79–87) creates a narrative formation that dramatizes the premise that the "white man" profaned the Word by imposing "his idea of God upon the everlasting Truth" (83).

The Calibanic word is Quickskill's (and Reed's) Hoodoo, his Canada, and his typewriter ("his drum he danced to" [89]) is the technological mechanism through which he mediates the Calibanic word. Through an auto-biographical act, Quickskill dances himself and his others, and as such he forms a natural insulation against diasporization. He, like his creator, Ishmael Reed, garners control of the Other's word and thus the power to define (to read and thus to curse) the Other.

The novel's readings of Native Americans and non-Southern whites concentrate on representative characters from these two groups who have become southernized.[6] Many Native Americans resisted Americanization, and the novel speaks sympathetically about those resistors and compares them favorably to those New World Africans (such as the Ibos [123]) who resisted and who still resist diasporization. However, the Native American subject the novel foregrounds, Princess Quaw Quaw Tralaralara, represents those Native Americans who succumbed to Americanization. Americanization has all but erased Princess Tralaralara's authentic ethnicity, and what remains of it has been whitewashed and thus deformed. She participates in her own deformation by attempting to become "universal" (95)—by selling her birthright as entertainment for whites. Like some of the Cherokees during the period of slavery, she is an ally of the slaves (signified in part through her romantic bond with Quickskill); and like some other Cherokees during the Civil War, this "Third World Belle" (123) is an ally of the slavocracy (signified in part through her marriage to the southernized Yankee Jack). She represents those Natives who either willfully or through coercion lost the power of their own word (language) and thus the ability to communicate with their gods. Their subjectivity became defined and deformed by the word of whites. (Pauline, a central character and one of the two narrators in Louise Erdrich's *Tracks,* is an excellent example of a Native American whose subjectivity is defined and severely deformed by the white Word/word.)

Two of the principal and representative non-Southern whites in the novel, Abraham Lincoln and Harriet Beecher Stowe, are also victims of southernization. Both are players in a confidence game in which they pretend sympathy for the slaves' plight but actually are supporters of the slavocracy. As the novel sees it, Lincoln's "Emancipation Proclamation" and

Stowe's *Uncle Tom's Cabin* are texts of history and literature, respectively, that collaborate in the deformation of black subjectivity. According to the novel, official biographies, literary biographies, and social histories fail to present an accurate portrait of the roles these people and their texts played in the deformation of New World Africans. As a corrective gesture, *Flight to Canada* purports to give an accurate reading of these two people and their texts and to show their complicity in the deformation of black subjectivity. The residual effects of Stowe's deformation of black male subjectivity have yet to be fully erased or negated.

The novel's reading of non-Southern whites emphasizes their affinity with (rather than distinction from) Southern whites and asserts that Southern white culture and character are the gauges by which one assesses white American character. Not only Virginia, but all of America, is Camelot (98)—"the Wasp's Jerusalem" (15). The novel's inscription of Yankee Jack is aligned with this reading. Reed accomplishes this in part by drawing upon the history of the nation's early colonial period, during which Virginia was a controlling metaphor for all English holdings in North America and the Virginia settler was the representative model for the white colonial. He also uses Southern white culture and character as the shaping forces of white American character during the nineteenth century, in which the novel is set, and the twentieth century, in which it is published.

Flight to Canada conforms to Linda Hutcheon's definition of historiographic metafiction: a form of the novel that is "both intensely self-reflexive and yet paradoxically also lay[s] claim to historical events and personages"; its incorporation of history, literature, and literary theory "is made the grounds for its rethinking and reworking of the forms and contents of the past" (5). The three domains (history, literature, literary theory) are intertwined around the nation's (particularly the South's) neo-feudalistic life and is one indication in the novel of how the present is merely an extension of the past. The nineteenth-century American slavocracy in which the novel is set is an extension of the European age of feudalism. The twentieth century in which it is produced is an extension of nineteenth-century America's age of neo-feudalism. What sets *Flight to Canada* apart from most other historiographic metafictions, including black ones, is the way it uses race to inextricably bind the domains of history, literature, and literary theory.

As author/narrator, Reed positions himself as a historian, and in doing so he questions the thin line that separates the history text from the literature text: "Who is to say what is fact and what is fiction?" (7). The novel argues implicitly that the historian constructs facts from events, then selects and arranges these facts to form an impression of persons, events, and periods.[7] What the historian does differs little from what the historical novelist does; both are fabulators and both manufacture reality. From the same events and periods the white historian and historical novelist use, Reed constructs a different set of facts and selects and arranges them in an order that forms a very different impression of historical times, persons, places, and events.[8] As part of *his* revisionist history, Reed foregrounds facts about a person's life that most historians and biographers subordinate or ignore. He uses some received facts of a person's subjectivity in a way that implies the person's essence and consequently contradicts the received historical portrait of that person—Stowe, Lincoln, and Jefferson Davis are the most prominent examples of subjects he inscribes (reads) in this manner.

Flight to Canada is a fiction that stands in opposition to white-authored fictions, whether the latter are cast in the form of literature, history, science, anthropology, or any other discursive format. Through referentiality and intertextuality, *Flight* repudiates specific and generic texts and their authors, particularly ones that purport to provide accurate portraits of the peculiar institution and its subjects, blacks and whites. Among these the novel foregrounds Tennyson's *Idylls of the King*, Stowe's *Uncle Tom's Cabin*, and Mitchell's *Gone with the Wind*, all of which, the novel contends, manufacture reality. From *Flight*'s perspective, Stowe and Mitchell and their novels are quintessential deformers of black subjectivity.[9] As part of its "rethinking and reworking of the forms and contents of the past" (to use Hutcheon's words), the novel asserts that an immersion in verbal reality is not confined to Southern white laymen (such as the Swilles) or to literary authors but includes southern and nonsouthern historians and their texts, such as Ulrich Phillips's *American Negro Slavery* and Fogel and Engerman's *Time on the Cross*.

The literary theory that *Flight to Canada* installs and most fully rethinks and reworks—that is, subverts—is that of Poe and the New Critics. As the novel sees it, New Criticism is largely an extension of Poe's "The Philosophy of Composition" and "The Poetic Principle." The formulators of New Criticism, of course, were southerners (the Fugitives),[10] and the theory's principles of literary composition and interpretation were preeminent in the white academy (principally a nonsouthern entity) at the middle of the twentieth century. New Criticism often deprecates the works of black writers, ostensibly because of the perspective on race and history these works advance. The form and content of *Flight* defy the white academy's received and prescriptive notions about literature and literary theory.

In his challenge to the white academy, Reed uses Poe as an exemplar and Canada as a trope to read him and certain contemporary critics. Among several other things, Canada is the imagination; it is whatever psychic space or geographic place that frees one from the constraints of another person's definition and imposition of reality. Targeting those contemporary critics who prescribe the creative process, *Flight to Canada* implicitly repeats a premise from *Invisible Man* (422) by asserting through its form and content that it is better to live out the absurdity of one's own reality than to die for that of others. Indeed, in writing his fictional slave narrative, Reed's imagination takes flight (as the saying goes) to Canada. His novel's form and content repudiate the academy's prescriptive notions about genricity (the historical novel, the slave narrative, realistic fiction) and debunk the academy's literary critics whose judgments are based on these prescriptions.

Reed's reading of (attack on) the white academy as part of his novel's narrative content begins a convention in contemporary fictional slave narratives whose roots extend from nineteenth-century African American novels such as Jones's *Hearts of Gold* (66–67). Though different in its form, this attack is similar in meaning to ones in *Beloved, Dessa Rose,* and *Oxherding Tale.* These three novels deprecate the white academy through its principal exponents (teachers and researchers) and their perpetuation of a sanctioned deformation of black subjectivity. In *Beloved,* it is Morrison's formation of the character called Schoolteacher, a pseudo-anthropologist who indoctrinates his "pupils" (his nephews) with the art and science of deforming black subjectivity. In *Dessa Rose,* it is Williams's formation of Adam Nehemiah, a pseudo-historian, pseudo-anthropologist, former teacher/tutor, and would-be novelist who asserts that "Science [and] Research" (255) have allowed him to know (to read accurately) Dessa's and thus slaves' and women's subjectivity.

Charles Johnson in *Oxherding Tale* reads the white academy through his construction of Ezekiel Sykes-Withers, a tutor and an intellectual, and through his formation of Andrew Hawkins, Sykes-Withers's pupil, as a countersubject. Johnson's attack lies principally in making the black pupil intellectually superior to the white teacher (the same narrative formation he uses in "The Education of Mingo"). Reed does not include in *Flight to*

Canada a white teacher per se as representative of the academy, but the relationship between Arthur Swille and Raven Quickskill intimates that Quickskill as pupil certainly learns from and intellectually surpasses his teacher, Arthur Swille. He does, however, include an anthropologist (Mitchell Swille, son of Arthur III) and singles out Columbia University as representative of the academy's institutionalized deformation of blacks and Natives.

One of this subgenre's conventions is its thematic and formal erasure of temporal and spatial boundaries. Reed puts his personal stamp on this convention. *Flight to Canada* concentrates on a conjunction of periods within historical time, which is consistent with its emphasis on reading the white Other. It inscribes the historical past in terms of the historical present, and vice versa, as a means of revealing the affinities between the Civil War period and the Civil Rights period and between Southern whites and non-Southern whites. For instance, in the decade preceding this novel's publication (the Civil Rights era), many Americans from all regions of the country viewed the nation and its first family (the Kennedys) as remanifestations of Camelot, just as many pre–Civil War whites considered the South as a new Camelot. In this instance, the Arthurian legend is the rubric under which the novel conjoins time and space and thus reads whites from the past, present, and future.

In other instances the novel conjoins time and space through symbols of technology (such as the television and the automobile) and through signifiers of social space and place (such as the Frederick Douglass Houses, a conjunction of nineteenth-century slave quarters and twentieth-century housing projects). Television was the technological invention Americans used to view the racial conflicts of the Civil Rights era as well as to view the military conflict known as the Vietnam War, and television is the mechanism antebellum subjects use to view the regional and military conflicts (predicated on race) of the Civil War.

Language, images, and symbols are the principal joiners of time and space in this novel. Reed's narrator often speaks of mid-nineteenth-century action (the novel's present) using language encoded with images and symbols generated in the mid-twentieth century. One of numerous examples is the narrator's description of Stray Leechfield "driving a carriage" in the mid-1800s outfitted with mid-1970s state-of-the-art automobile technology (36). Reed frequently inserts images, symbols, and personalities from twentieth-century culture into narrative formations about the nineteenth century. Tarzan movies (53), beauty pageants (59), "Crossbars of the Confederate [that] fly from pick-up trucks" (66), Air Canada's jumbo jets and Greyhound's buses (145), *Life* magazine (68), and broadcast journalists Barbara Walters and Harry Reasoner (69–70) are among the many examples. Along with references to the Frederick Douglass Houses and other signifiers of the present's (mid-1800s) extension into the future (mid-1900s), Reed shows how the legacy of the slave past thrives in the novel's and in the nation's future. Using the Arthurian legend as the controlling trope in his construction of this sociocultural and psychocultural phenomenon, Reed posits that diasporization is an unbroken continuum that began in historical time's remote past and continues into the present.

Responding to the assertion that on the scale of social evolution technology is the signifier of man's progression from savage to civilized, from "the raw to the cooked," the novel's retort is that the difference between the savage and the civilized is power (149), not technological advances.[11] Indeed, technology just makes it more convenient for man to engage in activities associated with the primal horde; it does not indicate that man has evolved significantly from a savage state. In fact, in this American Camelot, on "this unholy savage ground" (105), "Man [the gender] is in the last stage of his evolution" (106) and has progressed very little from man in the primal horde. The novel's formation of white subjectivity asserts that Man (white) in North America is still half-savage (104).

Flight to Canada as title bespeaks the diasporan subject's desire to return home and echoes Toomer's statement that the early African ancestors in the Americas charted the route for their descendants to re-turn home. Like other novelists writing in this subgenre, Reed draws upon the cultural myths about the walking Ibos and the flying Africans to name this desire. Typical for Reed, he inverts and expands the legend of the walking Ibos and applies it to Natives and to whites (123; 131–33).[12] Reed also calls this desire *Drapetomania* and draws from an historical and pseudoscientific myth for its definition: "that disease causing Negroes to run away" (18). Sherley Anne Williams installs a similar formation in *Dessa Rose* (16–19). Both Reed (explicitly) and Williams (implicitly) dialogically refute some basic premises of a specific contemporary text of history and "science" that seeks to define and to explain the behavior of slaves and the experience of slavery in the United States, Fogel and Engerman's *Time on the Cross*. Making Quickskill his mouthpiece, Reed decries such texts and their authors: "Revisionists. Quantitative historians. What does a computer know? Can a computer feel? . . . Look at those scars. Look at them. All you see is their fruits, but their roots run deep. The roots are in my soul. What does a fucking computer know about that?" (150–51).

As the novel repeatedly states, Canada is freedom and freedom assumes a variety of forms. Among these forms is the diasporan subject's self-transformation or self-reinvention through mastery of the word. Quickskill's control of the word effects his transformation from an object to a subject. Unlike the computer he decries, Quickskill (and Reed) can "feel" and therefore can dance the other and the self. As Senghor explains, "It is in his subjectivity" that the diasporan subject "discovers the [o]ther" and "in a centrifugal motion" is "*e-moved*" in a manner that allows him to "say, 'I feel, I dance the [o]ther, I am'" ("On Negrohood" 3, 6). The premise applies to the Reed-Quickskill nexus. In this instance, to feel and to dance the other is to reinvent the other and the self, and the vehicle for this reinvention is writing, as chapter 14 (85–89) of *Flight to Canada* makes clear. And though *Flight to Canada* devotes the majority of its textual space to reading the white subjects, text, and authors across centuries and continents, it does not neglect the theory and praxis of writing of the black Self.

Writing the Black Self as the White Other: Johnson's Oxherding Tale

In his *Being and Race: Black Writing since 1970*, Charles Johnson makes several poignant observations about the contemporary African American novel that are applicable to his *Oxherding Tale*. He correctly asserts that the black writer creates out of and within a tradition: "He must have models with which to agree, partly agree, or outright oppose, and these can come only from the tradition of literature itself" (5). The two most prominent models from the African American literary tradition with which aspects of *Oxherding Tale*'s form, content, and principal themes "agree, partly agree, or outright oppose" are the male-centered passing novel and the nonfiction slave narrative. The theory and praxis of black fiction that *Oxherding Tale* encodes—particularly in the formation of its centered subject—support Johnson's assertion in *Being and Race* that "black fiction is *about* the troubled quest for identity and liberty, the agony of social alienation, the longing for a real and at times a mythical home" (8; Johnson's emphasis).

Andrew's quest for an authentic identity is the novel's thematic and formal organizing principle. The biological circumstances of Andrew's birth endow him with a double identity that situate him between two racial and social worlds, what the novel calls the antebellum house and field. This double identity is the source of his social alienation. As a young adult he attempts to resolve his liminality by reinventing himself as a white man. However, the resolution to his identity crisis is not totally successful. Johnson inscribes Andrew's quest for identity and liberty and his "longing for . . . a mythical home" within the diasporan myth. At certain junctures the inscription revises (that is, agrees or partly agrees with as well as opposes) aspects of the tradition in black fiction in such a manner that the novel's production is, like that of several other contemporary black novels, "a fresh, original vision" (*Being and Race* 5) within the tradition.

Andrew resides in a social world—the West—that epidermalizes and genderizes Being (52, 55). Johnson observes that Bigger Thomas (from Richard Wright's *Native Son*, 1940) lives in a world in which "to *be* is to be white" (*Being and Race* 14; Johnson's emphasis). In *Oxherding Tale*, he agrees with Wright and others but emends this premise by demonstrating that in the Manichean world in which Andrew Hawkins lives, ontology is predicated on the premise that to *be* is to be white *and* male. Ostensibly, then, Andrew's transformation is not just from slavery to freedom, but from "thinghood" (70) to personhood, which means that it is a sociocultural transformation from black to white. Yet the transformation is incomplete. The freedom Andrew acquires is external rather than internal, and his Becoming is (somewhat ironically) a metamorphosis from authentic black to counterfeit white.

In the African American literary tradition, it is conventional in passing novels that racial transformation is more successful when the subject who undergoes the transformation is male rather than female. Typically, in the male-centered novel the subject's failure to complete his racial transformation stems from his inability to synchronize his exteriority and interiority. As the character Horace Bannon (the Soulcatcher) observes, it might be very difficult for one to accept his nature, but it is almost impossible to change "the nature you born with" (111). From the purview of the diasporan myth's theory of Being, one is born with a soul and the soul is the seat of one's essence. Though one can render the soul inactive, one cannot kill it. In the tradition of the African American passing novel, the black subject who passes for white often is not internally successful because he or she cannot erase every trace of the soul. This indelible trace of primordiality periodically surfaces as what Bannon terms "the Call" (115). The Call beckons the subject to admit and to affirm his or her essence. The conscious or subconscious response to the Call is the subject's conscious or subconscious desire to reactivate his or her soul.

In the tradition of the male-centered passing novel, James Weldon Johnson's ex-coloured man best exemplifies this premise. Moreover, he is the model with which Charles Johnson most fully agrees (and perhaps disagrees) in his construction of Andrew Hawkins.[13] In *The Autobiography of an Ex-Coloured Man,* the soulcatcher as concept—that trace of primordiality that the subject cannot effectively efface or elude—is manifested as manuscripts of spirituals, as discursive incarnations of the soul/spirit. These manuscripts emit the Call. In *Oxherding Tale,* the soulcatcher is Horace Bannon, who pursues Andrew and sends out the Call, stimulating Andrew's longing for a mythical home and thus activating his diasporan desire. As Bannon explains, the passer (racial or otherwise) is ever listening for the Call: "It's the Call he waited for his whole life. His capture happens like a wish, somethin' he wants, a destiny that come from inside him, not outside" (115). At the end (which is also the beginning) of *The Autobiography of an Ex-Coloured Man,* the protagonist still hears the Call but still fails to respond to it effectively. One can argue that the same is true for Andrew Hawkins. Because Andrew's narrative is a retrospective confessional, the novel's end is its beginning. Because Andrew has not successfully answered the Call, his diasporan desire has not been fully satisfied.

Andrew exemplifies the diasporan subject who is a biocultural amalgam of European and African. In the biocultural space that is his self, there is a war waging between the factions (house and field, black and white, European and African) of his subjectivity, and this war exacerbates his partitioning. It is that classic war of double-consciousness that Du Bois succinctly describes in *The Souls of Black Folk* (1903) and that is germane to the formation of centered subjects in several of the male-centered passing novels that precede *Oxherding Tale.* Du Bois defines double-consciousness as "two souls, two thoughts, two unreconciled strivings; two warring ideals in one dark body" (3). Johnson inscribes the concept as a battle within Andrew between the spirituality (blackness) and the materiality (whiteness) of his self—between the e-motion and the intellect, between the European and the African facets of Andrew's subjectivity. Torn between being "folks or white" (36), Andrew's attempts to reconcile these "strivings" in order to position himself comfortably in the Western world form a foundation for the novel's plot structure.

Johnson also inscribes these warring ideals as characters who are integral to the formation of Andrew's subjectivity. The contrast in the principles these characters represent precipitates Andrew's identity crisis. Progeny of a white mother and a black father, Andrew's biological duality begins with his conception. His conception is itself a violation of the slavocracy's social and moral tenets, and his birth automatically positions him as a social and racial liminal, a form of orphanhood. The cultural and psychological duality that commences in his childhood induces an internal duel (double-consciousness) that continues into his adulthood. During his maturation, adult males, black and white, function as mirrors that control and reflect his identity formation. Principal among these are George Hawkins (black) and Jonathan Polkinghorne (white), Reb (black) and Ezekiel Sykes-Withers (white), as well as Horace Bannon (both black and white). All of them function as forms of a father for Andrew. The paired males (George/Jonathan; Reb/Ezekiel) represent opposing sides of Andrew's internal warring ideals, and Horace Bannon is the principal mediation between these oppositions.

George, his biological father, encourages him to be himself (35)—to follow his nature as a black. The roots of his true nature are Allmuseri, and though the traces of his primordial Being are few, they are clearly discernible as he matures. For example, as a young adult Andrew can discern within himself traces of his plurality as a self, of his intersubjective nature, and of a shape-shifting ability endemic to the Allmuseri: "I was, or felt myself to be, several selves, like the Coffinmaker's polyhedral *kra,* which suffered all possible forms" (61). He also can discern a trace of *connaissance,* and the trace of this special power of seeing and knowing is evident when he realizes that he has the ability to "see . . . the interior of objects" (63). However, the "clairvoyance" (63) he experiences in this instance is more the product of a false nature induced by drugs (laudanum, a solution of opium in alcohol) than it is the activation of an inherent quality (true nature). The narrative formation recalls and partly agrees with one from Ellison's *Invisible Man,* in which for a brief period invisible man hears the Call and, responding, is transported outside the West's boundaries of time and space and Being (7–10). Under the influence of different surrogate fathers, Andrew, like invisible man, learns to suppress his true nature and to substitute instead a false nature.

George, Andrew's biological father, and Reb, his primal father, nourish the emotive qualities of his subjectivity. Jonathan Polkinghorne, his stepfather, encourages him to develop his intellect, and Jonathan employs Ezekiel Sykes-Withers as the instrument to accomplish this intellectual development. Because these two white surrogate fathers encourage Andrew to develop his mind to the neglect of his soul, they are in binary opposition to Andrew's black fathers. Though Bannon admonishes Andrew that a person cannot change his nature and that a person must know his nature, at the same time Bannon in effect threatens to annihilate Andrew if indeed he follows his true nature.

Andrew has been conditioned to see the Black World as "a style of being characterized by stasis, denial, humiliation, thinghood, and, as the philosophers said, 'relative being'" (70). He has been conditioned to see the White World as a style of being characterized by privilege, promise, personhood, and freedom. Forced to choose between these two worlds, Andrew chooses the latter in an attempt to liberate himself and to reverse his social alienation. Though he comes to understand that the freedom he gains as a member of the White World is relative and illusory, he tries to convince himself that it is real. It is real, if one accepts the novel's definition of reality as "a matter of consent, a shared hallucination" (49). Like ex-coloured man, Andrew attempts to justify his choice based largely on taste. Though "uneasy" (133) about his decision to reinvent himself as the white William Harris, he nevertheless chooses to privilege the exteriority of his Being over its interiority. In the example of ex-coloured man, he sells his "birthright [his spiritual nature] for a mess of pottage" (social freedom and materiality).[14] He reinvents a life (a self) that is "a living lie," one in which his knowledge, clothes, language, and other aspects of his subjectivity are "shamefully second-hand, made by, and perhaps for, other men"—white men (17). Though he chooses the white male as his ego-ideal, he is unable to negate the black male as a model for his Being. Such vacillations in his conscience and consciousness help perpetuate his partitioning.

Reb functions as Andrew's primal father, and Reb's personal history is a miniature version of the history of the Allmuseri and their diasporization. Born in Africa into "the ancient clan-state of the Allmuseri" (48), he is the great-grandson of "a powerful *osuo*" (49) named Rakhal, from whom he began to learn the special powers of seeing and knowing. In preparation for becoming a master sorcerer, Reb learned from Rakhal how to manifest his intersubjective nature—that is, how "to send his *kra* [spirit/soul] forth to dwell in" animals, plants, men, and women (49).[15] Before his training was complete, he became a victim of the Middle Passage. But his subjection to diasporization did not mute the intersubjective nature of his Being.

Throughout diasporization "his *kra* remained the same, unspoiled" (50); keeping the link with the Primordial Soul intact allows him to elude the Soulcatcher.

Reb's unbroken link with primordiality is what defines him as a survivor and distinguishes his ontology from that of most other diasporan subjects in the novel. Reb's son, Patrick, is one such subject who becomes so Westernized that he accepts the Western "belief in personal identity, the notion that *what* we are is somehow distinct from other things" (58; Johnson's emphasis). Thus, "the cause of death for these black men [is] . . . not physical at all" but a consequence of having effectively suppressed their souls by muting their palimpsestic nature (58). When this suppression occurs, the diasporan subject becomes a prime target for the Soulcatcher.

Johnson's perspective on the palimpsestic Self through his formation of Reb agrees with how other novelists treat the concept in their diasporan novels. Yet his inscription of this concept in his formation of Horace Bannon "outright opposes" that of other contemporary black novelists. Indeed, there is probably not a more imaginative, creative, and nonstandard inscription of the palimpsestic Self in black literature than Johnson's formation of Horace Bannon. On the Soulcatcher's body and still living are all creatures—insects, animals, persons—he has killed in the past and the present and will kill in the future. Though a profaned version of palimpsestic Being, the Soulcatcher literally and figurally embodies all living things; his body is a living "mosaic" (175) of the world. As part of his hermeneutic functions, the Soulcatcher is also the West and represents the Westernization or deformation of black Being in the West. He is Andrew's nemesis, his conscience and his consciousness, for Andrew eventually realizes that he "had produced him from myself" (170).

Among the women integral to Andrew's life and subjectivity—including Anna, Mattie, Flo, and Peggy—Minty is his most viable subject complement, the one who could lead him back to an androgynous state of Being and thus to primordial wholeness. Though she becomes the most tragic victim of diasporization in the novel, prior to her horrific brutalization the different parts of Minty's self appear to Andrew "to be purified features in a Whole." To him, all parts of Minty's self "fused together to offer a flawed, haunting beauty" (15). In this early description of her, Andrew draws particular attention to Minty's eyes, the window to her soul. Her eyes, like those of Toomer's Fern (*Cane* 27, 33), reveal that hers is a primordial soul, that she is a self/Self who "had been lifted long ago from a melancholy

African landscape" (15) and positioned in the West. Like Toomer's Karintha ("a November cotton flower" that blooms out of season [*Cane* 2]) and other women in *Cane*'s first section, Minty is "a sad, out-of-season beauty" (16) who suffers from a form of what Wideman in *The Cattle Killing* calls "the Ebo melancholy" (103)—a longing for "home."

Continuing to process Minty through the slavocracy, Anna Polkinghorne sells her. When Andrew meets her again (she is a commodity at a slave auction), Minty's body is "a latticework of whipmarks" (154). Her body, like Sethe's and Dessa's, is a virtual text of slavery's power to deform the body but of its inability to destroy the soul. Though she is physically deformed and eventually destroyed by the ravages of slavery, Minty's slow and painful death eventually returns her soul "home" to the primordial place of her spiritual origins, where she fuses with the African landscape—a landscape, Andrew says, that "had been planned at the instant of Creation to complement Minty, blues and browns to contrast the warm hues of her skin" (167).

In its form, content, and meaning, *Oxherding Tale* also agrees with, partly agrees with, and outright opposes some nonblack texts. Signifying this are three of the four epigraphs Johnson uses for the novel. One of them, from Saint Augustine's *Confessions,* is from a person whom Johnson identifies as "the first philosophical black writer" (119). That the novel is concerned with its centered subject's movement toward primordial (complete) wholeness is intimated in all four of the novel's epigraphs. When used as a gloss on the novel's content, the fourth epigraph, a quotation from Franz Kafka's *The Great Wall of China,* speaks to the palimpsestic and intersubjective nature of Being, concepts Johnson uses in his formation of Horace Bannon (discussed above), Reb, and Andrew Hawkins. The quotation asserts "the existence of different subjects in the same human being." These "subjects" are permutations of the principal subject's soul. For Reb, Johnson inscribes this permutation as Reb's *kra,* his "I," the essence of his Being, which he can implant in other human and nonhuman forms (49). Reb's *kra* is impervious to diasporization. Not subject to time, space, and circumstances, the *kra* can survive the deformation (50), even the destruction, of its host's physicality. Minty exemplifies the latter point.

Traces of Andrew's *kra,* his transcendental "I," are dormant through much of his narrative. When applied to Andrew, the second epigraph, a quotation from *Big Verda,* speaks to the fact that in the early chapters of his narrative Andrew indeed does "not know in relation to what [he] can say,

'This I am.'" The features of his discourse indicate that at this stage his self-definition would be Cartesian (I think; therefore I am) rather than Senghorian (I feel; therefore I am).[16] Indeed, diasporization has rendered him incapable of dancing/feeling the other and therefore incapable of dancing the self; thus, as the epigraph suggests, "bewildered and lost in thought," Andrew, like Toomer's Kabnis (*Cane*), wanders and his soul withers. Yet the traces of his primordial soul become more activated and manifest near the novel's end when Andrew experiences intimations of his palimpsestic nature—that is, the sensation or knowledge that "everything [is] mysteriously blended into everything else" (27). Johnson incorporates premises from sacred geometry to convey these intimations. As Andrew describes the revelation, "The profound mystery of the One and the Many gave me back my father again and again, his love, in every being from grubworms to giant sumacs, for these too were my father" (176).

Nevertheless, at the novel's end Andrew Hawkins is living as William Harris, a counterfeit white man. He is a facsimile rather than an authentic self. He has not achieved that original androgynous and primordial wholeness. When applied to Andrew, the third epigraph, a quotation from *Ten Oxherding Tales* (a source repeated in this novel's title), suggests that Andrew comes close but does not actually attain the object of his desire ("he is seeking an Ox he does not find"). In other words, he perhaps has attained wholeness from having reconciled his double-consciousness, but he has not achieved complete wholeness. His liberation is external, not internal; his freedom is vicarious, not real. The symbolic action that supports these conclusions is Andrew's "marriage" to Peggy Underwood.

From the purview of the diasporan myth's theory of Being, a wedding ceremony signifies the reunion of two formerly severed primordial souls ("the Woman [and] the Man"); it is a sacred ritual in which (Western) "Time" is suspended and a moment during which the "heart [knows] nothing of hours. Minutes" (140). Similar to the ritual nation dancing in Marshall's *Praisesong*, this ritual of complementarity is one of transportation/translation from historical time to primordial Time, and it is a ritual of transformation that reenacts in reverse order the "Platonic nous emanating from the One" (140). The wedding ceremony evokes in Andrew latent memories of primordial Time and Being: "We stood, I felt, translated, lifted a few feet off the ground, exchanging replies in old, old voices in a different tongue we borrowed from our better selves—the people we were intended to be—in some parallel world, where the absences of this life were presences, the failures here triumphs there, a realm of changeless meaning for which the only portal was surrender" (140). This feeling of translation, transportation, and transformation (metamorphosis) is short-lived, however. "After the ceremony this nearly mystical feeling of transport faded. We fell back into clock time" (140). What could have been a ritual for total liberation, a re-turn to primordial Time and Being, actually is not. In fact, Andrew's wedding ceremony signifies "a new, subtle, loss of identity" (139). That he has not fully liberated the authenticity of his Being and thus is not totally free of the Soulcatcher is indicated in the "final face" he sees on the Soulcatcher's body mosaic—"my own face, for he had duplicated portions of me during the early days of the hunt" (176). Because the Soulcatcher has not duplicated the entirety of Andrew's self, all is not lost and Andrew at the novel's end still has the opportunity to reform his authentic self.

As a reinvented self, what Andrew lacks most in order to be whole are love and a beloved. In his myth about the origin and nature of humankind as recorded in Plato's *Symposium*, Aristophanes states that "the desire for the whole and the pursuit of it is named Love" (88). A desiring subject's fusion with a kindred soul (a true subject complement) is fusion with his or her "very own beloved, which now few are able to do" (*Symposium* 89). Aristophanes states further that "Love . . . in the present gives us our chief blessing by bringing us home to our own, and for the future offers the greatest hopes; . . . [Love] will restore us to our ancient nature and heal us and make us blessed and happy" (89). Only if Andrew's marriage to Peggy produces love and Peggy becomes his beloved will he be restored to this ancient nature. The novel's end leaves this possibility open.

It is not Peggy's race that prevents her from being his true subject complement, but that Andrew marries her in order to seal his reinvention as a white man, as a counterfeit Other. Peggy is the mediation for the object of his misplaced desire; their marriage is one of social skins rather than of primordial souls. Like the male prototype in the passing novels that precede this one,[17] Andrew's reinvention of self is a calculated attempt to move closer to the center of Western (white) life. The principal requisites for this racial transformation are physiological, intellectual, and legal. Physiologically, Andrew looks like a white man and thus possesses the first prerequisite for reinventing himself as a white man. With the assistance of his white stepfather, he acquires the second prerequisite for being a white man, a white intellect. In fact, his intellect as an adult surpasses that of white male exemplars (Sykes-Withers and Marx) in the novel.

The third prerequisite for a black male to become a white male is to attain the legal status of a white man, which Andrew does when he marries Peggy Underwood, for in the context of the novel's historical setting only a white man can legally marry a white woman. While this third principal step makes him certifiably a counterfeit white man, it also, like his father's near-obsession with the historical and material world (43), signifies Andrew's "self-inflicted segregation from the Whole" (142).

The novel's ending suggests that there is another route by which Andrew still can attain complete wholeness—procreation, which yields (a form of) immortality. In the novel's second metafictional interlude, Johnson states that the "Subject of the Slave Narrative" is not a "perceiving Self" who "falteringly interprets the world, but a narrator who *is* that world" (152–53; Johnson's emphasis). From this perspective, Andrew's statement that after his body was emancipated he turned to the business of rebuilding the world/self can be read as his intent to reinvent himself again—this time as an authentic self. Thus, there is the suggestion at the novel's end that, in addition to complementarity, procreation is also a means for a partitioned self to achieve complete wholeness. Such a subject, Lacanian (via Aristophanes) in form, lacks and thus desires that original androgynous wholeness. According to Kaja Silverman, Lacanian "lack is sexual in definition; it has to do with the impossibility of being physiologically both male and female" (152). Metaphorically, the form of Lacanian lack applicable to Andrew's subjectivity is in part racial in definition and concerns the impossibility of him being psychologically both black and white. Silverman also states that "Lacan shares with Aristophanes the belief that the only resolution to the loss suffered by the subject as the consequence of sexual division is heterosexual union and procreation" (152). Andrew has secured a heterosexual union and has procreated; thus he is in a position at his tale's end to re-form himself.

To accomplish the reformation, he must realign his body (which has been liberated) and his soul (which has not been liberated), and this will be his "business of rebuilding the world"/self (176)—that is, the business of giving birth to self. Aristophanes's myth and Barlo's narrative of the mythic primal African parent (from *Cane*) offer a gloss on this androgynous characteristic of the diasporan male. The *Symposium* states that all men are pregnant in both body and soul (101). Those who are pregnant in body turn to women to beget children and "thus secure for themselves, so they think, immortality and memory and happiness." Those who are pregnant in soul and "who conceive in soul still more than in body, what is proper for the soul to conceive and bear" (that is, "wisdom and virtue") include "all creative poets, and those artists and craftsmen who are said to be inventive" (103). Andrew belongs to this group. His narrative is evidence of his artistic creativity. The product of his procreative act (his daughter, Anna) is an intimation of immortality ("all is conserved; all" [176]) and metaphorically a reproduction of his self. From this procreative act Andrew regains the primal parent's capacity to be both progenitor and progeny, which he reveals at the end of his tale: "I was my father's father, and he my child" (176). His soul is pregnant, and, like Barlo's androgynous mythic African, he now has the capacity to give birth to (to reinvent) his authentic self. The novel's end does not specifically indicate whether the product of his soul's pregnancy will be alive (an authentic self) or stillborn (a facsimile self or another counterfeit self). However, one can argue that, like ex-coloured man, Andrew's writing of his narrative, his exposé of self, is a (pro)creative act that intimates his ability to give birth to his authentic self.

The Arithmetic of Black Male Subject Formation

Though in both of his fictional slave narratives Charles Johnson states conceptually the arithmetic of Western black Being (the Many from the One), the concept is dramatized more fully in other contemporary fictional slave narratives, especially in Wideman's *The Cattle Killing.* In this novel Wideman uses the terms "peculiar arithmetic," "cunning arithmetic," and "the madness" (112, 113) to refer to whites' racist attitudes toward and treatment of blacks in Africa, in England, and in the United States during and after the peculiar institution. A product and instrument of diasporization, this peculiar arithmetic ruptured the spiritual intersubjectivity of black Being as well as partitioned the black self. Subject formation and related thematic and formal properties in *The Cattle Killing* and in some other novels in this subgenre are predicated on utilizing sacred arithmetic to reverse the peculiar arithmetic's debilitating effects. The reversal can be accomplished by repositioning diasporan subjects within the unity of Being.

Arithmetic is the science or art of adding, subtracting, multiplying, and dividing positive or real numbers. Sacred arithmetic endows these arithmetic functions with spiritual and philosophical properties, and it is integral to reading the Other and writing the self/Self in contemporary fictional slave narratives, especially in ones that are male-centered. This study uses sacred geometry as a concept inclusive of the spiritual properties associated with numbers (arithmetic), with forms and shapes (geometry), and with spaces and places (geography). Though all three of these (and other) sacred sciences are interrelated in the diasporan myth as theory and praxis in contemporary fictional slave narratives, sacred arithmetic has some properties distinct from those of the other sacred sciences.

A sacred arithmetic perspective on black male subjectivity within the context of the diasporan myth yields the following premises (abbreviated here). The subtraction of the black male Self from the Primordial Soul produced a bisected black male self in that the Self was split from the Primordial Soul and then the Self was divided into a male self and a male other.[18] (The same ensued when the common gender Self [the androgyne] was split from the Primordial Soul, producing a male self and a female other.) The divided/split male selves were multiplied in time and space to produce many other divided/split male selves. The addition (or reunion) across time and space of the components of the primordial male Self effects wholeness of the Self and potentially the Self's complete wholeness (reunion with the Primordial Soul). With the itinerant preacher as the focal subject, *The Cattle Killing* dramatizes this concept as effectively as any novel.

In *The Cattle Killing*, the components of the male Self exist in historical periods that span three centuries and in geographical places that include three continents, but as victims of the peculiar institution's peculiar arithmetic they all share basically the same psychosocial "condition" (13). In his role as a narrator, and himself a component of this plural male Self, Wideman asks early in the novel, "What is the name of the space they [the component selves] occupy now. All of them" (13). The "black male" names the ontological space in the West that these selves occupy in the past, in the present, and in the future, as the novel aptly demonstrates.

Formation of the Western black male as a plural entity assumes a variety of inscriptions in male-centered texts. Several novels fuse (or reunite) the author and his centered subject by aligning their intellects. In such novels the narrative's level of language usage and its (usually) extensive and explicit use of referentiality and intertextuality are the vehicles for this alignment. Whether spoken/written in the first person or the third, these male-centered texts rarely employ the vernacular as their centered subject's language. One intent is to empower the speaking subject through his mastery of the Western (white) word.

In *Flight to Canada,* there are only slight differences in the level of language Reed and Raven use, and their language differs demonstrably from the vernacular language that characterizes (negatively) most of the other blacks in the novel. Though *Flight* is primarily third-person narration, Raven's direct speech employs the same kind of referentiality (a marker of the intellect) that Reed's and the narrator's speech employ. A similar situation obtains in *Oxherding Tale* and in *Middle Passage.* In these first-person narratives the respective centered subject's speech is not vernacular and is on par with the author's learned speech.

Referentiality and intertextuality are more subtle in *The Cattle Killing* than in *Oxherding Tale* and *Middle Passage.* Nevertheless, it is clear that the principal subject's (the preacher's) intellect is synonymous with Wideman's and with that of some other black males (such as Liam and Bishop Allen) who speak in the novel. Their language usage distinguishes them intellectually from some of the novel's other speaking black males, such as the ex-slave Mr. Rowe (see 66) and the black watchman (185–86) at the orphanage. Yet while the watchman's language signifies his subtraction from the plural black male Self, Mr. Rowe's language does not.

Whereas the focal subject in the female-centered contemporary fictional slave narrative frequently is a reconstruction of a historical person (Dessa, Sethe, and Tituba are examples), the focal subject in the male-centered narrative typically is a composite of several males, including slaves, ex-slaves, free men, historical persons, and creations of the author's imagination. Forming the focal subject as a composite is another way to emphasize that this subject is part of a plurality. Again, *The Cattle Killing* is exemplary.

Another group of contemporary fictional slave narratives whose narrative form is quite different from *The Cattle Killing* build upon the same principle of a black male plural Self. Exemplary of this group are Calvin Baker's *Naming the New World* and Caryl Phillips's *Higher Ground.* Both novels begin with a slave's narrative and then proceed to foreground the narratives of other black males (and females, black and nonblack, respectively) in different geographical places and in different historical periods. By making the male slave's narrative the novel's generative formation, these two novels and similar ones argue that while the male slave does not share the same temporal and spatial zones with other black males, they all share the same condition—diasporization. In some instances the nexus among the components of this male Self is genetic (as in Phillips's *Crossing the River*), in some instances it is sociogenic (as in *Higher Ground*), and occasionally it is both genetic and sociogenic (as in *The Cattle Killing*).

In most instances the formation of the black male as a plurality is a positive statement about the primordial and spiritual bond among the black males. Occasionally, however, authors use this sacred arithmetic to bespeak a lack of spiritual bonding among black males or a rift in a black male's spiritual nature. Wideman's preacher "watches a spectral part of himself separate from his body, himself split in two," creating a self and a "second self" (*Cattle Killing* 27). This second self is a negative form of the first self. The trope extends to Wideman's inscription of Bishop Allen, whom initially the novel identifies as a component of the Self to which the preacher belongs. Later, however, the novel separates the preacher and Allen because Allen is wedded to Christianity and leans toward choosing the whitemale as his ego-ideal (158–60); thus, Allen is a negative form of the black male self. In *Middle Passage,* Johnson uses the same concept of the "split" male self that Wideman uses for the preacher when Johnson inscribes Rutherford Calhoun and his brother Jackson as the negative and the positive, respectively, of the same self. In Rutherford's words, his "brother [was] like a negative of myself" and "I was *his* shadow-self" (112–13; Johnson's emphasis). Jackson is the positive in that he repudiates Westernization and embraces the spiritual plurality of his black Being. Rutherford is the negative in that he embraces the West's concept of the madness of multiplicity, the *me* versus the *thee,* until he is transformed during his reverse Middle Passage. In instances such as the ones above, the authors use what Wideman refers to as a "cunning arithmetic" (*Cattle Killing* 113); it is "cunning" in that its overarching rubric is racism (though the practitioners are blacks). In the collective examples above, the formation of the black male as a plural Self indeed utilizes in various ways the arithmetic functions of addition, subtraction, multiplication, and division.

Speaking to a contemporary audience about the gender of numbers is about as problematic as associating gender with the intellect (male) and with the emotion (female). Nevertheless, even numbers are female; receptive, passive, sensitive, created, and nurturing are their associative properties. Odd numbers are male; initiative, active, creative, and positive are their associative properties (West, *Serpent* 52). The first female number is Two and the first male number is Three. The union of Two and Three is a return to One (Unity, the Absolute). Complementarity as a narrative formation in the black masculinist project requires the fusion of Two and Three, of male and female, to effect complete wholeness.

In the diasporan myth, the subtraction of the common gender Self from the Primordial Soul and the consequent bisectioning/division of this Self produced a male self and a female other.[19] The addition or reunion of the male self (represented by the number Three) and his female other (represented by the number Two) is complementarity and a re-turn to a primordial state of Being (represented by the number One); the addition yields complete wholeness. The addition of Three and Two yields both One (unity) and Five (the number for love/desire) (West, *Serpent* 52).

As I stated earlier, in a typical masculinist novel's treatment of complementarity as part of the diasporan myth, the diasporan subject rarely fuses with a female subject complement. In his quest for whitemaleness, his object of desire often is a white woman and one who usually is not his other self. He may engage in sexual intercourse with a black woman, but spiritual fusion with a black woman is very rare. Given the psychological and social circumstances that sustain his partitioning, he automatically rejects a black woman as his subject complement and consequently he forgoes opportunities to achieve complete wholeness. Johnson's Andrew Hawkins and Phillips's Cambridge are variants of the type. Cambridge's desire for whitemaleness is so thorough that he considers only a white woman as his other self. His relationship with (marriage to) the black woman Christiana is perfunctory. Pursuing whitemaleness (in whatever form) as a model of Being, subjects such as these privilege their European heritage over their African heritage rather than effect a healthy balance of the two.

Again, *The Cattle Killing* is an exemplary exception. In fact, Wideman inscribes Mrs. Stubbs, white, as an extension of the female half of a primordial common gender Self, and thus from this perspective Liam is an extension of the male half of the primordial common gender. The fusion of the two extensions is effected through love. From the same perspective, the preacher and the patient (who ostensibly is black) are extensions from, respectively, the male and female halves of a primordial common gender Self. As the novel's plot structure indicates, once these two selves achieve wholeness, they can reunite as one Self, an intimation of complete wholeness. By the novel's end, the preacher has moved from a partitioned to a whole self. The patient is in the process of becoming whole, the process of being "cured" of a disease that is diasporization. Once the cure is complete, the two will be "free . . . to love" (297): Two and Three will become One.

Male-centered diasporan novels are rather uniform in asserting that the roots of primordial black Being are in Africa. In its allegorical and metaphorical functions, Africa represents the site (more psychological and spiritual than geographical) on which the diasporan subject's desire for wholeness and complete wholeness can be satiated. It is an arithmetic site on which the addition (fusion) of Two and Three yields One. Characters such as Nash Williams, Cambridge, and Rutherford Calhoun literally travel to geographical Africa. But in the cases of Williams and Cambridge, the journey and sojourn, respectively, are nontransformative, even incarcerating. Williams and Cambridge approach Africa in the psychological state and social guise of Western white men. Both go as missionaries to the continent, a social role that prevents both from inculcating the spiritual sustenance of Africa as "home." Though both eventually come to understand the deforming nature of whitemaleness, neither abandons the generic white male as his ego-ideal, and this elevation of the Europe of their minds over the Africa of their souls eventually leads to their spiritual and physical demise.

Among post-1975 fictional slave narratives, Rutherford Calhoun represents the exception. Though Calhoun's journey toward primordiality is inadvertent, it eventually is transformative; he achieves wholeness and moves close to achieving complete wholeness. His transformation (or liberation from diasporization) is evident at the novel's end. Having come into direct contact with the Allmuseri, he returns from his inverse Middle Passage with a changed attitude toward his subject complement, Isadora Bailey. His intent to continue in the old ways of the New World—to make love rather than to love—is thwarted. His experiences having changed his attitude toward Isadora, he now views her as his beloved rather than as his lover. In his words, "My memories of the Middle Passage kept coming back, reducing the velocity of my desire, its violence, and in place of my longing for feverish love-making left only a vast stillness that felt remarkably full, a feeling that, just now, I wanted our futures blended, not our limbs, our histories perfectly twined for all time, not our flesh. Desire was too much of a wound, a rip of insufficiency and incompleteness that kept us, despite our proximity, constantly apart, like metals with an identical charge" (208). Expressed arithmetically, at the end of his journey-quest, Two and Three fuse as/into One and Five.

The reading, the writing, and the arithmetic of black male-centered discourse assume a variety of thematic and formal configurations and emphases in contemporary fictional slave narratives. All of the novels are concerned thematically with inscribing the black male self's authentic Being; several give considerable attention to the reading of the white male as Other; and a significant number explore the arithmetic of black male subjectivity under different but related rubrics.

5 Textual Androgyny, the Androgyne, and the Many-Tongued Chorus of the Common Memory

In a metafictional statement about *The Cattle Killing*'s blending of facts with fabulations and its departure from the academy's standard and prescriptive notions of novelistic discourse, Wideman characterizes his novel as a "hybrid" text (8). This form of hybridity is endemic to contemporary fictional slave narratives. Yet *The Cattle Killing* is also a hybrid within this subgenre. It is one of a relatively small group of contemporary fictional slave narratives and diasporan novels that this study considers textually androgynous, principally because they blend salient features of womanist and masculinist discourses (see chapters 3 and 4, respectively) and draw upon the diasporan myth's concept of the ideal Being—the androgyne—to construct their centered subjects and to delineate their plot structures.

Formally and thematically, fusionism is a defining criterion of this group of textually androgynous novels. Formation of the self centered in these texts characteristically fuses ontologies in that the centered self shares the same soul or a twin soul with his or her subject complement(s). Concomitant with this melding of selves is a fusion of epistemologies, which gives the centered subject firsthand access to the interior and exterior lives of his or her subject complement(s), even when the centered subject is separated from his or her complement(s) by centuries or continents or both. Consequently, temporal and spatial fusion conjoins the beginning with the end. Past, present, and future meld into one time. Geographically, near and far and here and there become the same.

The fusion of ontology, epistemology, temporality, and geography significantly defines the nature of Western black Being as these novels inscribe it, and thus ontology, epistemology, temporality, and geography meld with narratology. As Wideman expresses this premise in *The Cattle Killing*, story *is* Being (207–8). From the purview of sacred geometry, these fusions move the centered subject toward achieving his or her ultimate desire: a re-turn to the state of the androgyne. Thus, the concept of the androgyne helps configure subject formation in novels in this category and helps draw into focus each novel's grounding in the diasporan myth.

Perry's *Stigmata*, Brodber's *Louisiana*, Phillips's *Crossing the River*, and Wideman's *Cattle Killing* are representative novels that are textually androgynous. Novels in this group often proffer a nexus between author and centered subject and among subjects that is primarily emotive (as in *Cattle Killing* and *Stigmata*), and they convey this nexus discursively through a significant degree of intertextuality and referentiality (as in *Crossing the River* and *Louisiana*). However, this latter feature is not a narrative technique designed to foreground the author's and his or her centered subject's intellect. Elizabeth DuBose (*Stigmata*) and Ella Townsend (*Louisiana*) have a formal education, but neither Perry nor Brodber uses this fact to argue her subject's or her own intellectual equality or superiority to whites, as Johnson and Reed do for the subjects centered in their masculinist texts.

In *Stigmata* and *Louisiana*, the e-motion is the principal conceptual and narrative vehicle that facilitates the reunion of diasporan female selves. Referentiality and intertextuality are narrative techniques that support this reunion, more pervasively and obviously in *Louisiana* than in *Stigmata*. Each novel's referentiality includes persons, events, and texts that coincide with the novel's temporal setting. *Louisiana* also incorporates several references to Judeo-Christian and Greek mythologies; its major intertexts are the "story" of Zora Neale Hurston's life and career and the biblical story (actually merged stories) of Elisha and Elijah. Perry includes several references to contemporary fictional slave narratives that preceded *Stigmata*, and she uses *Cattle Killing* and the story of Jesus's crucifixion as her novel's major intertexts.

In *Crossing the River*, Phillips appropriates discourses and texts from eighteenth-century Britain and the United States and incorporates them into the novel's narrative fabric without calling attention within the narrative to specific authors and titles (see the novel's acknowledgments page). One of this novel's major intertexts, which Phillips does not identify in the text or in the acknowledgments, is a compilation of letters between a Louisiana slaveholder, John McDonogh, and a group of his former slaves whom he sent to Liberia as part of the colonization movement. In some instances the letters from Nash Williams to his former master, Edward Williams, are almost verbatim transcripts of parts of letters former slaves, especially Washington Watts McDonogh, wrote to John McDonogh.[1]

Wideman uses the same pattern in *The Cattle Killing.* On the novel's copyright page he acknowledges some of the "various texts [that] are 'sampled' in this narrative," including eighteenth-century letters, diaries, and sermons, as well as histories of the period, and he weaves these texts and others (including ones from the nineteenth and twentieth centuries) discreetly into the narrative. In addition, he incorporates the authors and subjects of some of the source texts into the novel's content by making them speaking subjects within the novel (his son D. J. Wideman, Benjamin Rush, Richard Allen, George Stubbs, and others). This latter form of referentiality and intertextuality is evident in several male-centered fictional slave narratives—Johnson's *Oxherding Tale* and Reed's *Flight to Canada* are exemplars. In the androgynous texts of Phillips and Wideman, the voices of a large variety of speaking subjects, therefore, join and expand "the many-tongued chorus of the common memory" (235).

While the plural Self is central to subject formation in the four novels foregrounded here, each novel inscribes and utilizes the concept differently. Indeed, discursive variations on the concept are almost as numerous as the novels that utilize the construct. In *The Cattle Killing*'s textually androgynous variation, the component male selves exist on different continents and in different centuries, are both sociogenic and genetic kin, and are connected through the repetition of a historical formation that Wideman names "the madness" (113). The same is true for the component female selves in this novel, except Wideman does not inscribe any of them as genetic kin in the same manner that he inscribes the Wideman males. (On one interpretative level, however, several of the black women are permutations of the same woman.) The ultimate desire in the novel, as its thematic and plot structures indicate, is the fusion of the male selves (represented by the preacher) and the female selves (represented by the patient) into one Self, into the androgyne.

In womanist and in masculinist post-1975 fictional slave narratives, subjects formed under the rubric of the multiplicity of Being typically are of the same race, are of different genders, exist in the same time and space, and have a spiritual nexus that is conjugal. Sixo and Patsy in *Beloved* (see 272–73) and Rutherford Calhoun and Isadora Bailey in *Middle Passage* (see 208–9) are exemplars. The usual variant in this construct is race, which in most novels in this subgenre draws into question the spirituality of the conjugal interracial nexus and thus indicates (or at the least suggests) that the two subjects are not true complements. Prominent examples include Andrews Hawkins and Peggy Underwood in *Oxherding Tale* and Nathan and Rufel in *Dessa Rose.* As does the plural Self, the multiplicity of Being also has variant formations in the subgenre, most of which can be found in the subgenre's textually androgynous novels. Phillips utilizes the construct (with significant variations) twice in *Crossing the River*, once with an interracial conjugal couple of different genders (Travis and Joyce) and once with an interracial conjugal couple of the same gender (Nash and Edward). In both instances, the members of each couple are extensions of halves severed from a primordial Self. Wideman also uses the multiplicity of Being as a rubric in *The Cattle Killing* for his formation of Liam and Mrs. Stubbs and of the preacher and the patient, and he forms Mrs. Stubbs (white) as a component of a plural female Self whose other components in the novel are black.

A centered subject's quest (conscious or subconscious) for complete wholeness motivates plot structure in womanist, masculinist, and textually androgynous contemporary fictional slave narratives. An actual or a potential reunion of the female selves and of the male selves to signify the acquisition of wholeness and of complete wholeness is a standard narrative formation in most of these texts. When the reunion is of two selves of different genders, it is often an instance of conjugal complementarity. Yet rarely does a womanist or a masculinist text include a formation of conjugal complementarity in which the subject's other is of a different race (Fred D'Aguiar's *The Longest Memory* is one exception) or of the same gender. Such formations typically are confined to textually androgynous novels.

In several womanist, masculinist, and textually androgynous novels included in this study, the formation of the centered subjects is inextricably bound to the stories of their interior and exterior lives—that is, in these texts ontology and narratology merge, especially in the textually androgynous ones. The plural Self, the multiplicity of Being, and complementarity as conceptual rubrics in textually androgynous novels advance the premise that because diasporan subjects are components of the same Self/Being, their stories are parts of one master story. Wideman states the premise as narrative theory in *The Cattle Killing* when he asserts that the "different stories" of diasporan subjects who belong to different genders and historical periods are all part of "one story" (207). Phillips's dramatization of the premise in *Crossing the River* includes race with gender and historical period. In *Higher Ground,* he expands the concept of the master story by using the biblical Diaspora as trope. *Higher Ground*'s title derives from a Christian concept of an ideal state of Being. Each of the novel's three focal subjects (non-Christians) longs to re-turn to what each considers an ideal existence. The three (two black males and a nonblack female) exist on different continents, in different historical periods, and are of different ethnicities. They all, however, are diasporan subjects who experientially share essentially the same status or "condition" (Wideman's term) in the Western world.

The first subject, an unnamed African whose story is the first to be told, is a slave in Africa during the era of the transatlantic slave trade. The second subject, Rudolph Leroy Williams, is a black inmate in the United States during the 1960s. The third subject, Irina, is a Jewish refugee from Nazi-dominated Poland who migrates to England. The three are sociogenic kin whose stories are parts of the same story. Imagistic language, narrative formations, and the biblical Diaspora as trope are among the fictive devices that conjoin the subjects and their stories. This is particularly the case in the center story about Rudi Williams. Language, images, allusions, and tropes in his epistolary narrative reveal that his experience is a repetition of both the black African diaspora and the biblical Jewish Diaspora.

The interfacing of thematic and formal features that are typically womanist and ones that are typically masculinist results in revisions (whether slight or extensive) of these gendered features in textually androgynous texts. By thematizing point of view in *Dessa Rose,* Sherley Anne Williams sorts through competing perspectives on the same events in order to separate the truest truths from other truths and from falsehoods. Phillips uses a similar narrative strategy in *Cambridge* by offering competing stories about the title character's experiences and subjectivity. Because Cambridge's version of his "story" is as suspect as other versions the novel inscribes, his subjectivity remains inauthentic at the novel's end. Through the thematization of point of view, Williams and Phillips illustrate how difficult or impossible it is to negotiate competing truths and falsehoods in order to discern any absolute truth about the past. To arrive at a fuller (though perhaps not absolute) truth about the slave experience and the slave as subject, Phillips in *Crossing the River*, however, provides complementary vistas from which one views the same events. He discerns the black subject not just through diasporan eyes of the self and the self's black others, but also through the eyes of the white others and Others.[2] D'Aguiar's *Longest Memory* and Baker's *Naming the New World* also utilize this narrative strategy. Chiefly through narrative structure and content, these and other novels argue that the Others (the victimizers) helped shape the Western black subject's Becoming and thus the subject's Being, and in the process were themselves reshaped.

Fatherless and Alone: Diasporan Desire in Phillips's Crossing the River

In its survey of the slavocracy's evils, the nonfiction slave narrative typically cites the forced rupture of the black family unit. A child's separation from his or her mother and an unknown or absent father are usually the narrative formations of this rupture. The contemporary fictional slave narrative continues this convention and aligns it with other revisions it makes to its precursor model. Female-centered novels that install the formation usually foreground the slavocracy's rupture of the bond between mother and daughter, and male-centered novels that inscribe it usually concentrate on a breached father-son relationship (the father is more often surrogate than biological). In both groups the centered subject lacks, therefore desires, a nurturing parent-child bond. This desire is the foundation of narrative formations in *Dessa Rose*, of which the Mammy episode (75–127) is most representative. It is even more pervasive in *Beloved*, significantly shaping subject formations, plot motivation, and several kinds of narrative formations.

Male-centered novels provide a wider variety of and more extensive revisions to this nonfiction convention than do female-centered novels in this subgenre. One revision is the amount of attention they focus on and the significance they give to the father, whether he is unknown, absent, estranged, dead, or the white master. This amount of attention and significance is typically not found in nonfiction slave narratives or in female-centered diasporan novels. Other revisions include the expansion of the "father" to include different kinds of surrogate and symbolic fathers and the foregrounding of tensions between "father" and "son." Johnson's *Oxherding Tale* and *Middle Passage* are exemplary in this regard. The male-centered novel is also more expansive than the female-centered novel in how it connects the parent to the concept of "home," especially when the novel inscribes home as geographic Africa and genders the concept to align with the centered subject's gender (that is, Africa the Fatherland).[3] More often than female subjects, male subjects either travel to Africa (as in *Middle Passage* and *Crossing the River*) or one of the male Self's selves is situated in Africa (as in *Naming the New World* and *The Cattle Killing*). *Beloved* is a womanist fictional slave narrative that exemplifies the exception to this masculinist convention by situating one of Sethe's and Beloved's other selves in Africa.

In *Crossing the River*, the parent-child formation and its conceptualization evolve into a trope for desire that permeates the novel and that foregrounds the ruptured bond between father and children (male and female). The trope interfaces effectively with narrative devices and strategies characteristic of contemporary fictional slave narratives. These include the subgenre's treatment of memory and rememory, of time and space, of self and the other (self), of being and Being, of race (the other and the Other), of intellect and e-motion, and of wholeness and complete wholeness, among other conventions. *Crossing the River* also charts in some instances and expands in other instances narrative territories for the subgenre, including but not limited to its treatment of Europeanism as a defining criterion of Western black subjectivity, Africans' complicity in the diaspora, and homosexuality in the slavocracy.

The speaking black male subject in the prologue and the epilogue to *Crossing the River* is a plural Self.[4] His component selves (the others) are an African father, the African Primordial Father, the novel's author, and the novel's narrator. Situated simultaneously in the past, present, and future, the speaking subject is African black and Western black, flesh and spirit, primal and primordial. Joining—but not fusing with—this black male "chorus of a common memory" (1) is the voice of an Other, the European slaver Captain James Hamilton. Unlike the black male voices that fuse into one, Captain Hamilton's voice is in italics, which signifies not only that his voice is a written text but also that it is separate from though it complements the black male chorus. The black voices and the white male voice form a composite voice (a chorus) that narrates complementary segments of the same experience—namely, the diasporization of three African Selves.

Speaking from and in the historical past (the 1750s) in the prologue's first paragraph is the voice of an African father who sold his children into slavery as well as the voice of Captain Hamilton, who bought these children. In the novel proper the section devoted to Captain Hamilton fills in gaps and silences in the biological father's narrative about his children, the novel's three focal black subjects. In fact, Captain Hamilton's voiced memory of these three African Selves is fuller and more detailed than the father's. This complement or composite of African and European voices is part of the novel's dramatized argument that the fullest narrative of Western black subjectivity requires the combined voices of the others (blacks) and the Others (whites).

Boundaries of time are erased in the prologue's second paragraph as the voice of Africa the Fatherland (the primordial parent) joins the male chorus and fuses with the voice of the biological African father. For "two hundred and fifty years" the primordial/biological father has been listening to the voices of the many who were forcibly transported from Africa. "And occasionally, among the sundry restless voices, [the biological father has] discovered those of [his] own [three] children" (1), whose souls now inhabit human hosts in the West named Nash, Martha, and Travis (this construct excludes Joyce). As incarnations or extensions of the three African Selves from the mid-eighteenth century, these three exist in the West in the nineteenth century (Nash and Martha) and the twentieth century (Travis).

The composite voice of the others and the Other continues to speak in the novel's epilogue and, therefore, connects the novel's end to its beginning, connects the three African Selves to their Western extensions, and gives the diasporan experience expansive wholeness. Joining them are the written, sung, and spoken voices of several primordial souls who inhabit human hosts from different times and spaces in the West. This commingling of voices to constitute an eclectic chorus of memory (genetic, sociogenic, and common) is germane to the narrative strategy Phillips uses to discern the subjectivity of the three focal black diasporan subjects in the novel.

More than most diasporan novels, particularly contemporary fictional slave narratives, *Crossing the River* emphasizes that Western black subjects are formed from a syncretism of biological, sociological, psychological, and cultural features that are both African and European. The diasporan subject and the narrative voice that speaks him or her into textual existence are formed from different races, genders, nationalities, historical periods, discourses, and geographic spaces. What Phillips's overall novelistic project reveals in *Crossing the River* is that a plethora of voices in a variety of discursive formats (journal, diary, letter, linear narrative, documentary history, and autobiography, among others) is necessary to begin to re-member the history of the diasporan subject and to narrativize his or her Being and Becoming.

The integration of different discursive formats in this novel constitutes a discourse of desire and speaks directly to all of the subjects' (male and female, black and white) lack of/desire for wholeness and, in some instances, complete wholeness. The prologue introduces the father's (primordial, primal, biological) desire for his lost children. Each section of the novel proper explores to some extent the respective focal subject's lack of/desire for his/her father. Though the degree of exploration (and therefore, desire) varies from one subject to another, the prologue establishes and the text proper dramatizes all five focal subjects' (Martha, Nash, and Travis, blacks; James and Joyce, whites) lack of and therefore desire for the stabilizing influence of a father (whether biological, symbolic, surrogate, ancestral, primordial, political, or religious), which will help move each toward wholeness.

The haunting first four sentences that open the prologue contain the novel's thematic and hermeneutic core. The biological African father is the speaker: "A desperate foolishness. The crops failed. I sold my children. I remember." With this desperate act the father fractured his children's bond with himself and with the Primordial Soul, creating in them and in himself a lack/desire that traverses time and space. The opening sentences introduce the absent father as trope, which pervades each of the novel's four divisions and helps shape both primary and secondary characters. The father trope not only links the three focal African American subjects across time and space to each other and to their respective primordial African forms, but it also links the novel's principal white subjects (James Hamilton and Joyce Kitson) to the three diasporan black subjects and all of these Western subjects to the primordial African father and to the Primordial Soul.

This form of intersubjectivity has a firm grounding in sacred geometry's purview on Being—specifically the premise of the Many from the One. Nash, Martha, and Travis are divisions (Western extensions) of three respective African Selves, and all six of them are subtractions from the Primordial African Father. The ultimate desire of Nash, Martha, Travis, and the plural male Self who speaks the prologue and epilogue is a reunion of selves with the primordial African father (and thus the Primordial Soul), the source of their Being. Implicitly, this is also the ultimate desire of the novel's focal white subjects. To be sure, the biological/primordial father's ruling desire in the novel's epilogue is for reunion with all of his lost children, which includes Joyce (237).

The novel's first section, "The Pagan Coast," centers Nash Williams as one of Africa's "lost children" (8), and it tropologically uses a father-son relationship to inscribe Nash's diasporan subjectivity. Orphanhood (fatherless and alone) is the concept that overarches the narrative that centers Nash, and the concept aptly describes Nash's tenuous position in the Western world. As a social being, Nash is the product of an asexual, almost amoebic reproduction by his "father" (which is quite different in form and meaning from the androgynous siring and birthing of diasporan subjects in other novels). His father as a plural entity has several permutations: his Primordial African Father (what Toomer calls "that Great Self called Deity" [*Wayward* 428]); his biohistorical African father whose voice frames the novel; his biological African American father; his surrogate and Great White Father, Edward Williams; his sociopolitical and symbolic father, a collective entity known as the Founding Fathers of the United States; and his religious father, the Judeo-Christian God. From Nash's purview at the close of his narrative, all of his fathers have forsaken him and induced his orphanhood. The question he asks at different junctures in his narrative—"Father, why hast thou forsaken me?" —is directed explicitly to one or more of these fathers and implicitly to all of them.[5]

First, the Primordial African Father (what in "Conversion" [from *Cane*] Toomer calls the African Guardian of Souls) abandons Nash by capitulating to the Judeo-Christian God and allowing Nash in his native African form to be converted from person to property. Next, his biohistorical African father, who commodifies his son (and two other children) because his crops fail, abandons Nash by selling him into slavery. Once he becomes a diasporized native son of the United States (a slave), the Founding Fathers abandon him by excluding him from the rights and privileges reserved for whites. Given the circumstances of the peculiar institution, his biological African American father (also a slave) in effect abandons him. He then becomes the surrogate child of his master and surrogate father, Edward Williams. But Edward, it appears to Nash, eventually abandons him. Having become a Christian convert seeking protection in the bosom of the Judeo-

Christian God the Father, God, too, eventually forsakes him. After returning to the primordial source of his origin, Nash repudiates most of these fathers. Fatherless, alone, and unpositioned in the world, Nash succumbs to his orphanhood. His repeated question and admonition to his "father," therefore, structures the narrative of his subjectivity, his Becoming, and makes his story (his Being) representative of a large group of native Africans who became victims of diasporization.

In several ways Phillips casts Nash and Nash casts himself in the image of his "father" Edward: like surrogate father, like surrogate son. Edward is Nash's ego-ideal and he copies several of Edward's behaviors and desires (a form of Oedipalization).[6] In effect, Nash Williams is a colonized black in that he imbibes the cultural, racial, and sexual ideology of his colonizer and consequently sees himself through the colonizer's eyes. As a colonized black, Nash does not significantly challenge the slavocracy's status quo; instead, he reinvents himself within the parameters of the slavocracy's reigning ideology. Thus, his distress stems primarily from being expelled from the colonizer's fold, from being exiled from America, which he considers his home (35).

Nash also is an example of the colonized become colonizer. His return "home" (geographic Africa) is to an alien geographic place rather than to a psychospiritual space. As an exponent of the American Colonization Society, Nash's mission in Africa is to Westernize the native African, which in this instance means to teach the African what the colonizer deems his or her proper place in a global social hierarchy, as Nash himself has been taught formally (in college) and informally.[7]

Having been reinvented (or reinvented himself) in the image of the colonizer by undergoing a "rigorous program of Christian education" (7), Nash in his relationship to native Africans is seen and, more important, sees himself as a "master" and thus as a "white man" (32). He becomes an ironic duplicate of the kind master, the "father" who views Africans as childlike, who sexually exploits the dominated while professing himself to be of "sound moral character" (7, 33), and who uses Christianity as a ruse for subduing and civilizing the so-called savage (19). In the context of the peculiar institution, "father" is a generic term that slaves and ex-slaves use in reference to their white male masters or former masters. Phillips draws from historical sources when in the novel he equates "father" with white and male and slaveholder. His most prominent source are letters former American slaves colonized in Liberia wrote to their former slave master,

John McDonogh.[8] Salutations in these letters typically are "Dear Father," "My Dearest Father," and so forth. For his own novelistic purposes, Phillips expands the meaning of this sociolinguistic formation (father-son) to inscribe a homosexual relationship between Edward and some of his male slaves, especially Nash (discussed in chapter 6 of this study).

Metaphorically lost in the African wilderness, Nash Williams comes to understand more fully the extent of his diasporization (62). Consequently, he rejects his Western fathers (Edward, the United States, God), feeling they have forsaken and exiled him, and he rejects what they represent. He abandons his role as colonizer, vowing never again to use education as a weapon against the African. He repudiates Christianity, having come to see it as a theology of oppression rather than one of liberation. Though he disavows his Westernness and "freely choose[s] to live the life of the African" (62), the narrative is not clear about how successful is Nash's attempt to re-turn to his primordial home. Indeed, Nash's narrative seems to support the novel's contention that the diasporan subject cannot re-turn home because there are no paths to guide him across the water (1–2). In effect, Nash remains one of Africa's "lost children." Traveling in space but not in time back to the primordial source of human origin, Africa, surrogate son and surrogate father suffer the same fate, primarily because of the rift in their love bond: "He was alone. He had been abandoned" (69). The two sentences apply equally to Edward and to Nash.

Abandoned (fatherless) and alone is also the fate of the novel's second original African child lost to the West. Entitled "West," the novel's second section focuses Martha Randolph, the most recent incarnation (within the novel's time frame) of the young African girl whose father sold her into slavery in the eighteenth century. The absent and abandoning father as trope is not nearly as pervasive and as explicit in Martha's story as it is in Nash's story. Instead, Phillips privileges the West tropologically to center the narrative of Martha Randolph's diasporization.

In time and space Martha is farther removed from the place of her origin than Nash is, but her desire for complete wholeness is no less poignant than Nash's. Her forced journey ever westward—from Africa to Virginia, from Virginia to Kansas, from Kansas to Colorado, and from Colorado toward California—comes to symbolize her desire for primordiality, for home. Her westward journey moves her toward wholeness and complete wholeness. If in the United States one continues to travel westward and beyond the nation's geographic border, one eventually arrives in the East. Given this teleological path, Martha eventually would arrive in her native home, Africa. She does re-turn home, but spiritually rather than physically.

Martha's last masters move from Virginia to Kansas and intend to move from Kansas westward in order to improve their lot in life. For them, the symbolic and mythic West represents freedom and a better life, and Martha's continued enslavement is a key to the better life they seek. The relationship between slaveholder and slave in this representative instance poignantly conveys the irony and contradictions embedded in life in the mythic West, particularly in the United States. Freedom and slavery, creation and destruction, and life and death are among the binaries that define the West as myth and symbol. For Martha, the West signifies slavery in perpetuity—until she frees herself from slavery's bonds and inverts the West's symbolic meaning. After she escapes from the slaveholders, the American West for Martha eventually symbolizes freedom and a space for spiritual renewal, as it does for the fugitive slaves in *Dessa Rose.* Martha then sets her sights on California, the farthest point west in this country in the nineteenth century, as a space where she finally can be free and reunited with her daughter, the last remnant of her American family.

During the course of her physical journey westward, Martha comes to realize that home is not a physical place but a psychospiritual space, that the journey toward California is a means rather than an end. With this knowledge she realizes at the end of her life and of her journey that "she would not be going any place. She would never again head east. To Kansas. To Virginia. Or to beyond [Africa]. She had a westward soul which had found its natural-born home in the bosom of her daughter" (94). Though now at the end of her life "she no longer possessed either a husband or a daughter, . . . her memory of their loss was clear" (78); and memory and desire convey her home to primordiality. In Martha's case East eventually becomes West, and vice versa, and both East and West become Africa. Martha's end is her beginning—Africa as home.

Having come to the end of her incarnation as Martha Randolph, she reunites with the original African girl from whom she has been extended and looks back on the different junctures of her westward journey. Martha activates her genetic memory and "through some atavistic mist," she peers back through time and space to the origin of her diaspority—"back east, beyond Kansas, back beyond her motherhood, her teen years, her arrival in

Virginia, to a smooth white beach where a trembling girl waited with two boys and a man. Standing off, a ship. Her journey had been a long one. But now the sun had set. Her course was run" (73).

Martha is a diasporan subject in the West, and Phillips constructs her subjectivity betwixt and between traditional African religion and Western Christianity. She retains only traces of the former but she does not embrace the latter. "Martha could find no solace in religion [Christianity], and was unable to sympathize with the sufferings of the son of God when set against her own private misery" (79). Neither Christianity nor a traditional African religion is sufficient to sustain her in this new world; neither can "reassure her that, having served her apportioned span, she would now be ushered to a place of reunion" (89). Her lack is her family and thus her desire is for reunion with her family, both her family in the West (represented by her daughter) and her family in Africa (two brothers and a father). Martha's "apportioned span" refers to the historical period during which this primordial female soul is housed in a human host named Martha Randolph. The "reunion" she desires refers to the fusion with the same female soul (or twin souls) that have been housed in other human hosts during historical time. This fusion would occur in and re-turn Martha (and her others) to primordial Time. To the godhead of her native African religion, to her biohistorical African father, to the Judeo-Christian God, to the Founding Fathers of the United States, Martha, like Nash, poses the question: "Father, why hast thou forsaken me?" (73). For Martha as for Nash, there are no paths in water.

In constructing *Crossing the River*'s third focal black subject, Travis, Phillips's narrative strategy is the opposite of that in *Dessa Rose*. As the narrative of *Dessa Rose* progresses through its tripartite division, Williams gradually privileges Dessa's perspective on events that shaped her life. In the novel's third part Dessa's voice, her perspective, fills the narrative's textual space. To discern Travis and his extended self (Travis's son Greer) as subjects, Phillips decenters Travis and uncenters Travis's extension, Greer. He constructs their Western selves primarily through the perspective of Travis's subject complement and Greer's mother, the white Joyce Kitson. Among fictional slave narratives this is an unconventional approach to black subject formation in that it privileges (rather than merely includes) a white Western purview on Western black subjectivity. In effect, Phillips forms these two black subjects in absentia.

It is not just privileging the white European component over the black African component in the inscription of a Western black's subjectivity that makes Phillips's construction of Travis and Greer a significant departure from convention in contemporary fictional slave narratives. Rather, it is how and why he does this. Indeed, several post-1975 fictional slave narratives use white European and white American intertexts and subjects to arrive at a fuller truth about Western black subjectivity. In most instances, though, these texts and subjects are negated rather than corroborated as valid or complementary perspectives on Western black Being. The formation and function of Adam Nehemiah (*Dessa Rose*) and Schoolteacher (*Beloved*) illustrate the point. Narrative strategy in *Crossing the River* and D'Aguiar's *Longest Memory* argues that to discern a fuller truth about the diasporan black subject in the West, one needs to consider complementary black and white perspectives. After all, biologically (in most instances) and culturally the Western black is an amalgam of black African and white European. Phillips's narrative argument of this point is more thorough than D'Aguiar's. Viewed through the lens of the diasporan myth, because Travis and Joyce are extensions of halves severed from an original whole Self, to know one is to know the other. In the interfacing of ontology and narratology in the typical womanist novel, black subjectivity is inscribed through the voiced memory of a black woman, whether author, character, or both. Phillips revises this strategy in *Crossing the River* in that Travis's subjectivity is revealed overwhelmingly through the voiced memory of two white Europeans, Joyce Kitson (primarily) and James Hamilton (secondarily).

In his discursive formation of Travis, Phillips demonstrates the premise that the fuller the story of any life, the more that story incorporates the stories of other lives. Because one's lived-world is inseparable from the lived-worlds of others, one's story is bound to the stories of others. Typically, when one writes (biographically or auto-biographically) the story of a self, one centers the self who is the subject of the story, as Phillips does in the respective sections on Nash, Martha, James Hamilton, and Joyce. In his narrative about Travis, however, Phillips uncenters the black subject, and his novelistic theory and praxis argue and demonstrate what is true about the narrative of any life: what to include and what to exclude about events and persons that help shape a self is a highly selective process, even when the subject is centered in the narrative. One might argue that the portrait of Travis is incomplete when compared to those of Nash, Martha,

James, and Joyce. This is true. Yet the portraits of these four also are incomplete, for the selection process necessarily has excluded numerous events that and persons who helped shape the subjectivity of these four.

To form Travis, Phillips concentrates on those nonblack or Western forces, persons, and events that helped shape Travis and that in turn Travis helped shape. Positioning Joyce center stage in the narrative of Travis is consistent with components of the diasporan myth and its theory of Being. The myth posits that Europeans (whites) also originated in Africa and thus are also diasporan subjects. Though Charles Johnson states the point in *Middle Passage* (65),[9] Phillips's *Crossing the River* is one of the very few contemporary fictional slave narratives that explores it through the formation of a white diasporan subject. The theory of black Being posits that one's other can be of a different race. Thus, Joyce and Travis are extensions from components of one primordial Self, and to know one is to know the other.

Phillips employs the absent father as trope to discern the subjectivity of Joyce, Travis, and Greer. Their lives and thus subjectivities are intertwined as one. Joyce's father is absent because he was killed in World War I (132). Nevertheless, Joyce's mother considers her husband's death as abandonment (132). Greer's father (Travis) is absent because he was killed in World War II. England's racist policies concerning biracial children in effect considers Travis's death an abandonment of his child. The county council declares Greer an orphan, takes him from his mother, and places him in the government's custody. Both Joyce and Greer lost their fathers when they were babies and thus have "no memory of him" (133). The traces that survive of Joyce's father are a picture of him and his name on a bronze plaque in the town hall. As Joyce sees it, the bronze plaque "is merely a place to find him, but not to discover him"; the "photograph," however, "might help [her] to discover him" (133). In other diasporan novels, however, either of these traces would be sufficient for the subject to (re)discover the self through (re)discovering the other of whom he or she is an extension. Greer, however, lacks even these traces of his father, for Joyce "destroyed . . . letters, pictures, everything" when she met her last husband, an action she later regrets (224). And, of course, Travis manifests as Greer's absent father, which continues the legacy of diaspority and orphanhood into the present generation.

Phillips constructs Greer's subjectivity through the voiced memory of his mother, Joyce.[10] Thus, Joyce's imprint on Greer's cultural and psychosocial Becoming is as strong as, if not stronger than, Travis's, and thus her imprint on his Being is as indelible as Travis's. Because both sources were integral to Greer's Becoming, both are integral to discerning a fuller truth of his Being. What Phillips demonstrates through the narrative strategy that constructs Travis and Greer is that the European component of Western black Being is not less valid than the African component. Like Andrew Hawkins, Greer is biracial. Yet Phillips, unlike Johnson, gives very little attention to the biological and cultural evidence of this facet of Greer's subjectivity. Unlike for Hawkins and Nash Williams, the white male is not Greer's ego-ideal, and thus Oedipalization is not a factor in Phillips's formation of Greer's subjectivity.[11]

That Western black Being is a biological, psychological, and cultural amalgam of African and European is a premise Phillips readily conveys through his formation of Greer. When Greer enters the narrative (his birth), his father is dead but his mother is alive. Nevertheless, the Western madness defines Greer as an orphan and places him in a physical and social space (an orphanage) reserved for biracial children in England born to white mothers. Orphanhood, then, literally and figurally defines Greer's position or condition as a Western black subject. Like Nash, Martha, and Travis, Greer as an heir to diaspority is fatherless and alone.

Story and/Is Being: Wideman's The Cattle Killing

On its most basic level of story, Wideman's *The Cattle Killing* recounts a young itinerant preacher's (an ex-slave's) experiences in late-eighteenth-century Pennsylvania. While traveling through the Pennsylvania countryside, he encounters an elusive and seemingly suicidal young African woman who has such an effect on him that after she disappears he relentlessly pursues her.[12] The pursuit brings him into contact with an array of other people and it eventually leads him to plague-ridden Philadelphia.[13] His desire to find the woman precipitates and perpetuates his geographical journey, which evolves into his spiritual quest for Self. In effect, she becomes his spiritual guide during this journey-become-quest. At his narrative's end, which is also its beginning, the preacher is telling the story of his experiences to a woman (ostensibly black) who is sick and who moves in and out of a comatose state. The intent of his storytelling is to heal her body and her soul.

The stories the preacher tells the patient and intends as a curative are of his encounters with people who told him stories of their experiences, stories that contained stories about others and Others. Story and storytelling, then, are at the hermeneutic heart of *The Cattle Killing.* In this novel, story expands well beyond its basic meaning of what is told and assumes a variety of meanings and functions, one of the most significant of which is that story is Being. Each subject in the novel has a story and, in Wideman's words, "each *is* a story" (207; emphasis added). Moreover, all are part of one story, many are components of one Self, and their voices blend into a chorus that narrativizes a common memory (experience).

Narratology and ontology fuse in this novel. Most of the women's stories (blacks and a white) fuse into one story, and therefore most are components of an original African female Self. So, too, do most of the black men's stories fuse into one story, and most of them are components of an original African male Self. As the novel moves toward closure, its stories move toward a fusion that would reunite the original female Self and the original male Self into one Self. From the purview of the diasporan myth and its theory of Being, the first and second fusions would reconstitute, respectively, the female gender and the male gender; the third would reconstitute the original manwoman or common gender. The three fusions would reestablish the original state of primordial Being. *The Cattle Killing*'s thematic structure, therefore, is firmly anchored in the diasporan myth.

The novel's narrative design is integral to its meaning. Except the designations "Part One," "Part Two," and "Epilogue," the novel lacks titles for its divisions. Thus, one story flows into another story, just as one self flows ("bleeds" is Wideman's term) into another self. Typographical spaces and symbols indicate pauses or interruptions in the narrative flow without designating narrative beginnings and endings and thus without separating one story from another or (in most instances) definitively distinguishing one self from another self.[14] This is an instance of narrative rupture—an insertion of gaps and silences in the narrative that themselves are germane to the novel's exploration of black subjectivity in the West. In the context of the diasporan myth, the black subjects the novel inscribes (with few exceptions[15]) are intersubjective selves, though victims of bisectioning and partitioning.

The novel focuses on stories the preacher tells, but its title comes from an event—a cattle killing—that occurred among the Xhosa people in nineteenth-century South Africa.[16] The story of this historical event occupies a very small amount of the novel's textual space, but its meaning permeates the novel and justifies its title. The cattle killing as story and as trope functions in part as a bridge to connect and to give meaning to the spaces (geographical, temporal, typographical) between different selves and their stories in the novel's narrative flow.

On one of its tropological levels, a cattle killing is the destruction or near destruction of a person's or a group's essence, a person's or a group's ethnicity. Whether it is willful or unwillful, partial or total, this self-destructive act is induced by the madness (Wideman's term for white racism and its effects) that has afflicted, continues to afflict, and will continue to afflict blacks (and some whites) across temporal and spatial zones.[17] Particularly for blacks in the United States, the madness dictates that "only those who kill all their cattle will be welcomed in this new world" (146–47). The novel's narrator sounds a warning: "Do not kill your cattle. Do not speak with your enemy's tongue. Do not fall asleep in your enemy's dream" (147). The watchman at the orphanage and Bishop Allen are examples of blacks who fall asleep in their enemy's dream. A convert to white Christianity (a form of cattle killing for blacks), the preacher himself falls asleep in his enemy's dream. However, as the novel's narrative structure reveals, he awakens. The sleep is not permanent for the preacher, nor does it have to be for other blacks. This is one of several instances in this novel that are referential and intertextual echoes of or parallels to Ellison's *Invisible Man.* As invisible man contends, "All sickness is not unto death" (11). This premise overarches plot structure, narrative formation, and subject formations (the preacher, Allen, and especially the patient) in *The Cattle Killing.* The solution the preacher offers to those blacks who have killed their cattle is consistent with a component of the diasporan myth that invokes the legends of the walking Ibos and the flying Africans. The solution is to re-turn to the African primordial state of Being: "We must return to the old ways. The sacred path the ancestors walked" (146); we must "fly away, fly away home" (205).

The cattle killing as trope also signifies the geometric symmetry of the novel's narrative design. The novel is a compilation of interrelated stories as well as a composite portrait of intersubjective selves. Its geometric narrative structure is a circular series of stories contained within other stories, and all of these stories are part and parcel of (contained within) one story. As a narratological trope that connects past, present, and future realities and selves, the cattle killing as event connects the *Lebenswelt* (lived-world) of diasporan blacks in eighteenth-century urban England to urban and rural blacks in eighteenth-century Pennsylvania to native South Africans of the nineteenth century and to diasporan blacks in urban centers of the United States during the twentieth century.

On this tropological level the cattle killing interfaces diasporan subjectivities within the narrative. It connects the novel's centered subject to Liam (black) and Liam's wife (white), to the African woman who disappears into the lake, to a female slave/servant named Kathryn, and to several other blacks contemporary with the centered subject's time and place. It also connects all of these eighteenth-century subjects one to the others and links all of them to future diasporan subjects, especially ones who resist the madness: to Mandela, Ramona, Mumia, Huey Newton, Goodman and Chaney, and Gabriel Prosser. Each of these subjects has a story and "each is a story, a celebration and mourning and letting go and gathering, different stories over and over again that are one story" (207).[18] The story that encompasses them all is of the madness that effects diasporization, and the madness is a principal tie that binds one diasporan subject to all and all to one. The stories of these different diasporan subjects are also the story of the novel's author and of its principal third-person narrator (who probably is John Edgar Wideman), and in effect the author and narrator are inseparable from the subjects they inscribe.

The novel's metafictional prologue collapses and traverses historical time and geographic space and establishes an emotive bond between the perceiving author and the perceived centered subject that melds present and past realities. In the author/centered subject nexus, perceiver and perceived fuse into the novel's narrating and narrativized "Eye/I." A fiction writer and thus a creator, Wideman has epistemic powers that allow him to *know* this perceived subject (and other subjects) as "intimate[ly] as a second skin" (12). Wideman privileges memory and the e-motion over the intellect as epistemological and ontological vehicles to move him back in time and to enter "into another skin," becoming successively a fifteen-year-old version of himself and a version of his father, melding his subjectivity with that of two destructive and self-destructive late-twentieth-century black boys in Philadelphia, with a "generic [black male] kid," and eventually with an eighteenth-century "young African man" (4, 11, 12) who is the novel's centered self.

What the author shares "with this eighteenth-century African boy whose story he wanted to tell" is diasporization: "The thing he would try to write, the thing that must replace names only the boy could give to what it felt like to be moving through clangorous streets, dead for two hundred years, what he could construct, would be testimony witnessing what surrounds them both this very moment, an encompassing silence forgetting them both, silence untouched by their passing, by the countless passings of so many others like them, a world distant and abiding and memoryless" (13). Through memory and e-motion, then, the author (re)discovers, (re)creates, and (re)writes past and present realities. He refashions the world of the past and of the present and (re)positions himself in these refashioned worlds. The text he writes, therefore, is the world and is a being in the world.[19] His text is his story and the stories of his subjects, all of whom are extended component parts of one primordial Being.

Through the process of rememory, the author utilizes a narrative strategy conventional in black novels of the United States: to discern his own subjectivity he must determine how he came to be.[20] Story is the discursive site on which he accomplishes this. From the purview of the diasporan myth's perspective on ontology, he is an extension of those diasporan subjects who preceded him, and those who will follow him will be extensions of him and of his predecessors. What the perceiving author does, then, is to enter into the complexity of his self and his others. He dances them: "All of them. The black boy always fifteen, the two boys freshly dying, the long-gone African, [and] his [own] father." In this instance, dancing the other is an emotive, auto-biographical act of subject (self-)formation: "And who is he anyway, interchangeable with these others, porous, them running through him, him leaking, bleeding into them, in the fiction he's trying to write" (13). From this metafictional statement (and ones similar to it) it is clear that epistemology, ontology, and narratology are amalgams in the formation of diasporan subjectivity. The statement is one example of how *The Cattle Killing* incorporates into its content theoretical premises that govern the novel's production and its interpretation.

Story also is the site on which the novel's innominate centered subject establishes an emotive, intersubjective bond with those diasporan subjects (male and female) whose stories are contained within his narrative. In speaking these subjects into being, he (like the novel's author) speaks himself into authentic Being. He "bleeds" into them and they "run" through him. This is especially the case in his nexus with black male subjects, for at the ontological level he is "interchangeable with these others." The emotive, ontological relationship is indeed porous. Story becomes the mechanism to effect his own rebirth, his transformation from a facsimile self to an authentic self, and story is the curative he uses to effect a rebirth of a patient who is listening to his story and to the stories he tells about others.

The cattle killing as story is also a metaphor for art. The story is the author's novel, an invention to "expose the lie of the madness" (127), to tell a truer truth about the diasporan subject's *Lebenswelt.* It is storytelling as a ritualized healing ceremony, and in this regard the author and his centered subject share the same mission—"to save [diasporan] souls" (24). Wideman as author rescues the black self from diasporization by giving voice to the subject's silence, by writing the subject into authentic Being, in the same manner that the novel's centered subject gives the character Liam back his voice (see 129–31) and speaks Liam and other diasporan subjects into authentic Being.

Accepting that the novel's centered subject is the itinerant preacher and assuming that the itinerant preacher is a fictive version of Bishop Richard Allen (Wideman is ambivalent about the identification[21]), then Wideman (re)met Allen through a text, much like Williams (re)met Dinah and Morrison (re)met Margaret Garner. In fact, Wideman (re)met Allen (as Morrison did Garner) while engaged in an editing project.[22] And like Williams, he turned this (re)meeting into a short story ("Fever") before casting it in novelistic form grounded in the diasporan myth and its theory of Western black Being.[23] The (re)meeting and fusion of Wideman and the itinerant preacher is duplicated in the (re)meeting and fusion of the preacher and Liam.

The (re)meeting between the preacher and Liam is an instance of the (re)meeting and fusion of subject and subject complement. Liam confesses to the preacher: "I didn't know how deeply I missed another like myself beside me until you arrived" (131). Indeed, the (re)meeting is a liberating act, and story is the site on which this liberation occurs. After the (re)-meeting, Liam's "voice returns" after a long self-imposed silence and he is "ready to take up the conversation [he had] fled" (129)—that is, he is ready to speak the past as a mechanism for the reformation of self. For story to be effective as a self-induced curative, there must be a storyteller and a listener. In this instance, Liam is the teller and the centered subject is the listener. As Liam tells him, "I couldn't begin to talk, son, till I learned you were willing to listen" (131). And Liam's "talk" is a continuum of stories about his lived-world, narratives that link his remote African past to his recent European past and to his American present and that speak and bespeak his Being. As Liam the storyteller speaks his self he also speaks and bespeaks his listener, moving both of them toward primordial wholeness. To be sure, Liam and the young preacher are interchangeable selves who share the same story. As the preacher observes, "I knew I must be in the Africa of Liam's stories. I was the boy he'd been before he was snatched away forever" (143). He also is in the Europe of Liam's stories. Their (re)-meeting is a reciprocal liberating act, for the centered subject "thaw[s]" Liam "just as surely as [Liam and his wife] thawed" him (101). This intersubjective nexus between the preacher and Liam (perceiver and perceived) replicates one between Wideman and the preacher.

This reciprocal thawing that moves both subjects toward primordiality evokes morphological features of the diasporan myth. Wideman endows certain of the novel's black subjects (especially the composite or generic male) with epistemological and ontological characteristics that duplicate those of Charles Johnson's Allmuseri tribesmen. For example, in Africa Liam's father "was a renowned wizard" with powers to "change his shape or disappear instantly" and to "be many different places at once" (104). An apprentice to his father, Liam would have become "a healer of soul and body" had he "not been stolen from Africa" (104). Diasporization muted but did not destroy Liam's inherent powers. His dormant capacity to use story as a palliative to heal soul and body is rejuvenated ("thawed") in his association with the preacher, who through this association begins (or continues) to transform into an authentic self. It is not that Liam endows the preacher with these special powers, but that their association allows the trace of those powers that inhere but are dormant in the preacher to become more fully activated. Those moments of "the clarity" the preacher experiences are exemplary of the rejuvenation, the thawing, of his *connaissance.*

The novel asserts that a trace of these primordial powers are innate in many Western blacks, a part of their ontology inherent in the tribal bloodline, endowing them with "an acuteness of ear" and with other epistemological powers that "no other race can match" (35). The innominate subject affirms this ontological and epistemological feature as a tribal (racial) characteristic when he recalls his first encounter with the African spectral woman at the lake, who functions as both the guide and the metaphorical object of his spiritual journey-quest. When he meets her again, she is in the form of a worshipper at a religious gathering. In this form she is primordiality manifest, and she exercises her powers to heal soul and body when she ministers to the preacher during one of his episodes of "the clarity."

Recognizing her healing powers, he ponders, rather rhetorically, if she, "like the other presences crowding" the scene that day, belonged "to the world of special seeing" (76). His encounter and re-encounter with the spectral woman, as in his association with Liam, rejuvenate this primordial facet of his Being and allow him to exercise his special powers of healing in his association with the patient, whom he endeavors to heal through the power of story, which in essence is the power of rememory.

As he does for most of the black males, Wideman constructs most of the black women in the novel as components of a plural female Self, whose subjectivities he fuses into one. These female selves include the ghostlike African woman whom the preacher encounters in the wilderness and who with her child disappears at (or into) the lake (36–39); the ethereal "young woman in the blue dress" who ministers to him during one of his "fits" (76–78); Kathryn, the African servant whose master sexually abuses and impregnates her; and the woman patient to whom he tells his story. These women, along with others, share parts of the same story and thus are components of the same Being.[24] In the novel, descriptive details about one woman overlap with descriptive details about another, just as the story the subject tells of one woman blends ("leaks") into the story he tells of another. Indeed, the women's stories and the women's selves bleed into one another and thus fuse narratology and ontology.

On another level of this fusion, the women and their stories bleed into the "porous" centered subject, for his Being, which is the totality of his lived-world, is intersubjective. With this composite of the African female Self and her permutations, the centered subject shares some features other than diasporization. For example, both he and the ethereal "young woman in blue" have the power to heal soul and body. He also shares with her the epistemological gaze (a signifier of *connaissance*). In effect, they represent the respective male and female extensions from the halves of an original Self that was serially bisected. When they (re)meet, he bleeds into her and she bleeds into him: "He knows her face only from inside out. As if he's slipped into the quiet chamber inside her skull where she sits and looks out at him" (78). Powers such as the epistemological gaze inhere in those descendants of the Ur-tribe that Charles Johnson calls Allmuseri.

To appropriate Johnson's terms and ideas and apply them to the preacher, one can say that the undiluted Allmuseri Self is an intersubjective Being and therefore is the world (*Oxherding Tale* 153). To partition the self is to fragment the world. For the diasporan self to move from partitionedness to wholeness is to move toward reuniting the world's fragmented parts. The epistemological gaze (a vehicle for this reunification) that links the centered subject to the woman in blue (her brush arbor permutation) also links him to other subjects.[25] For example, in observing Mrs. Stubbs naked, the preacher observes his self. He steps outside of himself to see his self, and he sees his self through the gaze of the object-subject of his perception, a liberating act that at least for an instant reveals the perceiver's and the perceived's authentic subjectivity: "As in a mirror my eye finds my eye. Or as in another's gaze I find my self. The play back and forth. A simple fellowship, each freeing the other, making the other real" (74). His observation of Mrs. Stubbs bathing is an observation of a birthing ritual, a fleeting moment of "the clarity" when he sees her and his self being reborn. For him, Mrs. Stubbs's "naked body" becomes an "anchor," and through his gaze he blends her "floating parts," reconstitutes her as a timeless (whole) self, and thus "slowly piece[s] a world together" (94). Simultaneously, he reunites his own disparate parts and for this fleeting moment he reconstitutes his self as a whole self. During this instant of "the clarity," the gazer, the object-subject of his gaze, and the world are reunited as one (an instance of complete wholeness). The phenomenon produces in the perceiving subject "the absolute peace of knowing the world's whole again. The infinite parts miraculously reassembled. In an instant. Seamlessly . . . each separate, lonely thing connects for an instance with its lost brethren" (74).

In yet another narrative formation the diasporized male self in the form of Liam experiences the fracturing of his Being and thus the fracturing of the world. Stolen from his native Africa and transported to England, Liam eventually becomes the property and the apprentice of the anatomist/medical illustrator George Stubbs Jr. Stubbs belongs to a group known, ironically, as "resurrectionists," "body snatchers who trafficked in corpses" (115) and thus who realized profit by commodifying the black body alive or dead. In this particular narrative formation it is the corpse of a pregnant African woman that is placed on the auction block and white men bid to own her and her unborn child. Accompanying his owner to the auction and witnessing the event, Liam discerns his intersubjective relationship to this "ideal form of woman rendered in ebony" (134). She is his "sister, mother, daughter," and he is the unborn child in her womb (137). Thus he is one with the female cadaver, and her fate is his fate. Already severed from her native land, she will become the object of the highest bidding resurrectionist, whose "knives would slice her open, hack her to bits" (137), literally severing her different parts from the whole. As Liam observes, the woman's "heart" is "the world's heart" (137), and the literal and figural fragmentation of her is the literal and figural fragmentation of the world.

The novel's centered self is an extension of both Liam and the female cadaver, and thus from the purview of the diasporan myth they are his primal parents in the West. Viewed through the lens of the diasporan myth, they also are diasporized parents who can give birth only to the facsimile self and not to the authentic self. The female cadaver's fragmentation and death result in the fragmentation and death of her unborn child, who is both Liam and the centered subject (137). As a diasporan self in the West, Liam's "African seed shrivels," "grows stunted and twisted if it grows at all" (130), and this primal parent produces a progeny who is stunted, twisted, diasporized. To be sure, Liam, who functions as another helpmate to assist the preacher on his quest to reverse his diasporization, identifies him as a "son" whom he has fathered in his "fancy" (131), an emotive procreation. Liam assumes the primal parent's role of charting for the preacher the route from partitionedness to wholeness. Story—the voicing of rememory—is the vehicle that Liam provides to convey the preacher on his spiritual journey. As the preacher declares, since their (re)meeting Liam's stories already have begun to accomplish their task of reunifying his (the preacher's) and thus the world's disparate parts: "I'm not who I was when the storm dropped me here. The world's different. I'm different in it. You taught me the shape of this different place" (132).

Using orphanhood as a conceptual rubric, the novel continues to explore diasporan intersubjectivity by linking the centered subject to other diasporan subjects. In one narrative formation the novel inscribes this diasporan intersubjectivity through the itinerant preacher's identification with the historical Bishop Richard Allen.[26] Estranged because of his race (his tribal identification) from the nation's social center, Allen ponders why he has "been orphaned in this strange land, in this unimaginable city [Philadelphia]. Divided first from others, then from himself" (158) in this city of brotherly love. Allen's partitionedness typifies diasporan subjectivity in the West. Moreover, Allen kills his cattle.

Another narrative formation, a deposition from one (or more) of Philadelphia's black orphans during the plague, makes the figural orphanhood more literal. The deponent is a narrating voice that blends with and extends other diasporan voices in the novel. This narrative episode (or story) underscores the repetition of historical formations in the lived-world of diasporan subjects by metaphorically inscribing an updated version of the Middle Passage and revising through repetition and corroboration narrative formations from Toomer's *Cane*. Like Richard Allen and all other African brethren who are marginalized because white Christians believe the African's skin "bore the mark of Cain" (154), the black orphans suffer the manifold consequences of the "plague" (a term the novel uses synonymously with the madness and diasporization).

In recalling the experience of being confined with others like him in a dark, cold, and damp cellar, the orphaned deponent "remembers the watchman's tale" about the Middle Passage and in effect he relives this phenomenon. The watchman, himself a diasporized African who now in his relationship to other blacks functions like a slave driver, recalls the Middle Passage and its aftermath by using basically the same metaphors and images Barlo uses in *Cane* in his inscription of the mythic African (*Cane* 38–39). In the watchman's tale, the pre-diasporan African belonged to a tribe whose members were literally and figuratively larger than life. Slave traders, the "white ants" of the European tribe fortified by what Toomer calls in "Conversion" a "white-faced, sardonic God" (*Cane* 49), captured the African giants, deformed ("Taken us apart") and then reinvented their subjectivity ("puts us back togedder again") as part of the diasporization process (185–86). The process created both literal and figural orphans in the West, subjects, in the example of Richard Allen, divided from others (bisected) and from themselves (partitioned). In the voice of the itinerant preacher, who, like Allen, is a convert to a new religion and an alien God, "the unspeakable experiences" of the Middle Passage and slavery altered the diasporan subject's understanding of himself, of the world, and of the life he lived in this strange new world (32).

Part of the sacred geometry of *The Cattle Killing*'s narrative and of the formation of black subjectivity is a series of "circles within circles within circles" that sometimes simultaneously and sometimes alternately expand and contract (144). The novel's narrative progression is a series of stories within stories within stories, beginning with the outer stories of the author and the author's father, the stories of their lives as well as of the lives they are reinventing in narrative. Within the boundary of these outer circles is the story of the novel's centered subject, whose story itself is a circular design consisting of stories within stories (which themselves contain other stories). Alternately contracting and expanding as the narrative progresses, these inner stories eventually circle penultimately back to the centered subject and ultimately back to Wideman. Thus, all stories become one story—of the African diasporan subject in the West.

The narrative contracts to include the stories of Liam and of his wife, within which are the stories of George Stubbs, the resurrectionists, and the female African cadaver, among other subjectivities. The narrative expands to include the stories of the Xhosa people of South Africa, of the "generic kid[s]" in present-day Philadelphia, and of the author (Wideman), the author's father, and the author's son (D. J. Wideman), among other selves. The stories and subjectivities of the three Widemans bleed into one another in the novel's opening and closing sections.

As the novel asserts, stories are beings, and thus subjectivities in the novel also expand and contract, particularly through the novel's use of sacred arithmetic. The itinerant preacher's subjectivity arithmetically expands (addition) and contracts (division) to include the author, Liam, Liam's wife, the female African cadaver, the orphans, the spectral woman, and other subjects, all of whom are components of a primordial African Being.

Through its form the novel demonstrates that each life, each subjectivity, contains a myriad of other lives, other subjectivities, other stories. In constructing the centered subject's *Lebenswelt,* the narrative's author (Wideman/the preacher) reinvents his subject(s) as well as himself as a compilation of other lives, other subjectivities, other stories. These other lives/subjectivities/stories are of Africans and Europeans, of males and females, of genetic and sociogenic kin, of ancestors and of generations to come. The novel's author dances these others, all of them, and in doing so he extends the emotive boundary of the author-centered subject nexus characteristic of womanist novels such as *Dessa Rose* and *Beloved.* Concomitantly, he renegotiates the intellectual parameters and perimeters of the author-centered subject nexus characteristic of masculinist novels such as *Oxherding Tale* and *Flight to Canada.*

Unbreaking the Circle: Sacred Geometry and Intertextuality in Stigmata *and* Louisiana

Sacred geometry is integral to the form and meaning of *The Cattle Killing, Stigmata,* and *Louisiana.* Employing different tropological perspectives on the circle, Wideman offers diasporan subjects a means for *unkilling* their cattle, and Perry and Brodber show diasporan subjects how to *unbreak* the circle. These and other authors give "directions" (Jean Toomer's term) for re-turning to the unity of Being.

"Will the Circle Be Unbroken" is a dirge or funeral hymn[27] whose chorus (the lines of which might vary slightly from one version to another) reads thus:

> Will the circle be unbroken
> By and by, Lord, by and by.
> I've got a better home awaiting
> In the sky, Lord, in the sky.

These lyrics express a desire that several diasporan novels (such as *Louisiana*) and most contemporary fictional slave narratives (such as *Stigmata*) dramatize as a desire for wholeness and for a repositioning in the unity of Being. It is a desire grounded in the precept of sacred geometry's symbolic circle. When the preacher in *The Cattle Killing* merges with one of his other selves (Liam) and is spiritually transported to Africa as a sacred space, this desire overtakes him: "Beneath that African sky I tried to will my body to rise, rise closer to the energy uncoiling from the stars, the circles within circles within circles nearly reaching me, almost audible. If my body would take me just a little higher, I'd hear the song, become part of it, the stars, that blackness over my head" (144). The preacher's comments recall lines from another religious song: "Just above my head I hear music in the air," lines that James Baldwin uses to advantage in his novel *Just Above My Head* (1979).

The preacher wonders "if [the stars] all together sang lonely and separate as the many things of this earth must sing until the day the broken kingdom is restored" (144). To restore the broken kingdom (that is, the world or the universe, terms the writers often use interchangeably) is to reunite harmoniously all things in the universe. Prerequisite to this reunification is the restoration of the partitioned self's wholeness and the reunion of the fragmented Self's component selves. The self/Self is the universe in miniature. To fracture one is to fracture the other, and to mend one is to mend the other. The innominate preacher in *The Cattle Killing* expresses this premise when, for example, a healing gaze that he fixes on Mrs. Stubbs reunites her "floating parts" and "slowly piece[s] a world together" (94).

As a symbol of the unity of Being, the unbroken circle signifies a state of existence when the universe's "infinite parts [are] miraculously reassembled," when "each separate, lonely thing connects . . . with its lost brethren" (*Cattle Killing* 74). The broken circle (the glyphs) as a symbol in *Cane* bespeaks the disconnectedness of diasporan subjects from self, from others, and from the universe. Wideman builds upon Toomer, and Perry (directly) and Brodber (indirectly) echo these predecessors by characterizing such diasporan subjects as exiles, orphans, and arcs of a broken circle (for example, see the epigraph for part 1 of *Cattle Killing*; *Cane* 88; *Stigmata* 95). The unbreaking of the circle that these four (and other) authors and subjects seek is what Toomer in *Cane* (39–40, 125) and Wideman in *The Cattle Killing* (67) express metaphorically as the Second Coming of Christ, which also is part of the dramatic content of *Stigmata* (the atonement theme associated with Lizzie) and *Louisiana* (the ascension theme associated with Sue Anna). For the purposes of this discussion, Perry's *Stigmata* and Brodber's *Louisiana* are complementary texts in that when considered together they exemplify female-authored and female-centered novels that are textually androgynous.

Set in Alabama between 1974 and 1996, *Stigmata* centers Elizabeth ("Lizzie") DuBose, who at age fourteen inherits from her grandmother, Grace Lancaster, a diary and a quilt. The diary is Lizzie's great-great-grandmother's (Ayo's/Bessie Ward's) slave narrative, which Ayo dictated to her daughter, Joy. The diary narrates key events in Ayo's life: her capture in Africa, her ordeal during the Middle Passage, and her life as a slave in Alabama. Grace made the quilt "and Ayo's whole story is set on it" (15); its visuals repeat Ayo's slave narrative. Lizzie's contact with these two forms of a slave's narrative precipitates emotive and physical memories of events in Ayo's and Grace's lives. Through the e-motion and through bleeding wounds on her body, Lizzie (re)lives Ayo's life in Africa and the pain of her experience during the Middle Passage and its aftermath.

The explanations her parents and doctors give for Lizzie's memories and wounds are that she is "crazy" and suicidal (3, 181), so when she is twenty years old they commit her for the next fourteen years to a succession of mental institutions. In 1986 a priest, Father Tom, gives Lizzie an explanation and precedent that she accepts as rational for her "mysterious physical trauma" (214). He tells her of "a devoted monk . . . [who] became so fixated on the passion and crucifixion of Christ that he was stricken with wounds on his body that corresponded to the Savior's torture and death. It's called stigmata" (213). Perry interfaces this Christian concept with a traditional African (especially Ibo) concept about reincarnation to explain the origin and nature of Lizzie's bleeding wounds, which replicate those slavers inflicted on Ayo. Innocent Onyewuenyi points out that "reappearance of bodily marks of a deceased person on the body of a newborn child is another basis for the Africans' belief in reincarnation" ("Philosophical Reappraisal" 160).[28] Though her doctors, parents, and others reject the priest's explanation and thus Lizzie remains institutionalized until 1994, the priest's story of the monk is a partial curative for Lizzie and from this point her physical, psychological, and spiritual healing begins. The novel is a retrospective account primarily of Lizzie's ordeal and secondarily those of her grandmother Grace and her great-great-grandmother Ayo—three lives that are one life; three arcs that become one circle.

Like Marshall's *Praisesong for the Widow, Louisiana* is a diasporan novel that contains several salient features of the theory of Western black Being. *Louisiana* tells the story of Ella Townsend, a graduate student in anthropology at Columbia University who in 1936 travels to Louisiana to interview the aging and infirm Susie Anna King-Grant ("Mammy"), a former civil rights activist. Mammy dies before Ella completes the interviews. While transcribing the interviews from the recording machine, Ella hears conversations between Mammy and another woman, Louise Grant ("Lowly"), and at times the two women speak through Ella. In addition, the tape recorder contains other voices and continues to record and to play Mammy's voice even after she dies.

This field experience begins Ella's transformation from a false nature to a true nature. The tape recorder becomes a medium that helps reactivate Ella's innate *connaissance*. Through it she learns the story of Mammy and Lowly's interfaced life, and in the process she learns more about her own life. As Ella states, "It was as if they were two halves of an orb. They were as amazed as I was by the wholeness which they made" (62). Eventually the three women merge: "In me Louise and Sue Ann are joined" (124). Three stories and three lives become one story and one life. In effect, three arcs are joined to make one circle.

As in *Cane* and *The Cattle Killing*, the circle in *Stigmata* and *Louisiana* is a preeminent symbol of the self/Self and "the join." In her dictated slave narrative, Ayo uses the circle to describe her pre-diasporan existence: "I come from a long line of forever people. We are forever. Here at the bottom of heaven we live in the circle" (7, 17). The Middle Passage breaks the circle. Taking her cue from this diary entry, Lizzie wants to "declare" to her mother and does declare to the reader: "I am the circle" (94). Lizzie, Grace,

Ayo, and other women in this matrilineal line are like the arcs in a broken circle. The novel's plot structure, therefore, turns on Lizzie's desire to return from spiritual death and exile, to unbreak the circle, to begin to reconnect each of the separate females selves in the matrifocal line with her other components, and to begin to restore unity and harmony in the universe. This desire is a mainstay of diasporan novels.

Though the triangle (Ayo, Grace, and Lizzie) has a significant symbolic place in *Stigmata,* the circle is the principal geometric form in the novel, and its spiritual and philosophical properties convey the unity of Being that (re)connects generations of female kin. Whereas in *The Cattle Killing* Wideman represents the plurality of black Being as a circle that contains other circles ("circles within circles within circles" [144]), Perry represents the plurality of black Being as different points on the circumference of a circle (a kind of dot matrix subject formation). Consider that an unbroken circle is an infinite number of points, and the spaces between the points are detectable only if the circle is magnified numerous times. If one were to locate three points on the circle's circumference that are equidistant one from the others and connect these points with a line, the resulting shape would be an equilateral triangle within the circle. Following a premise stated in *The Cattle Killing* (208), assign a name to the "space" that each of the points in the triangle occupies: Ayo, Grace, and Lizzie. Rotate the circle in any direction 120 degrees and, in effect, the spaces the three points occupy are renamed. For example, in a 120-degree rotation beginning with Ayo, Ayo becomes Grace, Grace becomes Lizzie, and Lizzie becomes Ayo. In a 240-degree rotation Lizzie becomes Grace, Grace becomes Ayo, and Ayo becomes Lizzie. In a 360-degree rotation Lizzie again becomes Lizzie, Grace again becomes Grace, and Ayo again becomes Ayo (see, for example, 47). These rotations provide the core of the narrative about the intersubjectivity of these three female selves. The rotations define the portions of the text in which each of these three selves becomes her genetic other(s) and thus each becomes all and all become each.

Though in the novel Ayo is the first point on the (unbroken) circle, she is not the beginning of the circle, because a circle does not have a beginning or an end; the end is in the beginning and the beginning is in the end, as the novel's formation of its centered subject as a plural Self indicates. Lizzie states and Perry dramatizes the premise thus: "The past . . . is a circle. If you walk long enough, you catch up with yourself" (117). As Wideman states and dramatizes through narrative structure in *The Cattle Killing,* one has to go backward in order to go forward (54). Perry dramatizes this same premise in *Stigmata* somewhat differently. In order for Lizzie to go forward with her life and Being, she must go backward to Grace and to Ayo and beyond. As the novel shows, Ayo extends from her mother and the matrifocal line that produced her mother. Lizzie is not the circle's end, for the novel indicates that at some future time Lizzie's granddaughter will be the human host for the primordial soul that her foremothers housed (63).

The spiritual and genetic nexus the novel demonstrates among these female kin can be found in traditional Ibo religious mythology. It is the belief that the Primordial Soul reincarnates in a human host one generation removed (for instance, from grandmother to granddaughter rather than from mother to daughter).[29] *Louisiana*'s installation of this formation is different in that it involves sociogenic kin and does not skip a generation. Nevertheless, from Sue Anna and Louise, the "transfer of souls" to Ella brings with it, as is the case in *Stigmata*, extraordinary knowledge; it is a "journey into knowing" that "first timers sometimes" resist, as do Ella and Lizzie (*Louisiana* 38). In addition to *Louisiana* and *Stigmata*, this resistance is detectable in *Cane* (Kabnis), *The Cattle Killing* (the preacher), and *Beloved* (Sethe), for example, novels in which story *is* Being. The "story" in *Stigmata* (to draw from Wideman and Morrison) is passed on directly in and to one generation removed.

Stigmata's formal configuration replicates three major forms of the antebellum and postbellum slave narrative. First, like *The History of Mary Prince*, it is a slave's narrative (Ayo's) dictated to and recorded by an amanuensis, Ayo's daughter, Joy. Second, like Jacobs's *Incidents*, it is a first-person narrative of a slave woman written by herself in that Lizzie, a twentieth-century subject, *is* the (former) slave Ayo. Third, like Sojourner Truth's *Narrative*, it is a narrative of a slave woman written by a third person in that the quilt Grace makes is a biography of Ayo, a visual (re)presentation of her life (similar to Jacob Lawrence's visual representation of Frederick Douglass's and Harriet Tubman's respective narrative). Perry's formation of Ayo, Grace, and Lizzie as separate human hosts who house the same soul is at the foundation of the novel's replication of these three major forms of the antebellum slave narrative as well as its replication of contemporary fictional slave narratives that preceded it.

Through its subtle referentiality and intertextuality, *Stigmata* repeats and revises several thematic and formal conventions of contemporary fictional slave narratives—female-centered ones by Williams, Morrison,

Jones, and others; male-centered ones by Johnson, Phillips, and others, but especially Wideman's *Cattle Killing. Stigmata*, therefore, is textually androgynous, but it does not contain the kind of balance between features of womanist and masculinist discourse that one finds, for example, in *Louisiana*. Though at times Perry references specific authors, titles, and events, for the most part the referential and intertextual features of this novel are subtle and unspecified. Typically, Perry references predecessor contemporary fictional slave narratives by installing conventions of the form or by revising specific formations from predecessor novels that the text does not identify. For example, Johnson's Andrew Hawkins asserts, "I was my father's father, and he my child" (176). Perry re-genders, expands, and dramatizes this premise by constructing Lizzie as a plural Self who is her mother's mother (Grace), and her mother (Sarah) is her child (230, 70, 71, for instance). Lizzie also is her great-grandmother's (Joy's) mother (Ayo), and her great-grandmother is her child (41, 70, 93, for instance).

The join, or unbreaking the circle, is more expansive in *Louisiana* than in *Stigmata*. Instead of returning to New York after Mammy's death, Ella moves to New Orleans where she uses her powers of *connaissance* to "join the world of the living and the world of the spirits," to "join the past with the present," and to "give [black] people their history" (124). Her principal clients are black men from the Caribbean, whose New World migration Ella describes as "another middle passage as unfathomable as the first" (118). Her interaction with these men helps propel her transformation into a primordial Self: "I am knowing more about my men and where they are from and in the process, I am becoming" (117). Ella's statement essentially repeats a premise about the perceiver-perceived nexus that Wideman demonstrates in *The Cattle Killing* and that Morrison states in "The Site of Memory" (115). As a signification of this transformation—her Becoming and Being—she changes her name from Mrs. Ella Townsend Kohl to Louisiana.

One meaning of the novel's title derives from a fusion of ontology with epistemology and geography to help form the novel's centered subject. Ontologically, the spiritual nexus between the internal text's author (Ella Townsend) and her text's principal subjects, Sue Anna and Louise, (re)-forms a plural female Self. This fusion gives Ella epistemological access to her subjects' thoughts, actions, and feelings. Silas, who is both Sue Anna's and Louise's other half, joins with this fused trio and thus constitutes the state of the androgyne as well as signifies the multiplicity of Being. The geographical site on which these fusions occur is Louisiana, the name Ella assumes for her transformed self. Her new name is an amalgam of ontology (Louise and Anna) and of geography. The three women derive from, are born of, and inhabit geographical spaces in the West whose names intimate their sacred nexus—Louisiana, St. Mary, in Jamaica, and St. Mary, Louisiana, in the United States. As do Louise and Anna (17), these two Western spaces sire and give birth (and rebirth) to the novel's title character. As the novel asserts, there is a joining not only of ontological spaces but also of geographical, epistemological, and temporal ones (124): "Two places can make children! Two women sire another?" (17). Therefore, the name Ella chooses for her new self indicates that, ontologically and geographically, the state of the androgyne is restored.

Consistent with the diasporan myth, Mammy and Lowly are extensions of the halves of a primordial female Self who was serially bisected. Their fusions, or unbreakings of the circle, signal a return to the state of the primordial Self. The first or penultimate one (wholeness) is of what Perry calls "visible people" and occurs on what Wideman calls "a highway [of] solid earth"; the second or ultimate one (complete wholeness) is of what Perry calls "invisible people" and occurs on what Wideman refers to as a "spirit road" of "air," a place "of the invisible ether where angels float" (*Stigmata* 211; *Cattle Killing* 76). The character Louisiana speaks of the fusion of these "two halves of an orb" from the purview of sacred geometry: "There is no clear information on the shape that this sense of their oneness took in their life time though the existence of Silas does indicate a shared chord, and certainly on the [tape recorder's] reel there is the suggestion that a physical orb has been transformed into a spiritual one which crossed the seas and earth and heaven and held in Mammy's translation the hope of a more productive bonding and subsequent action" (62). The "more productive bonding and subsequent action" is the ultimate unbreaking of the circle once Mammy joins Lowly as a member of the invisible world.

It is at a crossroad of the visible and invisible worlds that visible people and invisible people meet. Sometimes, as in the case of Mammy and Lowly, "wandering souls" (*Stigmata* 181) make contact in the invisible world, and often the souls housed in human hosts make spiritual contact in the visible world. In such instances ontology and epistemology merge. Typically, a diasporan subject experiences a physical trauma that forecasts this meeting of souls from "adjacent worlds" (*Stigmata* 53) and thus signals a reactivation of the subject's innate *connaissance*. In such a formation this reactivation of primordial or genetic memory often is inscribed as a vision (*Cane* 38, *Cattle Killing* 69, *Stigmata* 116, *Louisiana* xx, for example). Indeed, the preacher's fits are a prelude to the "clarity," an epistemological state that allows him to see and to know past, present, and future. His fits and the clarity they bring recall the preacher Barlo's physical changes that precede his "religious trance" and the subsequent "vision" he has about past, present, and future (*Cane* 37–40). *Louisiana* follows *Cattle Killing*'s lead. At the different narrative junctures in *Louisiana* when Ella, Sue Anna, and Louise fuse as one Self, in effect what applies to one applies to the others. From this purview Ella's epileptic fit (35) mirrors Sue Anna's epileptic "fits" (11, 60). The narrative formation of the epileptic fit that Ella experiences almost literally repeats one the preacher has in *The Cattle Killing*. The preacher has one of his periodic "fainting fits" (57) while in the white Church of St. Matthew. After his fellow black worshippers remove him from the church to a brush arbor, someone brings water and an ethereal woman in blue soaks a handkerchief in it and bathes the preacher's brow. While "in the church" preparing "for Mammy's final journey," Ella "shout[ed] out, . . . kicked, fought, foamed, stared, [and] had to be taken from the church and given water" (35). The preacher's fits forecast what the novel calls his "clarity" (see 69). Given how Brodber forms the plural subject of *Louisiana*, Ella's epileptic fits are a harbinger of what the novel calls her "clarity" (105–6). The novel also refers to this epistemological power as "pukkumina" or "getting the power," which in meaning is similar to what Marshall refers to in *Praisesong* as "*li gain connaissance*" (218). It is a spiritual experience that allows the subject to awake "whole and healed," if only for a brief period (see *Cattle Killing* 72).

In *Cane*, *The Cattle Killing*, *Stigmata*, and *Louisiana*, ontology and epistemology are inseparable from (sacred) geography. Sparta, Georgia, is the sacred space where for Toomer/Kabnis "things unseen to men [become] tangibly immediate" (*Cane* 31, 164) and the diasporan self's primordial "vision" is restored (31, 38–39, and elsewhere), if only for an instant, as is the case with Wideman's preacher during moments of "the clarity" or when spiritually he is transported to the soil of his primordial African ancestors (*Cattle Killing* 74–77 and elsewhere; 144). It is in the sacred space named Johnson Creek, Alabama, that the extraordinary powers of seeing and knowing endemic to Lizzie DuBose's primordial soul begin to reactivate and eventually to bring her full circle with her primordial Self. Though

Brodber inscribes this ontology-epistemology nexus differently than Perry, their meaning is the same. It is on the soil of her sociogenic foremothers in Louisiana (a name that has multiple meanings and applications in the novel) that Ella's innate powers of *connaissance* are rejuvenated.

In all four of these novels, and in slightly different ways, narratology is the catalyst for the joining of ontology, epistemology, and geography. Story and storytelling are effective mechanisms for unbreaking the circle. As is the case with Toomer, Morrison, Wideman, and others, in *Louisiana* the text (in this instance, an oral one on a tape recorder) is the site on which the author (Ella) fuses with her others. In this novel, story and Being are inseparable, as in *Flight to Canada, The Cattle Killing, Beloved,* and other contemporary fictional slave narratives. The research that an author conducts to rediscover and to reconstruct her or his centered subject is part of the narrative action of this novel. Ella, a graduate student and an aspiring writer, becomes one with the subject of her anthropology research project, who becomes the subject centered in the (nonfiction) text she produces.

One might say that Toomer's sojourn in Georgia was a kind of field research, the textual product of which is *Cane.* Years later, in "The Blue Meridian," he issued a call "for the joining of men to men / And man to God," for each American and each of "the seven regions of America" to "spiritualize"—for a spiritual merging of ontologies and geographies (*Wayward* 217). Dan, a character in *Cane* ("Box Seat"), states that he has "come to a sick world to heal it" (106). The same can be said for Toomer/Kabnis, for the stories of the diasporan subjects that he collects and narrates become a curative for him. Intratextually and extratextually, storytelling is a spiritual curative that can reverse the effects of diasporization. One of the best and most explicit intratextual examples of this premise is storytelling as performance that frames the core narrative of *The Cattle Killing.* Not only does the preacher intend his storytelling as a curative for the patient, but also the stories the preacher hears and collects are at the very least a palliative for him. Ayo's story interlocks with Grace's story in *Stigmata,* and both interlock with Lizzie's to heal her wounded body and soul. The formation is repeated in *Louisiana* in that the interlocking stories of Mammy and Lowly are a curative for Ella's ailing spirit.

Extratextually, storytelling has similar powers, for the stories authors of diasporan novels tell are intended as (and often are) a curative for diasporan readers' wounded spirits if, as Wideman says, they are "listening"

(208). In such instances the "story" becomes a guide for spiritually wounded readers to find wholeness and healing. Certainly, *Cane* has served this function for many contemporary readers and authors.

The interweaving of stories is the form this intended curative takes in *The Cattle Killing* and *Stigmata,* and this form is reminiscent of *Cane*'s eclectic form. The first quilt in *Stigmata* contains the story of Ayo, as filtered through her granddaughter Grace. There has been a rupture of the matrilineal bond between Grace and her daughter, Sarah (Lizzie's mother), and the second quilt in the novel, the one that Lizzie makes, is a narrative that tells Grace's story and ultimately rejuvenates the spiritual bond between Grace and Sarah and Sarah and Lizzie. The more Lizzie (eventually with the help of Sarah) completes her quilt, the more Grace's story is told; the more Grace's story is told, the more Ayo's story is told. It is a literal form of narrative quilting. As concept, narrative quilting also defines the discursive form of *Cane* and *The Cattle Killing:* the respective author/narrator metaphorically sews bits and pieces of stories together to make a whole—the respective novel. Story, teller, listener, being, Being, and other diasporan concepts interface in *Stigmata* under the rubric of the broken circle to chronicle Lizzie's progression from wounded in body and spirit to healed. As she states near the end of her narrative, "The circle is complete and . . . the gap is finally closed" (230).

6 The Third Gender among the Common Memory

Unspeakables Barely Spoken

The term *unspeakables* is one Morrison (*Beloved* 199), Wideman (*Cattle Killing* 32), and other authors sometimes use to characterize the horrific experiences to which slaves were subjected. The experiences include rape, incest, pedophilia, homosexuality, and other abusive (and some nonabusive) sexual behaviors that much of society then and now would consider deviations from a sexual norm. The authors incorporate these sexual deviations into their texts as part of the common memory of diasporan subjects.

A sexual liaison between a white male and a black female, whether one of abuse or one of conjugal bliss, has been and remains a conventional narrative formation in fictional and nonfictional discourses on slavery that treat sexual behavior. Sexual contact between a black male and a white female during the period of slavery is much less common in these discourses. Harriet Jacobs's *Incidents in the Life of a Slave Girl* is one exception among nonfiction slave narratives. One of the "incidents" Jacobs narrates is about the daughter of a slave owner who selects from her father's human property "one of the meanest" and "most brutalized" male slaves to be her lover, "over whom her authority could be exercised with less fear of exposure" (45). With this slave she has a child.

While speaking about the fate of children born to interracial unions,

Jacobs indicates that consummation between a white woman and a black man was not an anomaly during the slavocracy. Historical records support her statement. Indeed, the number of instances in which a white male petitioned his state legislature for a divorce from his white wife because she gave birth to a child or children whom a black fathered suggests how frequent such unions must have been throughout the Southern slave states from the 1770s to the 1860s. The white women came from all social classes and the men came from both the slave and the free black populations and ranged the spectrum of complexion.[1] It seems plausible that for social, financial, and other reasons, most instances of this kind of miscegenetic union would not result in a petition to a state legislature.

Several authors of post-1975 fictional slave narratives, however, give this formation thematic and structural focus in their texts. Chief among these are Johnson's *Oxherding Tale,* Williams's *Dessa Rose,* D'Aguiar's *Longest Memory,* Phillips's *Cambridge,* and Wideman's *Cattle Killing.* Nevertheless, the formation still is not as common in post-1975 fictional slave narratives as the formation of a sexual relation between a white male and a black female is in pre-1975 fictional slave narratives. During slavery and in the discourse on slavery, the latter kind of relationship seems to be considered a sexual norm.

As a group, nonfiction slave narratives avoid the topics of incest, pedophilia, and homosexuality. Again, Jacobs's *Incidents* is a notable (and perhaps surprising) exception, for among the slave narrators it is Jacobs who is perhaps most inclusive (though she abbreviates the "incidents") of different sexual behaviors during the slavocracy that deviated from the period's social norm. Jacobs mentions incest in passing when she notes that several slaveholders "violate their own [ostensibly black] daughters" (62). In the popular mind, incest typically is defined according to how close the blood relation is between the persons involved, and the definition varies among races, classes, and ethnic groups. For example, among European royalty (especially in the past) and certain ethnic groups in the Middle East, marriages between first cousins were relatively common and not considered incestuous.[2] Blacks in the United States, past and present, generally consider incest as sexual intercourse between persons with any known (or suspected) degree of blood relation. Since the early nineteenth century a few nonfiction discourses on slavery have included, usually in passing, instances of incest during the slavocracy. The relatively infrequent inclusions of incest in literary texts about the slavocracy primarily treat incest among whites, secondarily incest between whites and blacks, and very rarely incest among blacks.[3] In the latter two instances the inclusions usually are in the context of the consequences of the peculiar institution's disregard for blacks' humanity. Basically unrestrained by law and generally free from social censure, some white males during the slavocracy engaged in sexual relations with their black daughters or with close black and white female relatives.[4] Given the sexual freedom white males of the slavocracy enjoyed with black females and the system's general disregard for any sanctity of the black family, it seems a logical consequence that when unaware of their blood relation or when the slave owner forced the sexual union, incest between blacks occurred.

A white-authored fictional slave narrative, Hildreth's *Archie Moore* provides interesting twists to the statements above. In the novel's plot Colonel Moore opposes the marriage between the title character and a house slave named Cassandra (Cassy), while his wife promotes the marriage. The Colonel, his wife, and Archie Moore (a slave) are aware that the Colonel is the father of both Archie and Cassy, and the Colonel forbids the marriage because of his own incestuous desires and intents for Cassy, not because Archie and Cassy are siblings. Learning that Archie is her half-brother does not deter Cassy's conjugal relationship with him (see chapters 7 and 8 of the novel).

Though it is not a fictional slave narrative, Faulkner's *Absalom, Absalom!* is certainly one of the most sophisticated novels to treat the psychosexual complexity of whitemale subjectivity (the intertwining of incest, homosexuality, and miscegenation) during the peculiar institution and afterward, as is evident in his construction of Henry Sutpen (who wants to become his own brother-in-law) and Quentin Compson (centered in *The Sound and the Fury*), each of whom develops an incestuous attachment to his sister. Waters Turpin's treatment of incest, homosexuality, and miscegenation in *The Rootless* is without the sophisticated complexity one finds in *Absalom, Absalom!*

Among the rare instances in which incest is mentioned or explored in a contemporary fictional slave narrative are Reed's *Flight to Canada* and Jones's *Corregidora*. Reed seems to have European royalty in mind when he has his principal white male character in the novel, a Southern aristocrat, characterize his sexual relationship with his sister as "the royal love, the royal love" (110). Further, the novel's narrator inscribes this sexual relationship between Arthur Swille and his sister Vivian as incestuous necrophilia (60). The narrator also intimates an incestuous relationship between the "green-eyed" Vivian and her father, Arthur Swille II (172).[5] Reed uses these formations as a means of denigrating not only this family but also Southern white character in general by suggesting that such instances are not rare. An incestuous relationship between a white slave owner and two generations of his black female progeny is one of the thematic anchors of plot structure in *Corregidora* (59). Jones uses the formation to denigrate white male subjectivity but primarily to emphasize the psychological debilitation—"suppressed hysteria" is the term she uses (59)—and the extended residual effects of the white male's sexual exploitation of the slave woman.

Pedophilia, defined here as sexual relations between an adult and a prepubescent child, is a very rare inclusion in either nonfictional or fictional slave narratives. Olaudah Equiano mentions in his 1789 *Narrative* instances during which adult white males rape young black "females not ten years old; and these abominations some of them practiced to . . . scandalous excess" (77). Caryl Phillips, also in passing, notes in *Cambridge* an instance of a forced "*marriage*" between a thirty-year-old male slave and a ten-year-old girl. From then until he is sold three years later, this virile male brutalizes this prepubescent child because "she *refused* to produce children" (158–59; Phillips's emphasis). Wideman notes that the priests who buy ten young African boys from those who stole them from Africa subject these boys to physical, psychological, and sexual abuses. The sexual abuse is buggery (sodomy), which in this instance is homosexual pedophilia (*Cattle Killing* 110).

Homosexuality is another sexual behavior that society during the slavocracy considered taboo. Again, Jacobs stands out among slave narrators by drawing specific attention to the topic. In *Incidents*, she includes among her "Southern reminiscences" (148) a forced homosexual "relationship" (in that it is ongoing) between a master and his male slave, and she suggests that such a sexual liaison is not an anomaly. Given this slaveholder's sexual proclivities, Jacobs counts his desires among "the strangest freaks of despotism," adding that "some of these freaks were of a nature too filthy to be repeated" (149). She uses literal and figural symbols and images of chattel slavery and a language that at times seems intentionally ambiguous to describe the relationship. For example, the male slave, Luke, often is not allowed to wear any clothing except his shirt and is "chained to the bedside of [his] cruel and disgusting" master. Jacobs notes that the reason for Luke being partially clothed is that he remain "in readiness to be flogged" (149). However, in the same paragraph she points out that if Luke offers "the slightest resistance" to his master's wishes, he is forced to bare his back in order to be flogged by his master or by the town constable. Typically, floggings were inflicted above, not below, the waist, so Luke's chronic nakedness below the waist is apparently not in readiness to be beaten, given the standard meaning of flogged. The term *flogging*, therefore, carries a decidedly sexual connotation. Luke literally is chained to the disabled master's bed to provide him sexual "service" on demand (148–49). The ambiguity of the scene suggests both oral and anal intercourse (fellatio and sodomy).

In effect, Morrison repeats and expands this generic formation in *Beloved* through the experiences of Paul D. For "trying to kill Brandywine, the man Schoolteacher sold him to" (106), Paul D is sentenced to a chain gang in Alfred, Georgia. The formation is of forty-six blacks chained together with three white males standing guard. The white guards routinely force the black prisoners to service them with fellatio, both as a means for the guards' sexual gratification and as a means of denigrating the black male self. The guards, collectively personified as "Mr. Death" and then feminized ("her") as a "flirt," keep the men in their "cock-teasing hug," whether a particular black man is a veteran of the chain gang or a "New man" ("fresh meat" in homosexual prison parlance) (106–9). In *Corregidora*, Gayl Jones mentions a forced lesbian alliance between Mrs. Corregidora (the slave mistress) and one of her husband's concubines (13, 59), which is a rare inclusion even in contemporary fictional slave narratives that are of novel length. Johnson includes an even briefer allusion to Flo Hatfield's lesbian liaisons in *Oxherding Tale* (20, 29). He is more expansive, however, in his treatment of Captain Falcon's homosexual acts and desires in *Middle Passage* (26–27, for example), including his (supposedly) unconsummated sexual desire for Rutherford Calhoun (see, for example, 46).

Like the slave narrators, African American novelists before the 1960s also were reticent about discussing homosexuality. Though male-authored, the majority of African American novels published before World War I are female-centered. In the main, the few references to homosexuality among blacks in novels of this period are veiled allusions to one woman's unconsummated sexual desire for another woman. One of the earliest examples in the genre is J. McHenry Jones's *Hearts of Gold* (1896), which is representative of those very few African American novelists before the Harlem Renaissance who approached the topic but who treated it through indirection and innuendo (see, for example, *Hearts* 161). This pattern generally obtained from the 1920s to the 1960s, though it expanded to include homosexual desire or contact (mainly veiled references) between black males. Representative novelists who significantly embellished the pattern are Nella Larsen in *Passing* (1929) and Ralph Ellison in *Invisible Man* (1952), both of whom incorporate a relatively expanded though veiled narrative formation about male homosexuality (Larsen's is intraracial and Ellison's is interracial).[6]

It is notable that the epigraph Larsen chooses for *Passing* is an excerpt from Countee Cullen's "Heritage," a poem that evokes the diasporan myth and diasporan desire. She draws upon Greek mythology and uses a combination of images, allusions, innuendoes, and ambiguities to suggest the lesbian attraction between the two subjects the novel centers. For example, the color green traditionally has been associated with sexual desires and practices that deviate from an established norm, which includes homosexuality (within homosexual communities, however, the color signifies preference rather than deviance).[7] Green is a prominent image in narrative formations that involve Irene Redfield and Clare Kendry.[8] Combining this image with the knowing "gaze" and allusions to Greek mythology early in the novel helps establish the suggestion of lesbianism, which subsequent allusions and ambiguities support. The narrator's early description of Clare Kendry is of "a sweetly scented woman in a fluttering dress of green chiffon whose mingled pattern of narcissuses, jonquils, and hyacinths was a reminder of pleasantly chill spring days" (37). Though it is about heterosexual attraction, the story of Narcissus and Echo involves unrequited love, reflection, and self-reflection (the desiring gaze). A jonquil is a species (a cutting, if you will) of narcissus, just as Irene and Clare each is "a cutting" (Aristophanes's term in *Symposium* [87]) from the third gender. Though it is about two males, the story of Hyacinthus and Apollo is about Apollo's love for this youth, whom he accidentally slays. Larsen is not explicit about who or what causes Clare's death, but the novel strongly suggests that Irene kills her, whether accidentally or intentionally (184–89).

Through a combination of images, allusions, and ambiguities, Ellison's *Invisible Man* narrates a white male's (Emerson Jr.'s) sexual attraction to invisible man. The color green (and thus its sexual association) pervades the scene between the two. Indirect references to Walt Whitman's Calamus poems, direct references to Freud's *Totem and Taboo,* Emerson Jr.'s ambiguous language and gestures and invisible man's responses to his overtures—

these and other aspects of this scene suggest a white homosexual male's attempt to seduce a black male, and thus continue the usual manner in which African American novelists before the 1960s treat sexual desire and contact between males (see 136–48). James Baldwin reconfigures the pattern in the 1960s with direct treatments of black male homosexuality, though most of his formations are interracial ones. After Baldwin, black novelists (E. Lynn Harris is one) are less reticent than previous novelists to explore directly the topic of homosexuality generally and gay and lesbian relationships among blacks specifically. Nevertheless, on the whole the topic remains in the background of contemporary Western black novels, including fictional slave narratives.

Whether the setting in contemporary fictional slave narratives is entirely in the era of slavery or whether the setting extends to the contemporary period, narrative formations about homosexual relationships and homosexual acts, with very few exceptions, have a common set of characteristics. The participants are bisexual rather than exclusively homosexual. When the homosexual desire is consummated as a relationship or an act, it most often is between a black and a white (as in *Crossing the River*), occasionally between whites (as in *Middle Passage* and *Higher Ground*), almost never between two blacks (an exception is *Linden Hills*, in which the homosexual affair is between two contemporary black males), and usually between males rather than between females (*Corregidora* is an example of the latter). The authors most often portray the relationship or the act negatively, and they typically inscribe the interracial relationship or the act as a means whites use to denigrate blacks. A negative portrayal of whites who desire or who engage in a homosexual act is a means for the author to denigrate white subjectivity. Caryl Phillips (*Higher Ground*) is the most notable exception among the authors of contemporary fictional slave narratives in that he uses an enslaved bisexual black's homosexual desire for a white male (14–15, for example) as a means of castigating this African subject for his complicity in the slave trade. In the main, then, contemporary fictional slave narratives' depiction of homosexual acts between blacks and whites during the slavocracy is, in the example of Jacobs's *Incidents*, primarily an instance of a white (male or female) exerting power over a black.

Homosexuality and the Diasporan Myth's Theory of Being

Authors of contemporary fictional slave narratives often situate their formations of the homosexual self within the diasporan myth's theory of Being. The myth's theory of Being aligns with several features from non-Western and Western myths about the origin and nature of humankind without fully duplicating any single myth. It shares with several myths the premise that originally humankind consisted of three genders (male, female, and manwoman), the Supreme Being bisected each gender (compare to Aristophanes in *Symposium*), and the "cuttings" from these bisected halves seek reunion with their components selves in order to reestablish the whole Self and thus humankind's original state of Being. It also shares with several myths the idea that these cuttings or component selves are both opposite-gender and same-gender twins (in this context, twins refers to sameness and is not confined to number).

As it regards the homosexual self, however, the diasporan myth posits that male and female homosexuals (constituents of the third gender) are cuttings or twins, respectively, from the original male and female genders and that male and female heterosexuals are cuttings or twins primarily from the original common or manwoman gender. In diasporan novels (which are set principally in historical time), an extension of the cutting from the male half of the bisected primordial Self desires reunion with an extension of the cutting from the female half of the bisected primordial Self, and vice versa (heterosexuality). The same obtains for the male and female extensions of the cuttings, respectively, from the halves of the bisected primordial Selves that were male and female (homosexuality). Diasporan females and diasporan males who seek to effect a reunion through conjugality are heterosexual opposite-gender twins (Sixo and Patsy in *Beloved*, for example). Some heterosexual same-gender twins also are extensions from cuttings of both the primordial bisected male and female Selves. Their means for reuniting with their component selves is nonconjugal. Examples include diasporan females in *Beloved* and diasporan males in *The Cattle Killing*. When same-gender extensions from primordial cuttings seek reunion through conjugal fusion, they are homosexuals. In all three instances the genders' ruling desire is for complete wholeness, which would return them to the original state of the androgyne. (One should note that several narrative formations in contemporary fictional slave narratives and other diasporan novels indicate that complete wholeness is not the objective of all instances of conjugality, heterosexual or homosexual.)

The androgyne as a concept of Being can be found in several origin myths, non-Western and Western, and often these origin myths include it under the rubric of twinship, especially opposite-gender twinship. Robert Brain observes that "in the lore of opposite-sex twins [from several different cultures], the two are depicted as an original unit which split, a unit which strives to be reunited by sexual love" (141). From the purview of the diasporan myth, Brain's observation applies to what this study refers to as conjugal complementarity, whether the subject and subject complement (the "twins") are of the opposite or of the same gender.

Directly and indirectly, Judeo-Christian, African (central, western, and especially Egyptian), Greek, and Hindu myths are principal among the mythologies and cosmologies that authors of contemporary fictional slave narratives incorporate (and often interface) in their generation of the diasporan myth's theory of Western black Being. For example, Tananarive Due (*My Soul to Keep* and *The Living Blood*) combines Judeo-Christian with African (Yoruba, for instance [*Living Blood* 39]) religious mythology in her construction of the first group of Immortals, who become immortal after they drink the blood of Christ (*Soul to Keep* 61–62). Though quite differently, Naylor (*Linden Hills*), Perry (*Stigmata*), Reed (*Flight to Canada*), and Wideman (*Cattle Killing*) incorporate Judeo-Christian mythology and combine it with African mythologies in the formation of their black subjects. Charles Johnson's formation of the Allmuseri's Being (*Middle Passage, Oxherding Tale*) draws upon Egyptian and other African as well as Hindu and Greek mythologies. Reed is particularly attracted to (ancient) Egyptian mythology for the creation of his fictive worlds (especially in *Mumbo Jumbo* and *Flight to Canada*), and he interfaces Egyptian mythology, cosmology, and culture with those of other African and European groups. Indeed, Egyptian mythology and cosmology (specifically, sacred geometry and sacred mathematics) are principal sources for the contemporary fictional slave narrative's diasporan myth as an origin myth and for the theory of Western black Being embedded in this myth.

Several mythologies and cosmologies from which authors of contemporary fictional slave narratives draw include concepts of twinness and androgyny as endemic to human origin. In some of the myths, bisexuality (thus homosexuality) and hermaphroditism are simultaneous with human origin. This is the case in Dogon mythology. Nommo, whom the Dogon consider the "father" of humankind, was a hermaphrodite, "a complete being" who both sired and gave birth to the first group of humans as a social organization (Brain 137). In Greek mythology Night (Nyx), the female twin of the male Erebos, was born bisexual and later sired and gave birth to her own children, Day, Sleep, Death, and others (Brain 141–42); she also was the mother of children born from an incestuous relationship with Erebos. In Hindu mythology Ardhanarisvara and Tuisto are hermaphrodites; Tuisto sires and gives birth to Varuna.

In the diasporan myth some androgynous subjects are capable of nonconjugal reproduction but do not belong to the third gender and are neither homosexual nor bisexual. Parallels to this idea can be found, for example, in Hindu and Dogon mythologies. In Hindu mythology some versions of the stories of Brahma (the One) and Shiva (an androgyne) treat nonconjugal (Brahma) and conjugal (Shiva and Shakti) reproduction.[9] Much like some versions of Nommo in Dogon mythology, Barlo's "visioned African" in Toomer's *Cane* is a male who is both father and mother of Western blacks (39). In *Praisesong*, Marshall's formation of Lebert Joseph as an androgynous subject (179, 243) recalls Greek mythology in which the male Zeus sires and gives birth to Athena as well as Hindu mythology in which Brahma creates sons from his own thoughts. Joseph metaphorically sires and gives birth to his daughter, Rosalie Parvay: "She might have sprung whole from his head, a head-birth without benefit or need of a mother" (216). Mammy and Lowly in *Louisiana* are two women who figuratively "sire" and "[give] birth" to a third woman, the novel's title character (17, 32, 61).

When authors of contemporary fictional slave narratives form a third gender subject consistent with the diasporan myth's theory of Being and depict this subject as a homosexual (including bisexual) self, the formation usually is of a white subject and is decidedly negative. For the white subject, sex is a "despotic" mechanism (Jacobs's term) he or she uses to further dominate and demean the black self. The ostensible intents of such subject formations and their accompanying narrative formations are to textually reverse power relations between whites and blacks and to signify subject deformation—more often for whites than for blacks, more often for subjects who are uncentered than for centered ones. With few exceptions, the authors form the subjects as bisexuals (usually whites) who act on their homosexual desires or as heterosexuals (usually blacks) who are forced or seduced into homosexual acts. Mrs. Corregidora (*Corregidora*) and the chain-gang guards (*Beloved*) are examples of the former; their respective victims, Great Gram and Paul D, are examples of the latter. Rarely are such formations positive in that a respective author intends to depict different-race subjects who are homosexual twin selves attempting to reunite through conjugality and reconstitute the state of the androgyne.

Reading the Third Gender as Homosexual Other: The Example of Flight to Canada

As noted above, the language Jacobs uses in *Incidents* to narrate a slave master's homosexual exploitation of his slave Luke is certainly ambiguous, whether or not she intends such. However, several authors of contemporary fictional slave narratives that treat homosexuality (and other "nonstandard" sexual practices[10]) intentionally employ a vocabulary that slavery and homosexuality had come to share by the mid-twentieth century. Principal among these linguistic forms and formations are *master, slave, slave trade, servant, service, dominant, submissive, father (daddy), son, boy, girl, whips, chains, flogging,* and *sadism.*[11] Contextually, terms such as *peculiar, strange,* and *queer* also assume homosexual connotations in *Flight to Canada.*

In several ways *Flight* is one of the most unorthodox among contemporary fictional slave narratives in how it revises and embellishes the nonfiction slave narrative as master text, especially in how it treats homosexuality. Given the topic's pervasiveness in the novel's subject formations and narrative formations and its referentiality and intertextuality, one could argue that homosexuality, not slavery or the Civil War, is the topic of the novel's main text rather than of its subtext. Reed, through Lincoln's dialogue, asserts that the abolition of slavery is merely "a subplot in this war" (46). By analogy one could assert that the military and political tensions between the North and the South constitute this novel's subplot while homosexual attractions between the Northern "fathers" and the Southern "sons" constitute its main plot.[12]

Like most authors of contemporary fictional slave narratives, Reed uses homosexuality as a means of "reading" (denigrating) white male subjectivity. In gay parlance, "to read" a subject is to expose that subject's homosexual desires, tendencies, or nature. This meaning certainly is applicable to *Flight to Canada* as "more of a reading than a writing" (7). Through double entendre, referentiality, and subject formation, Reed applies this reading to white males on both sides of the Atlantic, but particularly to Southern ones. He positions three white males as key players in the Civil War games—Arthur Swille III (a fictional character), Abraham Lincoln, and Jefferson Davis.

The novel asserts that the males in the Swille patriarchy are direct descendants of King Arthur, that they are physically and morally deformed, and that their deformities and depravities are hereditary. Though early in the novel Reed describes "the first Swille [as] a zealous slave trader, breeder and planter [who] was 'indescribably deformed'" (15), he concentrates on the Swille dynasty's hereditary moral (that is, sexual) deformities. He cites Tennyson as his source when describing Uther, King Arthur's father, as "so 'sweet' some took him to be 'less a man'" (16); the former term connotes effeminacy and both connote homosexuality. Using hereditary markers, with particular emphasis on sexual depravity, Reed constructs the novel's principal white male character, Arthur Swille III, as a bisexual hedonist. Swille frequents "a private Richmond club called the Magnolia Baths" (16) "to shake [his] butt" (22) with his fellow "Planters."[13] At the Magnolia Baths and at private parties, Swille and these "gentlemen" indulge themselves sadomasochistically with whips and chains (58). Indeed, Virginia is known "as the Sadist's Canada" (127). Swille receives "the licentious Hedonist Award," is "known in London and Paris circles as a 'gay blade'" (16), and gets "indignant proposals" from some "boys" (58).

Swille is, however, a switch-hitter (in contemporary sexual language), in that not only does he have both female and male sexual partners but also he can switch between dominant and submissive roles in same-gender sexual encounters.[14] During his first encounter with Abraham Lincoln, Swille "takes the old keys from his right hip and fastens them to his left" (29). This symbolic action indicates that Swille wants to assume a dominant role in a sexual encounter with Lincoln. When Reed published this novel in the mid-1970s, same-gender sexual codes included wearing objects such as keys and handkerchiefs on one's rear. Wearing the object on the right side indicated that the subject desired a passive or submissive role; wearing it on the left indicated that the subject desired an active or dominant role.[15]

Early in the text Reed suggests that Swille assumes a passive or receiver role with one of his male slaves: "Swille's stud, Jim" (17). In homosexual encounters a stud usually is the dominant partner, the pitcher. In another allusion to Swille's homosexuality, Reed does not indicate whether Swille is the pitcher or the catcher. The allusion hinges upon a double meaning of white slavery (forced prostitution), and Reed suggests that the "white house slave," Mr. Moe (perhaps the most ambiguous of his character formations), is also one of Swille's sexual partners (22); he is a "house boi."[16] Through double meanings and suggestive language, Reed includes the slave Cato among Swille's homosexual partners. In addition to feminizing Cato through his attire and mannerisms, Reed has Swille in a Freudian slip refer to Cato as his "son" (54). Recovering from the slip, Swille explains that he intends the term "figuratively" (which compounds the double meaning). In the scene between these two (51–55), the father-son nexus is explicitly biological and implicitly homosexual. The latter instance would be one of miscegenetic homosexual incest, which would not be out of bounds for Reed's reading of Swille.

Reed constructs Swille as a "playa" (player) and a "pig," terms that in homosexual slang characterize a person whose sexual appetites and practices are excessive. *Playa* is a pejorative term that means slut; Reed undoubtedly intends the pejorative here. Included among Swille's variety of sexual partners are the gentlemen from the Magnolia Baths, his sister Vivian, his wife, male and female slaves, and "girls [who] are mere babies" (133). Swille is lord of his ancestral manse in Swine'rd, Virginia, a castle situated behind "mossy land and swamps full of so many swine" (15). He is a *pig*, a term that within the homosexual community is more pejorative than *playa* and refers to a person whose sexual appetites and behaviors homosexuals consider extreme deviations from a homosexual norm.[17] Indeed, "Swille's favorite hero of antiquity" is Caligula (52), whose sexual excesses allegedly included incest with his three sisters (especially Drusilla) as well as homosexuality.

Swille would not have to look to Caligula as a model for his own character. A contemporary fellow Southerner, James Henry Hammond, would provide the mold. A former governor of South Carolina and a U.S. senator, Hammond was a staunch defender of slavery. Historically, he is noted particularly for his "mudsill" speech to the U.S. Senate on March 4, 1858, and for his speech condemning Nebraska's stand against slavery. Among prominent slaveholders of his or any other era, he was one of the cruelest. Sadistic would not be too strong a term to describe him as a slaveholder. For him, slaves were merely "tools with life in them," to be used up and then discarded—literally, to be worked to death.[18]

It is more Hammond's sexual proclivities than his political views that align closely with Swille's. Hammond would have been a frontrunner for the "Hedonist Award" that Swille receives. Given his social and political prominence, diagnosticians today probably would consider him a sexual addict rather than a "playa." Among Hammond's (like Swille's) sexual proclivities were adultery, pedophilia, incest, and aggressive homosexuality. "Hammond took for his mistress an eighteen-year-old slave with a one-year-old child, and then when the child reached the age of twelve he made her his mistress as well" (Hammond xi). For a few years Hammond maintained sexual relationships with three of his nieces (171–72). More to explain than to justify his incestuous behavior, he cites other public men's (Henry Clay's, Daniel Webster's, and President William Henry Harrison's) incestuous liaisons.[19] One of his ostensible friends and sexual partners, Jeff Withers (who refers to himself as Hammond's "Stud"), suggests that Hammond's homosexual desires have "captured complete mastery over" him, so much so that he pursues "every she-male [he] can discover" in his "locality." Withers admits that he has "often had the honor of feeling" Hammond's "long fleshen pole." He cautions Hammond to curb "his lustful appetite" in order to avoid becoming exclusively homosexual. Characterizing Hammond as rough trade, he cautions that Hammond's aggressive sexual intercourse "roughen[s] the downy Slumbers of" a given "writhing Bedfellow" so much that some "awful results" inevitably will be "devastation, horror, & bloodshed, etc." (Duberman 87–89).

As a sexual switch-hitter, Swille closely resembles Hammond. As a political switch-hitter, he is noticeably different from Hammond. To construct Swille's subjectivity, Reed combines the politics of sex with the politics of the Civil War and sandwiches Swille between the commanders in chief of the opposing sides. The major scene between Swille and Lincoln turns on power relations, not only between dominant and submissive potential sexual partners but also between the North and the South. Swille suggests that at this point in the Civil War, neither the Union nor the Confederacy has the upper hand, that they are "even-steven right now" (32), which presents Swille the opportunity to exert his power and to exploit each side. Swille "hate[s] contemporary politics" (23), and thus his interest in the conflict ("these queer crises" [23]) is motivated more by money and power than by sexual desire. Though he is a slaveholder, his desire for power and control outweighs his sympathies for the Confederacy. He has helped finance the Confederacy, but now he agrees to provide Lincoln enough gold to bolster the Union's war effort and therefore turn the tide in the Union's favor. This political formation seems to invoke a homosexual parallel. In some male homosexual relationships, a desiring subject might provide his "trade" with remuneration for sexual favors. In the narrative formation Reed installs, Lincoln directly and Davis indirectly seek financial support from Swille for their war efforts. Thus, as a businessman and a power monger, Swille is, so to speak, in bed with two strange bedfellows.

Yet as Reed depicts this seemingly ironic and contradictory situation, the alliance is not so strange. Indeed, following popular thought of the mid-twentieth century, blacks do not perceive Lincoln as their Great White Father. Reed depicts him as a racist whose stance in the Civil War is motivated more by his desire to keep the Union intact and the North in power than to free the slaves, and principally by his desire to wield power and exert control over others. Using the homosexual-slavery nexus, Reed further paints Lincoln as less than a hero to or for blacks (except those blacks whom Reed also denigrates, such as Mammy Barracuda). To this end Reed suggests through the double meaning of language that Lincoln would not necessarily be an unwilling partner in a sexual encounter with Swille. In fact, he feminizes Lincoln. The yacht in which Lincoln travels to visit Swille is named *The River Queen;* Lincoln's voice is "high-pitched" (28); Swille associates him with the color green (25) and refers to him as "Marquis Lincoln of Springfield" (26). According to Swille, Lincoln tells "lewd jokes to the boys in the telegraph room," and "weird talk from the planters . . . strange ugly talk" circulates about his subjectivity (27). Ordinarily, terms, phrases, and narrative formations such as these would not connote anything beyond their standard meaning. Yet given Reed's use of homosexuality to denigrate white male subjectivity as well as the sexual content and connotations in this first scene in which Lincoln appears, such terms, phrases, and narrative formations assume homosexual connotations in regard to Lincoln's subjectivity.

Reed entitles part 2 of *Flight* "Lincoln the Player." One of the lexical definitions of *player* is a person who actively participates in a game or sport. Certainly, Lincoln is an active participant in the Civil War games. Moreover, in gay slang a *playa* is one who maintains multiple sexual relationships and has a grandiose image.[20] Reed's feminization of Lincoln and his reference to rumors of Lincoln's homosexuality support his formation of Lincoln as a playa, an active homosexual. When he published *Flight to Canada*, Reed no doubt was aware of suggestions in print that Lincoln was a practicing homosexual or at the least had homosexual desires. A recent and controversial biography of Lincoln more fully asserts this.[21]

The homosexual-textual politics of Reed's novel is consistent with his tendency to conjoin past and present realities. For example, one might note that for a white of Lincoln's era (and long afterward) to be accused of being a black person (as some of Lincoln's detractors accused him of being) carries the same kind of negative weight that would apply to a man (especially a politician) accused of being a homosexual during the time of the novel's publication. Swille's reversal of homosexual roles (switching of the keys) aligns with Reed's reversal of the subject roles often assigned to Southern and Northern white males. Typically, Northerners have portrayed Southerners as unintelligent, backward, buffoonish, racist, and shallow. In large part Reed reverses these roles in the major scene between Swille and Lincoln, and Lincoln exhibits subject characteristics often assigned to Southern whites. During the decades surrounding the novel's publication, television's portrayal of Southern white subjectivity through shows such as *The Andy Griffith Show, The Carol Burnett Show, Mama's Family, Dallas,* and others was basically negative. Reed uses television as one of the conjoiners of past and present realities.

Swille's desire to assume a dominant role in a sexual relation with Lincoln parallels his desire to assume and his belief that he has assumed a dominant position of power over both the Northern and the Southern factions in the Civil War. Certainly at this point in the novel, Swille seems to be more powerful than the two warring factions and their leaders and generals (Lincoln and General Grant, Davis and General Lee). Yet Quickskill, the novel's centered subject, undermines Swille's supposed dominant position through his poem and other subversive acts, and through the (homo)-sexual-textual politics of his subversive novel Reed undermines a power structure that white males, Northern and Southern, dominate. It is to be noted that in these sexual and textual power plays, Reed does not attach any homosexual connotations to Quickskill's subjectivity. When he does embed homosexual connotations in his formation of black male characters, such as Jim and Cato, he indicates that the homosexual acts in which they participate are interracial ones and that they are victims of power relations in which a white male, specifically the despotic Swille, dominates.

As he does for Abraham Lincoln, Reed "reads" Jefferson Davis as both the subject and the object of homosexual desire; he does the latter when he inscribes him as potential homosexual trade (25). Swille reports that one of his homosexual "friends recently visited this six-plus-foot tall specimen and said he just felt like stripping and permitting this eagle-eyed, blade-nosed, creamy Adonis to abuse him and . . . [pant, pant] humiliate him" (25; Reed's ellipses and brackets). From Swille's recollection of this conversation, it seems clear that he, too, wants to be the catcher for Davis as pitcher; he desires Davis as rough trade in a sadomasochistic encounter. Describing Davis's unsuccessful attempt to escape his Union captors by disguising himself as a woman, Reed uses double entendre to inscribe Davis as a cross-dresser, as effeminate, and perhaps as a closeted homosexual. Reed admits, however, that Davis's defenders claim the story of his disguise is a lie and that historians still debate the point (141–42). Nevertheless, Reed's reading of Davis in this regard is consistent with numerous political cartoons and commentaries of the era devoted to Davis's capture. As Neely, Holzer, and Boritt point out in *The Confederate Image,* many historians have missed these cartoons' "sexual connotations, and therefore their meaning" (232, n. 12). Reed does not miss the connotations and meanings of captions and phrases such as the "bearded lady," "the un-manning of Jeff," "Jeff in petticoats," "the exposure of Jeff's ram-parts," "the belle of Richmond," and similar ones, nor does he miss the "boldly sexual overtones" (Neely et al. 87) of several of the cartoons' graphics. As a satirical iconoclast, Reed levels a strong blow at Davis, one of the white South's most revered icons.

Through his formation of Davis as a feminized male and his formation of Swille as a bisexual hedonist, Reed generalizes to the white male South.[22] Through an alignment of white male subjects and a conjunction of temporal and spatial realities, he generalizes from the South to the North and to Europe. The novel asserts that Southern white male subjectivity is the gauge by which one assesses white American and European male subjectivity. Reed conjoins these regions and subjectivities in part by drawing upon the history of the nation's early colonial period during which Virginia was a controlling metaphor for all English holdings in North America and the Virginia settler (the Swille patriarchy in this novel) was the representative model for the white colonial. He also uses Southern white culture and character as the shaping forces of white American culture and character during the nineteenth century in which the novel is set and the twentieth century in which it is published.

As Reed suggests, Northerners and Southerners are players/playas in war games that have different levels and dimensions. One dimension, he asserts, is certainly homosexual, for in these war games or "queer crises" (23) the "fathers" of the North are the active players and the "sons" of the

South are the passive players. In the novel Abraham Lincoln, the Great White Father, epitomizes the Northern fathers and Jefferson Davis, a Southern "Adonis" (25), epitomizes the Southern sons. Referring to the white South as a "Fairy Kingdom" (49), Reed uses Oscar Wilde as a referential context to contend that "the South is dandyish, foppish, pimpish; . . . its assassin [Jefferson Davis] left behind a trunk in which was found: 'clothes in fine silk velvets; silks, ermine and crimson; and also hats, caps, plumes, boots, shoes, etc.'" (141–42).[23] According to Reed, what appealed to the "fair youth" of the South was not "the idea of winning" the war but "the idea of being ravished," an idea or desire that subsequently is ritually reenacted in "the New Orleans Mardi Gras, that great Confederate pageant, the cult of Endymion" (142).

The Greek mythological figures Endymion and Adonis are noted for their youthful physical beauty; Reed merges the two. In *Flight to Canada*, both Endymion and Adonis signify same-gender male attraction. As highly desirable homosexual trade, Davis in Swille's and other Southern males' imagination resembles Adonis (25). Following his capture, one cult that formed around Davis was devoted to him as a military and ideological icon; *Flight* contends that another was devoted to him as an icon of homosexual trade. It is the latter devotion, the novel intimates, that is reenacted as the cult of Endymion during the New Orleans Mardi Gras.

Historically, Mardi Gras is a carnival imported to the colonial American South in the 1690s directly from France (whose celebrations date back to the Middle Ages) and indirectly from ancient Greece and Rome. In modern times the carnival (and the term Mardi Gras) has come to be associated in part with a kind of wanton sexuality identified with ancient Greece and Rome, including homosexuality. It also is noted for the elaborate costumes parade participants wear, including men in female attire. Perhaps Reed has the history of Mardi Gras as well as nineteenth-century graphics about Davis (see Neely et al. 81–92) in mind when, having inscribed him at one point as rough trade, he later inscribes him as a cross-dresser and a drag queen.

Flight fuses past and present realities, including homosexuality, through a variety of fictive devices. Reed often uses a layered pattern of language, image, and allusion to emphasize especially the sadistic nature of the "peculiar" institution and its supporters. In one example he conjoins slavery and homosexuality by combining images of whips, chains, and floggings with allusions to Lord Gladstone and Marquis de Sade, not only to suggest the sadistic nature of slavery and its supporters but also to portray Southern male slaveholders and their supporters, such as Lord Gladstone, as sadomasochistic homosexuals (25, 108, 127).[24] With references such as "Marquis Lincoln of Springfield" (26), he positions President Lincoln in this group. When one recalls Jacobs's ambiguous use of the term "flogging" in *Incidents,* Lincoln's characterization of Swille as a "slave-flogging pea-picker" assumes decidedly homosexual dimensions and gains support from narrative formations in the novel that indicate Swille has sexual relations with his male slaves.

To be sure, it is with deliberation that Reed chooses historical white males from across the centuries and from both sides of the Atlantic as referential subjects and speaking subjects who have been rumored to be or accused of being or admitted to being homosexual—Jefferson Davis, Ezra Pound, Walt Whitman, Alfred Lord Tennyson, Lord William Gladstone, Oscar Wilde, Caligula, and Abraham Lincoln, among the best-known ones. Reed exempts few fictional or real-life white males included in the novel from a homosexual reading. A historiographic metafiction, *Flight to Canada* is satirical and often humorous, and it uses double entendre to underscore the serious nature of its homosexual readings of selected white male subjects.

As setting, Swine'rd, Virginia, is the place from which Swille III does "his business from the tower of a Castle he built on the grounds, said to be the very replica of King Arthur's in the Holy City of Camelot, the Wasp's Jerusalem, the great Fairy City of the old Feudal Order" (15). In effect, it is the South's capital seat for "endless games" (15) of sex and war. Male effeminacy and homosexuality are integral to Reed's inscription of the South as a replica of the legendary Camelot, and much of this he suggests through double entendre and referentiality.

Like homosexuality, Camelot is a major metaphor that Reed uses to conjoin past and present realities, past and present fantasies, the South, the North, and Europe. For example, the neo-feudalistic antebellum South envisioned itself as a replica of Camelot; during the Kennedy era of the 1960s, the nation envisioned itself as a replica of Camelot. Through this metaphor Reed erases boundaries of time and space. His conclusion is that not only Swine'rd, Virginia, but all of America is "Camelot. Camelot West. Camelot East. Camelot South. One big fucking Camelot" (98). To be sure, on one hermeneutic level *Flight to Canada*'s "story" is a fairy tale about a "Fairy Kingdom" (Reed's term, 49).

Loving Her, Loving Him: Same-Gender Conjugality in Works by Shockley and Phillips

When applied to the contemporary fictional slave narrative, Caryl Phillips's phrase "the many-tongued chorus of the common memory" (*Crossing the River* 235) assumes additional significance when the chorus includes voices of diasporan blacks and European and American whites who are gay (male or female). In general, though, the voices of blacks who are gay or bisexual are absent from or muted in the subgenre. One might say that though they are among the chorus, rarely are they selves centered in these novels. Homosexuality and bisexuality are two of those "unspeakables" that are barely spoken (about) in the nonfiction slave narrative. Ann Shockley's short story "The Mistress and the Slave Girl" and the "Pagan Coast" section of Caryl Phillips's *Crossing the River* are fictional narratives about interracial same-gender love bonds that are set entirely in the slavery period and that center gay subjects. Both authors use double entendre to conjoin slavery and homosexuality as psychosocial and psychosexual formations that link past and present realities.

In forming her centered female subjects, Shockley assigns them sexual roles that conform to some contemporary notions that in homosexual relationships one subject's role is "male" and the other subject's role is "female." In the language of homosexuality, male and female roles are equivalent to dominant and submissive roles, respectively. In the language of slavery, these same roles are equivalent to master (a gendered term) and slave, respectively. Constructing Heather Blakely, the slave mistress, from the mold of the "good" male slave owner, Shockley masculinizes her and thus assigns her a male subjectivity. When Heather first appears in the story, she fits the mold of the liberal, Northern-educated Southern mistress of the plantation. After she sees, is sexually attracted to, and then buys the beautiful Delia to make her her lover, Heather speaks "huskily," dons her brother's "riding breeches, her favorite plantation attire," conducts business like a man, and has her hair cut short. In this context, a woman's long hair signifies her femininity. Ralph (her brother) sees Heather's haircut as "another link to wearing pants and buying a slave girl." The contrast between Heather and Delia (petite stature, soft skin, soft hands, beautiful long hair) emphasizes respectively Heather's masculinity and Delia's femininity and underscores the "role" each occupies in their sexual relationship.

In response to her brother's question—"What role are you trying to play, dear sister?"—Heather responds that she is "*not* playing *any* role" (Shockley's emphasis), which suggests that her masculinity is endemic to her Being. In contemporary gay culture, role playing is a conscious fantasy in which the player or players might choose to assume any of a wide variety of sexual and gender roles. The term "player," therefore, also carries a decidedly homosexual connotation, as it does when Reed applies it to Lincoln and others in *Flight to Canada.*

Shockley casts Heather from the mold of the male slaveholder who buys a beautiful slave girl for his sexual pleasure but then falls in love with her. The sight of the seventeen-year-old girl on the auction block causes Heather to experience "a familiar sharp sensation" of sexual desire, "an overpowering magnetism." She decides immediately "to buy that girl" and thus assumes "a male prerogative" of "bidding outwardly for slaves." She competes with and outsmarts slaveholding "males at their own game" of owning sex slaves. Having won the game, she feels "triumphant" that this "was one slave girl who wouldn't be thrown to the wolves for a white master's breeder or concubine." Heather abhors the idea of being "a firsthand slave owner." The story makes it clear, therefore, that given her antislavery sentiments, Heather does not buy Delia as a work slave but as a slave whose "services" will be "personal" (that is, as a "concubine"). The story's formation of Ralph as a gay male intimates that males of the slaveholding class also bought male slaves to use as sexual servants: "Too bad she [Delia] doesn't have a brother of comparable beauty," states Ralph.

Though Shockley uses external trappings to masculinize Heather and to feminize Ralph, she maintains that their homosexual proclivities are congenital and that Heather has acted before on her sexual desires. The initial meeting of the two women during which Heather experiences "an overpowering magnetism" recalls Toomer's concept of "perfect correspondence" from "Sing Yes!" (*Wayward* 205). Indeed, Heather considers Delia her subject complement, and thus her desire is much more than physical. In fact, through her formation of the story's three focal characters—Heather, Delia, and Ralph—Shockley asserts that homosexuality is congenital, that all three are cuttings from the respective female and male genders and can recognize this sexual aspect of the others' subjectivity. Though it is unspoken between them, Heather and Ralph recognize each other's true nature. "Their blood was the same, their sexual proclivities against the norm."

"They were two people in the wrong bodies for this age and time." Once seduced, Delia responds as though "she had been born with the knowledge of this loving."

The meeting and fusion of Heather and Delia is (as Toomer indicates in "Sing Yes!") an act of liberation. In this story the liberation takes forms that are social, sexual, and emotional. The union eventually liberates Delia and other slaves on the plantation in that it prompts Heather to free all her slaves and to sell the plantation. The proceeds from the sale allow Ralph to move to Paris, "where there was a heritage of those like himself," and allow Heather and Delia to move to Boston where, though keeping their relationship secret, "they share a house sheltered by love." This liberation is the same kind that Wideman expresses in *The Cattle Killing* in that the subjects of slavery anticipate a time when they are "free . . . to love" (207). Though Heather and Ralph free their slaves, the institution of slavery remains intact. And though Heather and Ralph achieve limited liberation to live their lives as gay subjects, the institutionalized repression of gay subjectivities also remains in force at the story's end.

The story of the love bond between Edward and Nash Williams (bisexuals) in *Crossing the River* is much more complex and much more fully grounded in the diasporan myth than is "The Mistress and the Slave Girl." Chapter 5 of this study explains how Phillips uses the concept of orphanhood (fatherless and alone) in the formation of *Crossing the River*'s focal subjects, black and white. The concept is probably most expansive in his formation of Nash's diasporan subjectivity and in the narrative that centers him. Among Nash's "fathers," his surrogate father Edward has the most influence on shaping Nash's Becoming. It is a standard narrative formation in discourses on slavery that a male slave owner who sexually desires one of his female slaves often moves her into his house as a servant. This is the formation Shockley adapts in "The Mistress and the Slave Girl" and that Phillips adapts in the narrative about Nash. When Nash is a young boy, Edward takes him from his parents and moves him into the plantation house as a servant. Yet he positions him in this space as "something more akin to son than servant" (21). In both "The Mistress and the Slave Girl" and the Nash Williams section in *Crossing the River*, the terms "servant" and "service" (among other terms) have meanings associated with both slavery and homosexuality. While the father-son relationship in this instance refers to Edward's unusually kind treatment of Nash and similar young male slaves, it also suggests Edward's pedophilic attraction to Nash and others like him. In the language of homosexuality, "son" connotes young, submissive, and (often) effeminate. Indeed, in the sexual language of contemporary society, a surrogate father-son nexus typically refers to a homosexual relationship between an older and a younger man, and this is one of the meanings that applies to Edward and his slave "man-boys." In the same contemporary language, a "master-slave nexus" refers to a dominant-submissive sexual relationship, particularly (but not exclusively) between persons of the same gender, and this double entendre of master-slave functions in both Shockley's text and Phillips's text to situate the treatment of homosexuality firmly within the context of historical slavery.

Captain Hamilton uses the terms "man-boy" (104, 110) and "woman-girl" (121) to mean adolescent. The novel's context assigns additional meanings to "man-boy." The term is a linguistic link between racial (slavery and its legacy) and sexual (specifically homosexual) relations. In the context of racial/social relations, the hyphenated term refers to whites' perception and treatment of black males (during and after slavery) as perpetual children who always need the guiding influence of a white male surrogate parent (a Great White Father or master). This linguistic formation contextualizes the social and racial relationship between Edward and Nash. Even after having left the United States, Nash remains dependent upon his surrogate "father" for both material support and psychological guidance. The hyphenated term also contextualizes and defines (in part) the sexual relationship between Edward and Nash as, respectively, father and son, master and slave, dominant and submissive sexual partners. Though the novel does not describe a sexual act that situates Edward in a sexually dominant role and his "man-boys" in a sexually submissive role,[25] the double entendre of father-son and master-slave suggests that Edward's sexual role is dominant. In addition, while the hyphenated term's first half connotes homosexuality, its second half connotes the role of black submissiveness within the homosexual relationship. In the language of slavery, Nash is Edward's male house servant. In the language of homosexuality, he is Edward's "house boi."

The story of Edward Williams helps explain Nash Williams's sexual Being (who he is) and Becoming (how he came to be). Phillips creates Edward as a slave master who deviates markedly from the norm that history and literature texts have established. As does Charles Johnson in his formation of Flo Hatfield (*Oxherding Tale*) and Sherley Anne Williams in her formation of Miss Lorraine (*Dessa Rose*), Phillips constructs Edward by speaking the unspeakables about his (and thus his class's) sexual proclivities. Edward

Williams is a man of "strange behavior and desires" (14). Indeed, homosexual desire defines his subjectivity. What members of the slavocracy would consider strange about Edward's behavior is his generally kind treatment of his slaves and his indulgence of a select few of his male slaves by providing them a college education (12 and 21, for instance).[26] Edward's strange behavior is connected to his strange desires, and his homosexual desires remain basically unspoken to the slaveholding class except to his wife, Amelia. Among Edward's desires are his cravings for "the unconditional love of a child" (55), which he satisfies in Madison, Nash, and other "man-boys" who are his slaves (45–46, 56)—and perhaps ones who are not, as an incident that occurs when he is in Africa suggests (47–51, 57).

Indeed, as a white "*master*" (48; Phillips's emphasis) in Africa, Edward's sexually desiring gaze fixes on the bodies of young black man-boys (47) and especially on a "colored American boy" named Charles, "whom he observed to be a decent specimen" (48). He retains Charles to help him find Madison, one of Edward's former lovers who now lives in Monrovia, and instructs that "should Charles want for anything," he should "reveal to Edward, without fear or embarrassment, the full nature of his needs" (51). The sexual play in this scene is clear. Yet after Charles has located Edward's former lover, Madison Williams, and brought him to Edward, Edward's interest in Charles wanes. Charles "looked a little forlorn and asked if there might be some other way in which he could be of service to the *master*" (57; Phillips's emphasis). After a moment's reflection, Edward states that Charles may "return tomorrow," if he wishes. The language and other aspects of these two scenes reference both homosexuality and slavery. In contemporary gay parlance, Edward would be considered a "dinge queen" because he is a white male who has a sexual penchant for black males.[27]

Like Nash's biological/primordial African father who is plagued with guilt over having sold his children, Edward also suffers from a "profound guilt" (52) over how his desire caused him to mistreat his surrogate "children" by abandoning them for new and younger lovers. Edward does not feel guilty for defying social decorum and loving them unconditionally. That is, "Edward's guilt [is primarily for] having surrendered to his own changing passions" (45), or rather changing the subjects of the sexual passion that rules him. This is especially the case in his relationship with Nash. Nash surmises that Edward's "shame" and guilt about having seduced him into a homosexual relationship have caused a breach between them (40) and that, after having used him to satisfy his sexual desire, Edward then "expelled" him "to the Liberian paradise" (62) and severed all ties of communication. While Nash may be partially correct in his former assumption, in the latter instance it was Amelia (Edward's wife) who broke communication ties between the two by destroying Nash's letters to Edward (56).

Though the novel implicitly censures Edward's sexual exploitation of his young male slaves, it does not condemn the love bond between Edward and Nash. Both Shockley and Phillips indicate that the interracial relationships they inscribe are ones of love rather than of sexual exploitation. What began as Edward's gratification of his pedophilic desires with the boy Nash turned into his unconditional love for the man Nash, which Nash reciprocates. Indeed, within the purview of the diasporan myth, the novel suggests that each is the other's true subject complement, the other's beloved. However, nineteenth-century strictures on race and social morality coupled with each subject's personal passions cause this complementarity to create further partitioning in each subject rather than to effect wholeness and complete wholeness through their reunion as one. When speaking of "the old common sex," Aristophanes's observation about the male, the "boy-lover," the "beloved," and wholeness in the context of same-gender conjugal complementarity (87–88) is a useful gloss on Phillips's treatment of the relationship between Edward and his "man-boy" Nash.

Phillips does not create Edward as Nash's biological father, which would have been a logical formation in the context of time and place. Thus he avoids creating a homosexual relationship that is also incestuous and miscegenetic, what society then and now probably would deem the horror of horrors. Instead, Phillips indicates that the bond between Edward and Nash is love, and this love bond is the undoing of both. More than his inability to curb his sexual desire for "man-boy" slaves, Edward's inability to curb his love for Nash destroys his family life. As a plantation mistress, Edward's wife, Amelia (whom Nash calls Edward's "lady wife" [28, 29]), can adjust to most of his strange behaviors and desires. Edward "inherited from his father an aversion to the system which had allowed his fortunes to multiply" (13), and as a plantation mistress Amelia comes to share rather "fully in his unusually philanthropic fervor" (14) toward the improvement of slave life. Moreover, she comes slowly "to tolerate [his] strange behavior and desires" that signify his sexual preference for young black men that, the novel strongly suggests, makes him at the least a borderline pedophile. While she can tolerate all of his unorthodox behaviors and desires, perhaps as an inevitable part of the peculiar institution, his love for a man-boy slave is not a part of any system she can fathom, ostensibly because it precludes any possibility of her being his subject complement. Amelia considers the love bond between Edward and Nash so thoroughly a negation of her subjectivity that she goes insane and commits suicide (56).

Amelia's death causes Edward to consider more fully some of the deleterious effects of his desires, but it does not cause him to abandon them. Indeed, his wife's death frees Edward to pursue the most direct subject of his desire (Nash) more readily—her death frees him to love. In search of his lost love, Nash, Edward travels to Africa, a Kurtzian journey that leads him more fully into the dark recesses of himself. His journey inward is so intense and deep that he eventually loses contact with reality (69–70).

Edward's journey provides a gloss on Nash's journey into and eventual abandonment of his Western self. Following the lead of his various "fathers" who abandoned him, Nash's abandonment of his Western self includes abandoning his homosexual proclivity, in part because in Africa he does not have the opportunity to nourish it. He explains such to Edward: "You, my father, did sow the seed, and it sprouted forth with vigor, but for many years now there has been nobody to tend to it, and being abandoned it has withered away and died" (63). From a homosexual perspective, Nash is now fatherless and alone. This passage and others in the novel suggest that in Nash's case his homosexuality is a conditioned or learned desire (a product of Westernization), while Edward's is endemic to his Being.

Often in contemporary fictional slave narratives the black body functions as a text that is written (upon) and read. From the purview of the palimpsest, the writing/reading is positive. When the body-text's signs are scarifications from floggings, the writing is negative but the reading can be either negative or positive, as in *Dessa Rose* and *Beloved*. For example, Adam Nehemiah and Amy Denver read the scars on Dessa's body and Sethe's body, respectively, from the negative, while Harker and Paul D, respectively, read them from the positive. Perry incorporates this same kind of reading in *Stigmata* when Anthony Paul reads the scars of Lizzie/Ayo's back as signs of "horror" and of beauty (131, 147). Reading the black body in "The Mistress and the Slave Girl" and in the Nash section of *Crossing the River* evokes both positive and negative purviews on the slavery-homosexuality nexus.

To appropriate Reed's statement about the form and function of *Flight to Canada* (7), the black body as text in narratives that foreground the slavery-homosexuality nexus is indeed more a reading (in its sexual connotation) than a writing. Reed also uses sports as a metaphor for writing against an oppressive structure (*Writin' Is Fightin'*) and the concept of games to couch his treatment of homosexuality within the context of the peculiar institution (*Flight*).

Several fiction writers, blacks and whites, have suggested that erotic or homosexual "games," as Ishmael Reed would characterize such behavior, were a definite part of the peculiar institution and afterwards. For example, Faulkner inscribes such an erotic game in *Absalom, Absalom!* when Thomas Sutpen instigates a kind of battle royal boxing match between his male slaves that he joins, ostensibly to assert his "supremacy" and "domination" (29). The "fighting" match in this novel has a parallel in homosexual activities. In the gay community, wrestling is a sexual game designed to elicit sexual arousal from the participants and from the observers. Part of Ellison's battle royal scene in *Invisible Man* (14–21) is a variation on this formation, from which the white male observers and the black male participants experience erotic stimulation. Valerie Martin, perhaps expanding on *Absalom, Absalom*! and *Invisible Man*, opens her novel *Property* (2003) with a type of sports game between black males that a white male referees. Martin endows this sexual game with definitive homosexual dimensions; both the young black slaves and especially the slave master become sexually aroused. In Faulkner's, Ellison's, and Martin's respective novels, the black body as sexual text is more to read the gazer(s) than to read the object-subject of his/their gaze.

What is implicitly inscribed about the homosexual gaze in *Absalom, Absalom!* and *Invisible Man* is explicit in *Property*, "The Mistress," and *Crossing the River*. The latter three texts are indicative of how post-1975 fictional discourses on slavery more explicitly treat the slavery-homosexual nexus. Both Shockley (the desiring gaze Heather fixes on Delia) and Phillips (the desiring gaze Edward fixes on Charles) call attention to the black body as a site for the white gazer's erotic stimulation.

Though authors of contemporary fictional slave narratives have charted new directions in their discourses on slavery through their formulation of the diasporan myth and its theory of black Being, they are only beginning to explore gay subjectivities in the contexts of the slavocracy and diasporan desire. As both Shockley's and Phillips's respective texts indicate, the master-slave nexus in the context of homosexuality is fertile for fictional exploration. One should be reminded that during the era of slavery blacks were almost totally subjected to the power of whites with few legal and social restraints on whites' power and on the exercise of their sexual desires. One also should be reminded that the variety of human sexual proclivities other than standard heterosexual ones that have been documented since the beginning of recorded history did not go into remission during slavery. Indeed, the system of slavery in the West would have allowed almost unbridled freedom for those of the slaveholding class (and perhaps whites in general) to engage in homosexual activities with blacks that ranged (from a contemporary purview) from socially unorthodox to criminally abusive.

Conclusion
Diasporan Literacy, Sacred Geometry, and the Visual Arts

The critical paradigm this study derives from the diasporan myth and its theory of Western black Being is closely akin to what VèVè Clark calls "Diaspora literacy," which she defines as "the ability to read and comprehend the discourses of Africa, Afro-America and the Caribbean from an informed, indigenous perspective" (303–4). As I adapt the definition of Clark's term, diasporan literacy provides fuller interpretative access not only to literary texts but also to texts from other forms of Western black expressive culture that are anchored in the black African diaspora. Diasporan literacy facilitates interpretative insight into numerous works in the plastic arts, but especially murals, paintings, drawings, and related visuals from the Harlem Renaissance to the present. The philosophical and spiritual properties of sacred geometry are integral to diasporan literacy and largely define the approach certain contemporary visual artists take in their representation of the New World African and his or her World.

The works of Harlem Renaissance artist Aaron Douglas and contemporary artist John Biggers can serve as representative of several other black visual artists whose careers fit within this time frame. A blending of traditional African and Western religions, the use of sacred geometric formations, the influence of ancient Egyptian culture, the foregrounding of the black body/self, the blending of history and myth, attention to social issues, and the use of symbolic images drawn from black African and Western black cultural life are trademarks of these two artists. These are among the characteristics these two artists share with authors of contemporary fictional slave narratives and other diasporan novels.

As this study has argued, Jean Toomer's works, especially but not exclusively *Cane*, are foundational for several contemporary black novelists. So, too, are Aaron Douglas's works foundational for several African American painters who followed him and who in their visual representations of the black self/Self interrogate and visually narrate the diasporan experience of New World blacks. Toomer's literary representations of the sacred circle parallel Douglas's visual representations of this sacred geometric form. While Toomer and some of his literary descendants privilege a broken circle that should and must be unbroken, Douglas foregrounds the circle's wholeness and several of his artistic relatives and descendants foreground the wholeness embedded in other geometric forms, notably the triangle (Jacob Lawrence is a prime example).

When individual works in Douglas's canon[1] are ordered by chronological content, they in effect form a narrative of the origin, history, and nature of Western black Being. *Creation* (1926) and *The Creation* (1927) suggest the African origin of humankind.[2] Works such as *Congo* (1929) and *The Negro in an African Setting* (1934) depict blacks in their native Africa who are harmoniously situated in the unity of Being. His painting *Into Bondage* (1936) is a visual narrative of the capture and enslavement of African blacks and their transatlantic transportation on slave ships to the New World. This visual is a parallel to Morrison's narrative of the fracture of the unity of Being, the capture, enslavement, and middle passage of native Africans in the interpolated section of *Beloved* (210–13). *Harriet Tubman* (1930) and *From Slavery through Reconstruction* (1934) are representations of the black experience during slavery and its aftermath. *From Slavery through Reconstruction* is filled with images and symbols of familiar scenes and conditions that define these two periods in African American history. Works such as *An Idyll of the Deep South* (1934) and *The Fugitive* (1927) convey, respectively, the joy and pain of living black in the postslavery South. Douglas produced numerous works—especially textual illustrations for African American novels, stories, and poems—that visually narrativize the disaporan experiences of blacks in the Americas between the world wars.

The character Kabnis, an aspiring literary artist in Toomer's *Cane*, is torn between drowning in the pain and basking in the beauty of southern black life. Douglas's works in general concentrate not on what he characterized as the "pain" and "sadness" but on the "joy" and "mirth" of black life (Kirschke 31). During his career Douglas created illustrations for numerous literary and scholarly works by and about blacks. Among these many are Countee Cullen's *Caroling Dusk* (1927), Georgina Gollock's *Sons of Africa* (1928), Paul Morand's *Black Magic* (1929), and perhaps most notably James Weldon Johnson's *God's Trombones* (1927). The illustrations he provided for these books and several others, as well as the illustrations he produced for literary and cultural texts included in periodicals such as the NAACP's *The Crisis* and the Urban League's *Opportunity*, are indicative of the distinctive style he had developed in his paintings and drawings by the early 1930s.

Two signature features of a Douglas work are a series of concentric circles and the stylized black body. His concentric circles are a visual rendering of what Wideman refers to in *The Cattle Killing* as "circles within circles within circles" (144), and in some of his murals they bespeak the interrelation and intersection of stories/selves that are parts of one master story/Self. Within the context of the diasporan myth and its theory of black Being, these circles often represent the ideas of wholeness and unity that are associated with sacred geometry. Rutherford Calhoun in Johnson's *Middle Passage* observes that the Allmuseri's "perspective" on visual representations of the body/self is not Eurocentric "but rather the flat, depthless technique of Egyptian art" (75). The same can be said for Douglas. The stylized black body in a representative Douglas work shows the strong influence Egyptian paintings and West African wood sculpture had on his style. In an interview with L. M. Collins in 1971, he explained that he "used the Egyptian form" in his depictions of the black body/self (see Kirschke 77). The flat, angular, two-dimensional, silhouetted, even androgynous manner in which he inscribes the black body/self suggests a lack of individuated identity, much in the manner that Charles Johnson uses the lack of fingerprints to suggest that the Allmuseri are without an individuated identity (*Middle Passage* 61). His depiction of the black self through his representation of the black body aligns with the representation of the black self in contemporary fictional slave narratives.

From the purviews of diaspority, representations of the black self/Self, and the theory of Western black Being, Romare Bearden's visual inscription of the black self/Self in his collage compositions (notably the *Prevalence of Ritual* series) is as distinctive as Douglas's in conveying concepts that align with contemporary fictional slave narratives. In some of his collages Bearden forms a black body/self from parts of other black bodies/selves. He sometimes gathers parts from male selves and female selves of different ages, complexions, and walks of life and from different materials to form one male self or one female self. The result is a visual rendering of concepts such as fragmentation, partitionedness, wholeness, the plural self, the communal self, the multiplicity of Being, and the extended self that are evident in contemporary fictional slave narratives.

Similar to contemporary fictional slave narratives, Douglas's canon referentially incorporates through various symbols, images, and visual narrative formations a wide range of disciplinary subjects. In 1930, for example, he produced several works whose titles alone show his interest in the arts, sciences, history, and other disciplines: *Drama* (1930), *Music* (1930), *Poetry* (1930), *Dance Magic* (1930–31), *Science* (1930), *Harriet Tubman* (1930), and *Philosophy* (1930).

Building More Stately Mansions (1944) is one of Douglas's works whose content, composition, and visual style are not only representative of this artist's vision and technique but also align well with salient features of contemporary fictional slave narratives. Through a kind of superimposition of images (a visual form of intertextual layering), the painting blends past, present, and future realities. Its title derives from a line in Oliver Wendell Holmes's 1858 poem "The Chambered Nautilus" ("Build thee more stately mansions, O my soul"). Its narrative extends the narrative of *Into Bondage* and is an intertextual response to Holmes's poem adapted to a black diasporan experience. Just as Charles Johnson narrates the spread and influence of the culture and civilization of the Allmuseri in *Middle Passage* (76–77), so does Douglas trace the influence of Egyptian culture and civilization on the West. The painting foregrounds a large image of an Egyptian figure and juxtaposes it with Western skyscrapers and other symbolic structures. The seven black figures at the bottom of the painting (including two children) represent the arts, the humanities, the sciences, and the trades. The painting is a visual narrative not only of contributions blacks have made and are making to world civilizations but also of future contributions they will make. As do several of his diasporan works, *Aspiration* (1936) uses symbolic images of slavery, the sciences, the trades, education, and the arts to conjoin blacks' past, present, and future. As Kirschke points out, in his works Douglas "chose to use his own unique style of geometric symbolism to show blacks as a proud, majestic people with a very rich heritage. He included history, politics, religion, myth, and pertinent social issues in his work" (131).

Like Douglas, John Biggers blends subject matter from a variety of disciplines into the composition of several of his paintings, lithographs, drawings, and murals. Geometric symbolism largely defines his style, especially in works he produced after about 1980. The sacred geometry in his art reflects the "complex ideas and philosophical inquiry" with which he wrestled "throughout his life" (Thiesen 75). Following his trips to West Africa in 1957 and to East Africa in 1969 and 1987, Biggers "worked out a narrative [in his visual art] that reached back into African and Egyptian mythology" (Thiesen 113). These sojourns proved to be spiritually and artistically liberating ones.

The works he produced during the early decades of his career are characterized by "narrative linearity" (Wardlaw 55) and by images of "deep and somber impressions of the downtrodden, tragic expressions of the human condition" (Thiesen 55).[3] Shotgun houses, quilts, turtles, railroad tracks, washboards, elderly people, and other iconography drawn from his life in North Carolina are prominent in these early works. After each of his African sojourns, he began to blend "his understanding of Africa into his art and beliefs" (Thiesen 57) and to incorporate several symbols from African cultures into his works, particularly (after 1974) from the Dogon culture (see Wardlaw 55). From 1957 to about 1980 was a period of "transition from figurative form to geometric abstraction" in his art (Thiesen 90). During this period he gave additional and sometimes new meanings to several of the cultural symbols of African American life that were prominent in his earlier works, such as water, washboards, shotgun houses, the womb, and elders (see Thiesen 111–18).

At times symbols in his later works assume multiple meanings, especially when placed in spatial relation to other symbols and in the context of a respective work's philosophical and spiritual content. The washboard is one example. In *Washerwoman* (1940s), the washboard symbolizes the toil, strength, and fortitude of the black woman. In *Shotguns* (1987), it is also a ladderlike symbol that signifies preparation for the soul/spirit's ascent into Heaven (Thompson 109). Its symbolic function in this instance is much like that of the ladder (a reference to the biblical Jacob's ladder) in Brodber's *Louisiana* (35).

Narrative quilting as a conceptual discursive device in *The Cattle Killing* and other contemporary fictional slave narratives and diasporan novels has a visual counterpart in some African American art works. The patchwork quilt, one of the most familiar products of African American material culture and of Biggers's early works, assumes an important structural, thematic, philosophical, and narrative place in his later paintings and murals. His 1981 mural *Quilting Party* contains features that would distinctively define his art from the 1980s to the end of his life (2001). One of these features is his tendency to fuse African American geometric quilting patterns with geometric patterns of West African fabrics. As Thiesen observes, the "metaphoric imagery" of *Quilting Party* and of works that followed it incorporates "actual African sculptural forms," includes "scenes and stories recalled from his African visits," and adapts "quilt patterns as textural and structural unifying device[s]." The preparatory pencil drawings for *Quilting Party* "just begin to reveal the tantalizing mythology of [this] inventive storyteller" (81).

In reference to "the symbolism of the quilt design" in his works, Biggers offered the following explanation: "Putting together those pieces of materials that have been discarded, worn, . . . it's like putting life together again . . . building something together. It's a marvelous symbol of order, creativity" (quoted in Thiesen 85). In relation to the diasporan myth, it is also a symbol of wholeness and complete wholeness. Indeed, in his visual art Biggers parallels Wideman's literary technique in *The Cattle Killing* of weaving different stories into one story, into the same Story. In this regard one is also reminded of the function of appliqué quilts and quilting in Perry's *Stigmata* as well as the collagist technique of Romare Bearden (an artist whom *Stigmata* references).

Like contemporary fictional slave narratives that are womanist, Biggers's canon gives the black woman center stage. For his mural *The Contribution of Negro Women to American Life and Education* (1954), into which he "packed many stories" (Thiesen 44), he researched the lives of ex-slaves Harriet Tubman, Sojourner Truth, and Phillis Wheatley and foregrounded them in this mural. Following his 1957 trip to West Africa, he began to endow his depictions of black women with "the West African concept of *maame*, a word signifying great respect for women" (Thiesen 62).

Whereas Douglas privileges circularity over triangularity as geometric formation, triangularity is an artistic trademark of Biggers and is especially evident in his *Shotgun* series of lithographs and paintings. In this series and in several of his other works, early ones and late ones, Biggers uses the triangularity of the shotgun house to symbolize and to emphasize "the importance of the contribution women have made to the survival of his people" (Thiesen 93). The shotgun house, a common architectural structure in the black South and in the Caribbean (Thompson 108), "likely has its roots in Africa" (Thiesen 93). The triangularity of these physical structures and of aspects of African American material culture (particularly the patterns in clothing) in Biggers's works shows a strong African influence. As Robert Farris Thompson states, *Shotguns* depicts "more than a single aspect of black culture, traditional domestic architecture. Illuminating space and elevation with philosophy, the painting becomes a model of belief and practice" (108).

Much as theory and praxis conjoin in Wideman's *The Cattle Killing*, *Shotguns* is a model of theory and praxis in visual art. According to Thompson, the painting "illuminates numinous qualities in complex interaction; it carries us into process, where black Creole vision takes the poetic measure of three worlds—Europe, Africa, and America—and combines them. It does this in order to make a medicine, an *nkisi,* as artistic images and charms for healing and protection are called in Kongo" (108).

From this perspective, the shotgun house in some of Biggers's works has numinous qualities and medicinal, thematic, and structural functions similar to story and storytelling in *The Cattle Killing.* Each of the shotgun houses, each of the five black women, and each of the variety of other symbols and images in *Shotguns* is a story and all are the same story (compare to *Cattle Killing* 207). The railroad track that runs in front of these houses is like the crossroad in *The Cattle Killing* (76) where past, present, and future intersect. As Biggers explained, "*You ain't painting perspective, you're painting* shotgun blocks, *their own spatial concept, all the houses of the past, all the houses of the future, just let it roll*" (quoted in Thompson 110).

Biggers typically uses the black woman to explore the spiritual dimensions of the Western black self/Self in several paintings that can be classified as abstract. While some of his paintings foreground the postslavery experiences of blacks, some of his most notable ones trace this experience to its African roots. *Shotguns* is such a work. It chronicles the black female self/Self's evolution from African hearth and home to African American hearth and home. Concepts such as the plural self, the communal self, the extended self, and twinness are useful for understanding aspects of Biggers's representation of the female self/Self in this painting. Collectively, the women are one Self, as physical resemblances among them (that is, twinness) indicate. Details in this painting evoke a variety of experiences (including ontological changes) the black woman faced from the time of her African existence to the modern world. For example, when one reads the painting from left to right, each woman's skin becomes lighter than the previous one, no doubt suggesting miscegenetic mixing during and after slavery. Retentions of the African past are conveyed not only through the representation of the black female body but also through representations of aspects of material cultures. The triangularity of the African hut is retained and repeated in the triangularity of the shotgun house.

Geometric abstractions, symbols of spirituality, philosophical content, and the fusion of black African and Western black cultures became increasingly complex in several works Biggers produced after about 1980. Nevertheless, his continued use of familiar symbols and images in the re-working of his vision and visual narratives facilitates interpretative access to these works. The ceremonial African comb, a symbol of "the soul's transformation and ascension" (Thiesen 111), and the African balaphon, a symbol of music, work in tandem with symbols Biggers used in his early paintings. For instance, works such as *Rape of the Earth* (1994) and *Lift Us Up* (1994) center a black woman and include his familiar African American shotgun houses, washpots, and washboards along with the African ceremonial comb and the balaphon.

In several diasporan novels, elders are the source of wisdom and knowledge. For example, both Toomer (*Cane*'s Father John) and Marshall (*Praisesong*'s Lebert Joseph) use elders as sources and transmitters of epistemological powers. Both authors use metaphorical "threads" as re-connectors and transmitters. Toomer uses "threads of union" to re-connect the disparate parts of self and to "re-member ourselves" (*Wayward* 423). Marshall uses "slender," "silken," and almost invisible threads that extend from the "hearts" and "navels" of diasporan selves to re-connect them epistemologically, ontologically, and spiritually in a web of "confraternity" (*Praisesong* 190–91). Biggers's visual representation of these ontological and epistemological connectors, in works such as *Holy Family* (1984) and *House My Father Built* (1983), are visible threads, often presented in triangular formations, that connect young to old, past to present, and the one to the many. That they extend from the mouth of one self into the mouth of another self (as in *House My Father Built*) suggests, among other things, the transference of knowledge.

Many if not most of Biggers's post-1980 works (*Upper Room* [1984], *Wheel in Wheel* [1986], *Ascension* [1988], *Origins* [1988], and *House of the*

Turtle [1989], among them), especially the murals, are very complex works of symbolic abstraction and therefore their narratives are not easily accessible. Many of the meanings of his symbols also can be found in contemporary fictional slave narratives. Images of birds are prominent in Biggers's works, even more prominent than the avian imagery Ishmael Reed finds in antebellum slave literature and as one finds in contemporary diasporan novels such as *Louisiana*. From among the different perspectives that one can read Biggers's avian images are ones that coincide with these images in literary texts: flight home to Africa, as in *The Cattle Killing*, and ascension of the spirit/soul to its heavenly home, as in *Louisiana*. Robert Farris Thompson observes that the "washboards set like ladders" in the washpots of *Shotguns* signify preparation for the ascent (109), which is supported by other images (such as the birds) in this painting.

One of the more accessible works of Biggers's later period is *Climbing Higher Mountains* (1986), which foregrounds African women in a glorious state. Yet in the bottom right of the painting is a Western black washerwoman toiling with washtub and washboard, which is in contrast or conjunction with one of the African women over whose head hovers an iron washpot. The regality of the four African women and two children contrasts sharply with the labor-intense portraiture of the African American washerwoman. Geometric shapes (the circle and the square with especial emphasis on the triangle) abound in this painting. The color blue, the second most prominent color in this female-centered painting, is one of the symbolic (and thus philosophical) connections between the Western black and the African female selves, much in the manner that this color functions as a symbolic connector of sociogenic and genetic female selves, respectively, in *The Cattle Killing* and *Stigmata*.

As do other contemporary fictional slave narratives, *The Cattle Killing* and *Stigmata* interface aspects of Western and non-Western cultures, which suggests the global dimensions of the Becoming and Being of the Western black. Biggers's *Climbing Higher Mountains* seems to do the same. *The Cattle Killing* draws upon and integrates into its narrative some aspects of Native American culture. The symbolic "mountain" in *Climbing Higher Mountains* is in part suggestive of the Egyptian pyramid as well as the pyramidal shape of colossal structures indigenous peoples in Central America and South America constructed. One is reminded here of the diasporan myth's component that asserts the influence of African cultures in the Americas, as Charles Johnson relates in *Middle Passage* (76–77). In the bottom right of

Climbing Higher Mountains, Biggers includes the backs (primarily) of three turtles. When read in conjunction with other thematic, imagistic, and symbolic components of this painting, the turtle backs suggest the diasporan experience of Native Americans, who according to some Native American mythologies migrated from Asia to the Americas.

From the purview of sacred geometry, the diasporan myth, and the myth's theory of Western black Being, the increased use of geometric symbolism and geometric abstraction in Western black visual arts from Douglas through Biggers is quite similar to the development of the fictional slave narrative from the modern version to the contemporary version. Diasporan literacy allows one to comprehend the cultural hybridity essential to the production and interpretation of different forms of Western black creative arts. In their form, content, and meaning, most diasporan texts—literary, visual, musical, and otherwise—are cultural hybrids and many of them reflect the biocultural hybridity of the Western black self. This cultural hybridity, which is subject matter in contemporary fictional slave narratives such as Johnson's *Middle Passage* (a masculinist text) and Phillips's *Crossing the River* (textually androgynous), is at the heart of form, content, and meaning in a womanist diasporan novel such as Maryse Condé's *Hérémakhonon* (1976; 1982). The diasporan myth and its theory of Being give fuller interpretative access to Western black texts. Diasporan literacy gives fuller interpretative access to Western black and, as Morrison suggests in *Playing in the Dark,* nonblack texts. As it relates to black texts in different genres, diasporan literacy incorporates European, Asian, and some other cultures but accords African cultures a central place in the formation of the Western black self/Self and that self/Self's World.

Notes

Introduction

1. Calvin Baker (acknowledgments in *Naming*) states the influence of contemporaries D'Aguiar and Phillips. Intertextually, Wideman's (*Cattle Killing*) influence on Perry's *Stigmata* is obvious.

2. I use the term *mythographers* to refer to artists (black novelists in this instance) who collect and interface various myths in a work of art. Myth has various definitions and dimensions, as William Doty cogently explains in the opening chapter of his book *Mythography*, and I have selected ones that best fit the purposes of this study.

3. Hildreth published the novel anonymously in 1836 and a new edition, with some revisions, in 1839. Following the success of *Uncle Tom's Cabin*, he published an expanded (adding chapters 38 through 59) and revised edition with an introduction and a new title in 1855, and a final edition with a new introduction in 1856 under the 1855 title, *Archie Moore, the White Slave; or Memoirs of a Fugitive*. Textual references in this study are to the 1856 edition.

4. For example, Bell uses "neoslave narrative" (*Afro-American Novel*), and Rushdy (*Neo-Slave Narrative*) and Beaulieu (*Black Women Writers*) use "neo-slave narrative." Mitchell (*Freedom to Remember*) uses the term "liberatory narrative" and Keizer (*Black Subjects*) uses "contemporary narrative of slavery."

5. My use of the term *extension* is based on Vincent Mulago's perspective on African (particularly Bantu) concepts of Being in which he defines "living" or being as "an extension of the life of one's forefathers, and a preparation for one's own life to be carried on in one's descendants" (139).

6. Published originally in *Negro Digest*, the essay was reprinted in Addison Gayle Jr.'s landmark publication *The Black Aesthetic* (1971). Page references are to this reprint.

7. See Kerman and Eldridge 126.

8. Examples include Marcy Heidish's *A Woman Called Moses* (1976), Daniel Panger's *Ol' Prophet Nat* (1967), and William Styron's *Confessions of Nat Turner* (1967).

9. I use *mythoform* to refer to an object, person, action, idea, or utterance that carries a conceptual meaning. Malefi Asante defines mythoform as "the all-encompassing deep generator of ideas and concepts in our living relationship with our peers, friends, and ancestors," and as "the basal psychic patterns by which we organize our experiences" (96, 98).

10. Though several ideas and principles associated with ancient Egypt's sacred geometry can be found in other cultures, they do not appear to be as systematic, expansive, and inclusive as the sacred science of ancient Egypt. While the novelists incorporate ideas from other cultures, it is ancient Egypt that they collectively allude to most often.

11. In his study of African American visual arts, Richard Powell, for instance, posits that the blues have had an "impact" not only "on other Afro-American musical forms" but also on "much contemporary literature, theatre, dance, and visual arts" (*Blues Aesthetic* 20).

12. Linda Hutcheon's (*A Poetics of Postmodernism*) discussion of metafiction and historiographic metafiction can help illuminate the form and function of the contemporary fictional slave narrative.

1. *Mythopoeic Realities*

1. I use both terms here to refer to a collection of stories rather than to a single story.

2. Paramenides, Aristotle, and Plato are among the ancients; Nietzsche, Henri Bergson, and Gilles Deleuze are among the moderns. The philosophical writings of Gilles Deleuze and Félix Guattari, especially their *Anti-Oedipus: Capitalism and Schizophrenia*, are the foundation for several contemporary discussions of and perspectives on Becoming.

3. Using Ellison's *Invisible Man* as exemplary, I discuss this convention in *Blacks in Eden* (239–51).

4. The latter part of this sentence paraphrases a statement from Mircea Eliade's *Myth and Reality* (5–6).

5. Wideman admits that the statement is "mysterious" and "complicated." I read the statement to mean that all stories are truth.

6. Official history in this sense includes not only history texts but also texts in anthropology, philosophy, sociology, religious studies, and other disciplines.

7. I acknowledge that the term *African* is problematic, because the continent contains many groups of people who are racially and culturally different. My use of the term *black African* to distinguish between races is predicated on a Western definition or identification (including ones by Western black writers) rather than on how so-called black ethnic groups in Africa "racially" identify themselves. Yet even with the qualifier, "black" is not intended to mean that all "black Africans" are culturally the same, but to acknowledge strong cultural similarities among groups defined as black. In "The Theological Estimate

of Man" (83–84), Swailen Sidhom addresses problems inherent in scholars' use of the term *African*, and his observations obtain also for writers.

8. Note, for instance, Morrison's comment about one of the connections between *Beloved* and *Jazz:* "The next story [*Jazz*] has to do with the tension between being one's own Beloved and the lover" (Darling 255).

9. Johnson uses Hinduism rather extensively in his novel. For a discussion of this, see Little, *Charles Johnson's Spiritual Imagination* 80–108. Avey Johnson's first name, Avatara, recalls the Hindu belief that a deity can incarnate in human or animal form. Avatar also refers to the incarnation of a concept or quality. See *Cattle Killing* (68) for Wideman's reference to Hinduism.

10. See Little, "Interview with Charles Johnson" 230; the copyright page in *Cattle Killing;* and the acknowledgments page in *Crossing the River.*

11. Wideman acknowledges such research sources. See L. Baker 267–68.

12. Certainly through the middle of the twentieth century, the "races" of man often were associated generally with the "color" of people who dominated the population in certain geographical regions of the world. See also Mbiti 121 on the Shilluks' belief regarding the different colors of men.

13. Before the discovery of DNA, a human's fingerprint distinguished him or her from any other human. Charles Johnson notes in *Middle Passage* that the Allmuseri are without fingerprints and thus lack a separate identity (61).

14. In Ashanti mythology, "The first man enjoyed a position of great privilege," including exceptional epistemological powers (see Mbiti 123–24). Aristophanes tells of the humans' rebellion and its consequences. That those with white skins led the rebellion and that one result was a decrease in the rebels' epistemological and ontological powers are implicit in Western black novels; whites' rebellion against the Divine and social order, their removal to Europe, their wars against the black tribe, and other features of the diasporan myth have parallels in Yakup's story (the origin and nature of the white race) as contained in Elijah Muhammad's *Message to the Blackman in America* (68, 110–126).

15. Hereafter this study will follow the practice of several black writers who in their fiction and nonfiction (Phillips's *European Tribe* and Morrison's "Rootedness" [339] are examples) use the term *tribe* synonymously with *race.* It is to be noted that Aristophanes also uses the term *tribe* to refer to humans (*Symposium* 86).

16. Aristophanes tells of the bisection, and Toomer uses the premise in his poems "Split Men" and "Sing Yes!" The concept is a pervasive aspect of subject formation in the fictional slave narratives that are focused in this study.

17. Aristophanes's story about the origin and nature of humankind is also a story about the origin of love and desire. Using Aristophanes's narrative analogously, the discussion of the African diasporan myth in the remainder of this chapter and in subsequent chapters will include more of the myth's details and variations on its morphological features that can be found in the Western black novel.

18. The point is consistent with general knowledge about the geographical location of the races of man. Mbiti notes that all the races of man are indigenous to Africa (130).

19. In *Stigmata*, Ayo's soul/spirit inhabits Grace and Lizzie (70, 181, for instance) and the respective quilts Grace and Lizzie make (22–25, 57–72) as well as a portrait of Lizzie

that is simultaneously a portrait of Ayo (182). Through a genetic form of memory, Lizzie experiences Ayo's and Grace's *Lebenswelt* or lived experiences (87), and Beloved knows the lived-world of her namesake twin self in Africa, during the Atlantic crossing, and during slavery (213–17). The preacher in *Cattle Killing* knows Liam's lived-world when Liam was in Africa (143). The same premises are true in *Louisiana*. In this novel Mammy's soul/spirit inhabits Ella (a "transfer of souls" [38]) as well as a tape recorder (44–45, 59–60, for instance) and a pendant (125, 131, for instance), and Ella is able, through a form of atavistic memory or "a journey into knowing" (38), to *know* Mammy's lived-world (37–38). In *Oxherding Tale,* Reb transfers his *kra* (soul/spirit) to both animate and inanimate objects and is thus able to know these hosts' lived-worlds (49–50). In both *Cattle Killing* (104) and *Louisiana* (155), subjects are able to occupy different spaces simultaneously. I extrapolate the feature of humans walking on water and flying from the legends of the walking Ibos and the flying Africans that are incorporated into novels such as *Praisesong for the Widow* (37–39) and Earl Lovelace's *Salt* (3). I discuss the legends more fully in chapter 2 of this book.

20. *Oroborus, oroboros, oureboros,* and *ouraboros* are among the different spellings for this symbolic snake.

21. Ivan Van Sertima's *They Came before Columbus* is one of the best-known works to discuss an African presence in the pre-Columbian Americas. Anthropologist, historian, and novelist J. A. Rogers's two-volume *World's Great Men of Color* (1947) is little known. One of its merits is that it surveys African blacks and persons of black African ancestry who contributed to cultures and civilizations in many parts of the ancient and modern worlds.

22. *Middle Passage*'s plot includes the literal capture and enslavement of African subjects (the Allmuseri) as well as one of their gods.

23. The fragmented or partitioned self is germane to subject formation in several contemporary black novels. Jean Toomer's writings provide clear definitions and illustrations of the concept.

24. Several of Charles Johnson's black characters are Allmuseri, which means that they are the same as their African ancestors. This is consistent with those who consider blacks in the West the same as African people. Others, however, consider Western blacks as very similar to yet distinct from black Africans.

25. Though blacks in Brazil constituted perhaps the largest nation of New World blacks, this study is confined to English-language texts from the Caribbean, the United States, and Europe.

26. Chapter 2 includes further discussion of the ways novelists incorporate the legends of the walking Ibos and the flying Africans.

27. While identifying most of these terms and the fictional texts and critical essays from which they come, the discussion in this book will privilege one over the others.

28. I am referring here primarily to the liberation of a black subject. However, some novels, such as Phillips's *Higher Ground,* also treat the liberation of a diasporan subject who is not black.

29. Mulago's conclusions are based on his study of Bantu peoples—Bashi, Rwanda, Barundi, Bakongo, Baluba, Babira, and others.

30. Oduyọye 273–77.

31. The epigraph (from Ezekiel 12:3) preceding part 1 of Wideman's *Cattle Killing* speaks metaphorically of Western black subjects as exiles.

32. Keith Byerman uses the term *orphanhood* in his discussion of works by Leon Forrest and Clarence Major. His definition of the term (240) is in some ways similar to how I intend and use it in this study.

33. Senghor, "On Negrohood" 2–10; see also Onyewuenyi, "African Philosophy" 39–41.

34. In standard critical language that references race, "the other," whether lowercase or uppercase, typically signifies difference. For Sethe in *Beloved* and Dessa in *Dessa Rose*, the racial "other" when applied to a specific white woman (Amy Denver and Rufel, respectively) acknowledges difference but emphasizes sameness. The same principle applies to Liam (black) and his wife (white) in *Cattle Killing*, and to Travis (black) and Joyce (white), and Nash (black) and Edward (white) in *Crossing the River*. From one interpretation, it does not apply to Cambridge (black) and Anna (white), an interracial couple in *Cambridge*. *Middle Passage* acknowledges Tommy O'Toole's (a white's) racial difference but emphasizes his spiritual sameness with the Allmuseri (blacks).

35. This is not the case in other kinds of diasporan novels, nor is it the case in female-centered novels that are not diasporan. In several, if not most, female-centered novels that include this type of character, the character is female. But in *Praisesong*, for example, it is Lebert Joseph, not Aunt Cuney, who functions as Avey's primal parent.

2. *The Subject(s) of Diasporan Desire*

1. Cited in R. B. Jones 49 and in Rusch 26.

2. Though I take a different approach, my discussion of *Cane*'s geometric design agrees in part with Robert B. Jones's detailed discussion of the novel's spiritual design and plot structure (49–58).

3. According to Frederik Rusch, "In the original edition of *Cane*, Toomer placed arcs on separate pages before each of the three sections" (26n).

4. R. B. Jones points out, "While *Cane* is essentially a mimetic text, holding a mirror up to nature throughout its lyrical narrative design, the text also manifests metafictional impulses" (61).

5. R. B. Jones observes that this poem "expresses the poet's quest for unity of being and self-integration" (66).

6. See chapter 3 of this study for a fuller exploration of this concept.

7. See Senghor, "On Negrohood," especially 6–10.

8. It is this concept of dance and Being that undergirds Alice Walker's short story "Beauty: When the Other Dancer Is the Self." Walker notes the autobiographical nature of this story in "From an Interview" (*In Search of Our Mothers' Gardens* 244–72) in which she also speaks of Toomer's influence on her thinking and writing.

9. *Re-turn* is the orthography Toomer uses in "Split Men" (*Wayward* 426). The hyphenated term fits the meaning I intend.

10. In these instances, I use the term *self* to reference the subject as a singular entity and the term *Self* to reference the subject as a plural entity.

11. In his chapter "Friends as Twins," Brain provides a useful discussion of twinness in African and other societies (122–44).

12. The ship's name reminds one of the biblical St. Paul, who was the source of the text that slaveholders often preached to slaves: "Servants, obey your masters." Indeed, this character has obeyed his masters and thus has acquiesced in his own diasporization.

13. The term "*psycho*logical" is from Toomer's "Split Men" (*Wayward* 426).

14. Some critics consider the walking Ibos and the flying Africans as (versions of) the same legend, as does Sheila Smith McKoy in her article "The Limbo Contest" (see her footnote 4). This study considers them different legends rather than versions of the same. An extended and very useful discussion of the legend of the flying Africans in the cultures and literatures of blacks in the Americas is Wendy Walters's "'One of dese mornings.'"

15. For a more extended discussion of salt eating as an integral part of the legend of the flying Africans, see chapter 1 of Angelita Reyes's *Mothering across Cultures*. Among other things, Reyes connects "flying" to suicide and other forms of resistance to slavery.

16. I borrow the term *sous rature* from Gayatri Chakravorty Spivak's preface to and translation of Jacques Derrida's *Of Grammatology* and from John P. Leavey Jr.'s preface to and translation of Derrida's *Edmund Husserl's "Origin of Geometry."* I shift and bend the term slightly for an application to this study.

3. *Modalities of Rememory*

1. I use the term *empathetic*. Senghor uses the term *sym-pathetic* ("On Negrohood" 6).

2. Dana does not complete her undergraduate degree (*Kindred* 56), and Ella does not complete her doctoral degree.

3. Sartre weaves various distinctions between Europeans and Africans in his introduction to Négritude poetry, *Black Orpheus*.

4. The ritual merging of epistemology and ontology, of subject and subject complement through the act of writing, is essentially what Wideman explains as the emotive nexus between author and centered subject(s) in *Cattle Killing* (13), which I discuss in more detail in chapter 5.

5. Here and elsewhere in this chapter I use the prefix *(re)* to indicate, in accord with the diasporan myth, that subject and subject complement originally were part of one Being/Self and that the action or state referenced is not a new one.

6. For Dinah's name, see Mary Kemp Davis's article "Everybody Knows Her Name" (546) and her source, J. Weston Coleman's *Slavery Times in Kentucky* (178).

7. Several scholars of traditional African society define the nature of the black African self as communal rather than individuated. See, for example, Setiloane (9–16) and Mulago (137–45).

8. Fusion of form and substance expresses a primordial state of Being, and expressions of this fusion can be found in several black texts. Toomer (*Cane* 17) and Ellison (*Invisible Man* 90–91) speak of the fusion of the singer and the song. The fusion of the singer and the song also intimates the fusion of story and being, as Wideman expresses it in *Cattle Killing* (207) and as Reed expresses it in *Flight to Canada* (8). Wideman speaks of the

fusion of the worker and the work, the teller and the listener (109; 206–8), and Morrison speaks of the fusion of the laugher and the laugh (*Beloved* 216).

9. *Praisesong* 178, 218, 246; *Cattle Killing* 57–58; *Louisiana* 105–6. Writers often inscribe the phenomenon without naming it, as in Toomer's *Cane* (31, 164) and Ellison's *Invisible Man* (10). Elsewhere this study provides a fuller discussion of the phenomenon Marshall calls *connaissance.*

10. A. Davis, "Reflections on the Black Woman's Role" 11; Aptheker, *American Negro Slave Revolts* 287–88.

11. Chapter 5 of this study offers a detailed discussion of the conjunction of story and being in diasporan novels.

12. Such images—darky, coon, mammy, sambo, and others—persist into the twenty-first century.

13. For a lucid discussion of parodic intertextuality, see Hutcheon 124–40.

14. This is the case in *Dessa Rose.* The premise is not applicable to all diasporan novels. In cases where the male, black or white, is the black female's true subject complement, he can dance her as other. According to the diasporan myth, self and other do not have to be of the same race or of the same gender, a point I discuss more fully in chapter 6.

15. This is the stance Dessa Rose takes, not the stance this study takes.

16. In his *Appeal* (23–24), David Walker does not name the female slave who with seven male slaves actively rebelled. Mary Kemp Davis asserts that he ignores this female's actions (246).

17. As Douglass explains in the *Narrative* (106–11), he does not want to put these people in jeopardy nor to alert slaveholders to the mechanisms slaves use to escape from slavery.

18. Truth's full statement is thus: "I have plowed, and planted, and gathered into barns, and no man could head me—ar'n't I a woman?" (Gilbert 134).

19. Condé's comments below about the writing of *I, Tituba* are from an interview with Ann Armstrong Scarboro and are included in Scarboro's afterword that is appended to the English translation of Condé's novel.

20. The literature texts to which Condé refers are Ann Petry's novel *Tituba of Salem Village* (adolescent fiction) and Arthur Miller's play *The Crucible.*

21. The abbreviated account is contained in Middleton Harris's *Black Book* (10). Morrison was the editor at Random House who prepared this book for publication.

22. I adopt here Senghor's meanings for *re-creation* and *re-discovery* ("On Negrohood" 6, 10).

23. Morrison says that she "wanted Beloved to function" as both "spirit" and as "flesh." See Darling 247.

24. For an extended discussion of this concept, see Mulago.

25. One might take note here of how Zeus in Greek mythology gives birth to Athena, and Brahma in Hindu mythology gives birth to his sons (see Pattanaik 123).

26. Anglicized spellings of these terms vary. Christopher Okonkwo explains similarities between Ogbanje and Abiku in his article "Critical Divination" (653–55).

27. Martha J. Cutter cites this interview in her article "The Story Must Go On and On" (67), and she argues convincingly that Wild is an extension of/the same as Beloved.

28. In trying to determine exactly who Beloved actually is/was, Paul D asks Denver if the girl (Beloved) was her sister. Denver responds that at times she thinks so, and "at times I think she was—more" (266).

29. Among these are Barnett 418; Daily 144; Horvitz 163–64; Jessee 208; Rushdy, "Daughters Signifyin(g) History" 578; Sitter 29 n. 17; and Wyatt 479. Though from a perspective different from mine, Martha Cutter in "The Story Must Go On and On" surveys critical opinions on who Beloved actually is (62, 72 n. 1).

30. James Phelan leans toward, but does not arrive at, this conclusion in his article "Toward a Rhetorical Reader-Response Criticism" (711).

31. I reference here the character Wild in Morrison's *Jazz*. As I stated earlier, the 1870s marks the birth date of Wild, who appears in a "story" set principally in the 1920s and published in the 1990s.

32. In "Gods, Spirits and the Spirit World," Stephen N. Ezeanya points out that "in the world of spirits, Africans distinguish four main categories of spiritual beings: the Supreme God, a multitude of lesser divinities and spirits, the ancestral spirits, and evil spirits" (35).

33. For other characteristics, see, for example, Okonkwo 653–55 and Ogunyemi.

34. Butler xii; see also Beal 14.

35. In the main, I adhere to Spivak's definition of *sous rature* to mean "under erasure." Spivak discusses the term/concept in her preface to Derrida's *Of Grammatology* (xiii–xx).

36. Based on the biblical story of Abraham, the revised Abrahamic paradigm in these novels is of a man who destroys the lives of women in his obsession to beget a son who will ensure him a kind of immortality.

37. *The Autobiography of My Mother*'s (re)creation of Xeula's mother begins with only the head of Xeula's mother being visible. Willa's (re)creation of Priscilla ends with Priscilla's face being erased.

38. Liberation from a socially constructed "role" is also a thematic and narrative formation in *Beloved*. Morrison points out that when Sethe acquires "a taste of freedom," she "begin[s] to think of herself as a proper name—she always thought of herself as a mother, as her role" (Darling 251).

39. Though *Kindred*'s content reveals the subject's biological tie to a white male ancestor, the novel emphasizes the centered subject's emotive bond to her foremothers. In *Linden Hills*, the connection between Willa and a white male predecessor is part of a series of historical formations that also connects the Luther Nedeeds in a pernicious bond of Otherness that dominates the identity formation of the Mrs. Nedeeds.

40. Caryl Phillips uses a similar phrase in *Higher Ground* (24) to describe one of the debilitating effects of diasporization.

4. *The Reading, the Writing, and the Arithmetic of the Black Masculinist Project*

1. In general, several (white) critics have interpreted Melville's black characters negatively and his white ones positively. For a representative sampling of these critical opin-

ions, see Gross, *"Benito Cereno" Handbook.* Johnson's stance here challenges such interpretations, and this is a part of his reading of a whitemale-dominated academy.

2. In *Invisible Man,* Norton refers to this deformation of blacks euphemistically as his "first-hand organizing of human life" (33).

3. For a discussion of the disease trope in *Rootless,* see J. Lee Greene's *Blacks in Eden* (222–34). Reed's characterization of the Ibos (123) also is very similar to Turpin's characterization of the Coramantees.

4. Cartwright 707–9.

5. For a discussion of southern white civil religion, see Charles Reagan Wilson's *Baptized in Blood.* For a discussion of African American novels' use of this concept, see J. Lee Greene's *Blacks in Eden* 119–33.

6. As it is applied to *Flight to Canada,* "southernized" means essentially the same as "Americanized" in Johnson's *Middle Passage* (30), and the two terms are similar to what this study calls Westernized and diasporized.

7. See White 43 and Hutcheon 123.

8. For a discussion by southern historians and writers (including Ralph Ellison and William Styron) relevant to this point, see "The Uses of History in Fiction."

9. Reed's Mammy Barracuda seems more a corroboration than a negation of Mitchell's character Mammy. Yet *Flight* suggests that this is not Mammy Barracuda's true nature but a false nature induced by diasporization.

10. A useful study of this group is Rubin's *Wary Fugitives.*

11. In *Middle Passage,* Johnson inverts the anthropologist-savage subject paradigm by making the "civilized" the subject of the "savage's" study: "[The Allmuseri] saw whites as Raw Barbarians and me [Rutherford Calhoun] (being a colored mate) as a Cooked one" (75). He parodically evokes Levi-Strauss's study *The Raw and the Cooked* and echoes Sartre's contention that "being is black, being is of fire, [whites] are accidental and remote [and] 'undercooked'" (*Black Orpheus* 10).

12. In her inscription of the legend in *Praisesong,* Marshall's character Aunt Cuney recalls her grandmother's tale of and spiritual affinity with the walking Ibos: "Her body she always usta say might be in Tatem but her mind, her mind was long gone with the Ibos" (39). Reed's inversion of the adage is Arthur Swille's statement that "though my body inhabits the Swille Castle, my mind is in Europe" (131). *Flight,* of course, was published seven years before *Praisesong.*

13. Though from a different perspective than I use here, Vera Kutzinski ("Johnson Revises Johnson") writes perceptively about thematic and formal relationships between *Ex-Coloured Man* and *Oxherding Tale.*

14. J. Johnson, *Autobiography of an Ex-Coloured Man* 211.

15. Some scholars and some traditional African societies (such as the Ashanti) distinguish between the spirit and the soul. Others (societies and scholars) do not make a distinction and at times use the term "spirit-soul" as the English translation for *kra.* For a discussion of distinctions or lack of distinctions between soul and spirit among the Akan and other West African people, see Parrinder's *West African Psychology,* especially chapters 4 and 5. Parrinder notes that problems arise when one attempts to "import European and

Asiatic concepts wholesale into African thought" (29). Indeed, concepts of soul and spirit differ among African people, which makes English-language translations of these concepts even more problematic.

16. See Senghor's "On Negrohood" (6).

17. For a discussion of these novels, see chapter 3 of J. Lee Greene's *Blacks in Eden.*

18. Though this particular discussion focuses on the black male Self, the diasporan myth posits that one's other self can be of a different "race," for race is a social construct and thus is a product of historical time, not primordial Time.

19. From a womanist novel's perspective, this subtraction and bisectioning produced a female self and a male other.

5. *Textual Androgyny, the Androgyne, and the Many-Tongued Chorus of the Common Memory*

1. See Wiley's *Slaves No More* (115–54) and Starobin's *Blacks in Bondage* (173–88).

2. While the "Others" in this novel refers to whites, not all whites in the novel are assigned to this category.

3. Elizabeth DeLoughrey's very informative article "Gendering the Oceanic Voyage," which focuses on Anglophone Caribbean women writers, speaks to this general point about gendered discourse in contemporary Western diasporan novels.

4. The opening and closing sections of the novel are untitled, but they function respectively as prologue and epilogue.

5. The line is an echo from biblical passages (Psalm 22, Matthew 27:46, and Mark 15:34) and is applied to all five of the novel's focal characters.

6. My comments here about Nash's ego-ideal and his Oedipalization are informed by Silverman's discussion of these ideas (130–49).

7. In *Crossing,* Nash mentions having attended "college" (21). W. W. McDonogh, in a letter (dated "Oct 7th 1846") to his former master John McDonogh, whom he addresses as "Dear Father," mentions having attended college. The college probably is Lafayette College in Eaton, PA, where John McDonogh sent some of his slaves to be educated (see Starobin 179 and Wiley 121).

8. In the letters, several former slaves address McDonogh as "father" and refer to themselves as McDonogh's "son." See Starobin's *Blacks in Bondage* and Wiley's *Slaves No More.* For his own purposes, Phillips expands the meaning of this sociolinguistic formation (father-son) to inscribe a homosexual relationship between Nash and Edward (discussed in chapter 6 of this study).

9. The novel's narrator points out that "in their [the Allmuseri's] mythology, Europeans had once been members of their tribe" (65).

10. This is not to ignore the fact that everything in the novel emanates from the mind of its black male author.

11. For a relevant discussion of ego-ideal and Oedipalization (which I adapt), see Silverman 140–41.

12. In most instances, Wideman's term *African* coincides with the contemporary use of

the term *black* and does not, as current usage does, distinguish between African and African American.

13. There are numerous accounts of the Philadelphia yellow fever epidemic of 1793. One study from a medical perspective is Powell's *Bring Out Your Dead.* From a sociocultural and black perspective, see Jones and Allen's *Narrative . . . of the Late Awful Calamity in Philadelphia.*

14. The statement here applies generally to diasporan subjects, black and white. There are characters in the novel, most but not all of whom are white, who are individuated and therefore who are not included in the spiritual fold of intersubjective Being. Reverend Doctor Amos Parker and Mrs. Thrush, whites, and the watchman at the orphanage, though a black diasporan subject, are examples.

15. Among these exceptions is Mr. Rowe, who functions as a spiritual guide for the preacher (63). Mr. Rowe's story receives significant narrative space, but Wideman does not make him a component of the black male Self, as he does for subjects (such as the two boys on the Philadelphia street) whose stories receive a relatively small amount of narrative space.

16. A very useful study of this 1856–57 event is Peires's *The Dead Will Arise.*

17. From this perspective, Dessa's and Sethe's participation in their own denigration, though inadvertent, is a form of cattle killing. Several of the black characters whom Reed portrays negatively in *Flight to Canada* engage in a cattle killing.

18. A "gathering" as a concept in which several stories constitute one story controls content and meaning in Ernest J. Gaines's novel *A Gathering of Old Men* (1983).

19. Edward Said's statement that a "text is a being in the world" (33) in part informs my thought in this instance, though Said might intend a meaning different from mine.

20. For a discussion of this paradigmatic narrative convention in African American novels, see J. Lee Greene's *Blacks in Eden* (239–51).

21. See Laura Miller's interview of Wideman (8).

22. In chapter 3 I point out why I use the prefix *(re)* before such terms as *discover, creation,* and *meeting.* Wideman supports this position when he points out that the preacher's encounter with different women is actually his re-meeting of the same soul housed in a different body (see, for example, 48, 54, among several other instances).

23. L. Miller 1–2.

24. Wideman's reference to "young Lucy" (76) in a section in which the centered subject speaks of a meeting of generations past and present, corporeal and ethereal, seems more than coincidental. Lucy is the name given to the quintessential primordial African female Self—the first woman—from whom all other women (and men) have descended. Anthropology, archaeology, geography, and diasporan mythology dovetail in this reference.

25. The color blue is an "image," as Morrison uses the term ("Site of Memory" 114–17), that links several of the women in this novel as permutations of the same female Self. Perry uses the same image in *Stigmata* and for basically the same purposes as Wideman does.

26. A useful biography of Allen is Wesley's *Richard Allen.*

27. Ada R. Haberson's 1907 lyrics for this song (and Charles H. Gabriel's music) have

been adapted to several different musical genres, white gospel, black gospel, country, and bluegrass among them. Though the song's chorus has remained basically intact in the different adaptations, revisions to, deletions of, and additions of stanzas have characterized several of these adaptations. In the rural foothills of North Carolina where I lived until my late teens, the song, sung in a very slow tempo, was a favorite at funerals for women who were mothers. The stanza (in an adapted version) that speaks of the hearse coming to "take my mother away" invariably drew an intense emotional response from the deceased's family members and other mourners.

28. Though he uses the term "reincarnation," Onyewuenyi observes that this phenomenon in African society does not have exact or "proper translations in European languages" ("Philosophical Reappraisal" 157–58).

29. Obiego 192.

6. *The Third Gender among the Common Memory*

1. Such petitions can be found in the Race and Slavery Petitions Project at the University of North Carolina at Greensboro. The project's Web site includes, among other information, an abstract of each petition. See http://library.uncg.edu/slavery_petitions.

2. See Ottenheimer for comments about cousin marriages in Britain down through the centuries (81).

3. Faulkner's *Absalom, Absalom!* is the premier text that treats the psychological complexity of incest (unconsummated in the novel) and miscegenation that the system of slavery induced. Jones's *Corregidora* and Turpin's *Rootless* treat incest between whites and blacks, and Hildreth's *Archie Moore* treats incest between blacks.

4. Former governor of South Carolina James Henry Hammond is one example. See Hammond xi, 171–72.

5. As indicated below, green is a color associated with sexual deviancy and with, from a heterosexual perspective, homosexuality.

6. See Blackmore for a discussion of homosexual subtexts in *Passing;* for a brief discussion of homosexual motifs in *Invisible Man,* see J. Lee Greene's *Blacks in Eden* 219–22.

7. See Katz, *Gay American History,* 539, 661 n. 175.

8. Green as color symbolism and several aspects of this novel's plot structure resemble Helen R. Hull's 1932 novel about lesbian attractions, *The Labyrinth,* as Katz describes it in *Gay American History* (539).

9. Pattanaik 123–32.

10. I intend the qualifier "nonstandard" for sexual acts that are deemed socially unorthodox or that include an unwilling participant.

11. The vocabulary of gay sexual practices varies among gay communities and in different time periods, though several terms are standard ones. One of the fullest dictionaries of gay slang can be found at http://www.sex-lexis.com/Sex-Dictionary/gay%20slang.

12. The term *homosexual* as I use it in this chapter and as Reed implies its use in his novel refers not only to a subject who has a sexual relation with another person of the same gender but also to a subject who desires a same-gender sexual relation. The term also refers to a subject whose behaviors or mannerisms, denoted as masculine or femi-

nine, resemble those of the opposite gender. In this regard, the degree to which gender is a social construction must be kept in mind.

13. Private sex clubs and public bathhouses were popular in the gay community during the time Reed published *Flight*. It seems obvious that the Magnolia Baths is based on these facilities and is another way Reed merges past and present realities.

14. The language of baseball (such as pitcher, catcher, doubleheader, first base, home run, etc.), though perhaps less utilized in literary texts than the language of slavery, is also applied to (homo)sexual activities, as in William Melvin Kelly's *dem*.

15. For a statement about keys and handkerchief codes, see Hal Fischer's "Gay Semiotics," http://www.queerculturalcenter.org/Pages/HalPages/GaySemIndx.html, as well as "Keys and Handkerchiefs," www.ncf.ca/ip/sigs/life/gay/codes/keys.

16. In contemporary gay male lexicons, a "house boi" is a male (usually younger) whose principal duties for his employer (usually older) are sexual. This is the position Nash Williams and some other young black male slaves occupy in their relation to the slave master Edward Williams in *Crossing the River*.

17. A contemporary pig gets sexual gratification from eating feces and blood, for example.

18. In Charles Johnson's "The Education of Mingo," the character Harriett Bridgewater characterizes slaves as "tools with life in them" (10); compare Hammond xi, xvi.

19. Hammond 172. The *Diaries* gives only surnames. I assume the references are to Henry Clay, Daniel Webster, and William Henry Harrison.

20. "Gay and Black Glossary," http://mindprod.com/ggloss/playas.html.

21. See Tripp, *Intimate World of Abraham Lincoln*. In the book's introduction, Jean Baker mentions works by Sandburg, Tarbell, and Leech that suggest Lincoln's homosexual impulses. These works were in print before Reed published *Flight*.

22. In her doctoral dissertation Akiyo Okuda discusses southern writers (particularly Thomas Dixon, Charles Chesnutt, and Walter Hines Page) who responded through their literary texts to the image of a feminized male South. See her chapter 2, especially 106–12.

23. The "assassin" reference no doubt is to Jefferson Davis and a comparison of Davis to John Wilkes Booth, a comparison that some journalists of the era noted. See Neely, Holzer, and Boritt 83.

24. Some homosexual males have a penchant for abuse, humiliation, spankings, and other "kinky" behavior, usually with males they call "rough trade."

25. In the context of slavery, the term "man-boys" refers generally to a young male slave, which is how Phillips uses it in Captain Hamilton's section of the novel. When applied to Nash (as on page 124) and recontextualized by his sexual relationship with Edward, the term assumes another meaning, much like the term "lady wife" when applied in the sexual triad of Edward, Nash, and Edward's wife, Amelia. According to Ian Stevenson, there is a belief in traditional Ibo society that a person can change his or her gender when reincarnated: "Effeminate and homosexual men may wish to make a full transition and become reborn as women" (17). The man-boy, a primordial African self, whose father sold him into slavery reincarnates much later as Nash Williams. Nash does not undergo a full gender transition, but he does change his sexual orientation more than once during the course of his narrative.

26. According to Bell Wiley, John McDonogh sent some of his slaves to Lafayette College "to prepare them for a missionary career in Africa." See *Crossing* 12. In at least one instance, the slave, David McDonogh, did not go to Liberia. After leaving Lafayette College, he "attended medical school and became a successful surgeon in New York City" (118).

27. A definition of "dinge queen" can be found in "Tolerance in the News" at http://tolerance.org./news/article_tol.jsp?id=995.

Conclusion

1. Amy Kirschke reproduces several of Douglas's major works in her book *Aaron Douglas*. Color reproductions of some of the works I reference in this conclusion can be found in Richard Powell's *Rhapsodies in Black*.

2. *Creation* is an illustration in Locke's *New Negro* (1925), and *The Creation* is an illustration in J. Johnson's *God's Trombones* (1927).

3. A representative sampling of Biggers's works and most of his works that I reference in this conclusion are reproduced in Thiesen and in Wardlaw.

Works Cited

Adegbola, E. A. Ade, ed. *Traditional Religion in West Africa.* Ibadan, Nigeria: Daystar Press, 1983.

Aptheker, Herbert. *American Negro Slave Revolts.* 1943. New York: International Publishers, 1963.

Asante, Molefi Kete. *The Afrocentric Idea.* Philadelphia: Temple Univ. Press, 1987.

Baker, Calvin. *Naming the New World.* New York: St. Martin's Press, 1997.

Baker, Lisa. "Storytelling and Democracy (in the Racial Sense): A Conversation with John Edgar Wideman." *African American Review* 34.2 (Summer 2000): 263–72.

Barnett, Pamela E. "Figurations of Rape and the Supernatural in *Beloved.*" *PMLA* 112 (May 1997): 418–27.

Barthes, Roland. *Mythologies.* 1957. Trans. Annette Lavers. New York: Hill & Wang, 1972.

Beaulieu, Elizabeth Ann. *Black Women Writers and the American Neo-slave Narrative: Femininity Unfettered.* Westport, CT: Greenwood Press, 1999.

Bell, Bernard. *The Afro-American Novel and Its Tradition.* Amherst: Univ. of Massachusetts Press, 1987.

———. "Portrait of the Artist as High Priest of Soul: Jean Toomer's *Cane.*" *Black World* 23, no. 11 (September 1974): 4–19, 92–97.

Bernal, Martin. *Black Athena: The Afroasiatic Roots of Classical Civilization.* 2 vols. New Brunswick, NJ: Rutgers Univ. Press, 1987.

Beal, Frances M. "*Black Scholar* Interviews with Octavia Butler: Black Women and the Science Fiction Genre." *Black Scholar* 17, no. 2 (March–April 1986): 14–18.

Blackmore, David L. "'That Unreasonable Restless Reeling': The Homosexual Subtexts of Nella Larsen's *Passing*." *African American Review* 26 (Fall 1992): 475–84.

Bontemps, Arna. *Black Thunder.* 1936. Rpt. Boston: Beacon Press, 1968.

Brain, Robert. *Friends and Lovers.* New York: Basic Books, 1976.

Brodber, Erna. *Louisiana.* 1994. Rpt. Jackson: Univ. Press of Mississippi, 1997.

Brown, William Wells. *Clotel; or, The President's Daughter: A Narrative of Slave Life in the United States.* 1853. Rpt. New York: Collier Books, 1970.

Butler, Octavia. *Kindred.* 1979. Rpt. Boston: Beacon Press, 1988.

Byerman, Keith E. *Fingering the Jagged Grain: Tradition and Form in Recent Black Fiction.* Athens: Univ. of Georgia Press, 1985.

Byrd, Rudolph, ed. *I Call Myself an Artist: Writings by and about Charles Johnson.* Bloomington: Indiana Univ. Press, 1999.

Carabi, Angels. "Interview with Toni Morrison." *Belles Lettres* 10, no. 2 (Spring 1995): 40–43.

Cartwright, Samuel A. "Report on the Diseases and Physical Peculiarities of the Negro Race." *New Orleans Medical and Surgical Journal* 7 (May 1851): 89–165.

Césaire, Aimé. *Cahier d'un retour au pays natal.* Ed. Abiola Irale. 2nd ed. Columbus: Ohio State Univ. Press, 2000.

Chase-Riboud, Barbara. *Echo of Lions.* New York: Morrow, 1989.

———. *The President's Daughter.* New York: Crown Publishers, 1994.

———. *Sally Hemings.* New York: Viking Press, 1979.

Chesnutt, Charles Waddell. *The Marrow of Tradition.* Boston: Houghton Mifflin, 1901.

Clark, VèVè A. "Developing Diaspora Literacy: Allusion in Maryse Condé's *Hérémakhonon.*" In *Out of the Kumbla: Caribbean Women and Literature,* ed. Carole Boyce Davies and Elaine Savory Fido, 303–19. Trenton, NJ: Africa World Press, 1990.

Clifton, Lucille. *An Ordinary Woman.* New York: Random House, 1974.

Coleman, J. Weston, Jr. *Slavery Times in Kentucky.* Chapel Hill: Univ. of North Carolina Press, 1940.

Condé, Maryse. *Hérémakhonon.* 1976. Trans. Richard Philcox. Washington, DC: Three Continents Press, 1982.

———. *I, Tituba, Black Witch of Salem.* 1986. Trans. Richard Philcox. Charlottesville: Univ. Press of Virginia, 1992.

Cullen, Countee, ed. *Caroling Dusk.* New York: Harper & Brothers, 1927.

Cutter, Martha J. "The Story Must Go On and On: The Fantastic, Narration, and Intertextuality in Toni Morrison's *Beloved* and *Jazz.*" *African American Review* 34, no. 1 (Spring 2000): 61–75.

D'Aguiar, Fred. *The Longest Memory.* New York: Pantheon, 1994.

Daily, Gary W. "Toni Morrison's *Beloved:* Rememory, History, and the Fantastic." In *The Celebration of the Fantastic: Selected Papers from the Tenth Anniversary International Conference on the Fantastic,* ed. Donald E. Morse, Marshall B. Tymn, and Csilla Bertha, 141–47. Westport, CT: Greenwood Press, 1992.

Darling, Marsha. "In the Realm of Responsibility: A Conversation with Toni Morrison." In *Conversations with Toni Morrison,* ed. Danille Taylor-Guthrie, 246–54. Jackson: Univ. Press of Mississippi, 1994.

Dash, Julie. *Daughters of the Dust.* 1997. Rpt. New York: Plume, 1999.

Davies, Carole Boyce. *Black Women, Writing and Identity: Migrations of the Subject.* London: Routledge, 1994.

Davis, Angela. "Reflections on the Black Woman's Role in the Community of Slaves." *Black Scholar* 3, no. 4 (1971): 2–15.

Davis, Mary Kemp. "Everybody Knows Her Name: The Recovery of the Past in Sherley Anne Williams's *Dessa Rose.*" *Callaloo* 12 (Summer 1989): 544–58.

Delany, Martin R. *Blake; or, The Huts of America.* Edited with an introduction by Floyd J. Miller. Boston: Beacon Press, 1970.

DeLoughrey, Elizabeth. "Gendering the Oceanic Voyage: Trespassing the (Black) Atlantic and Caribbean." *Thamyris* 5, no. 2 (Autumn 1998): 205–31.

Delueze, Giles, and Félix Guattari. *Anti-Oedipus: Capitalism and Schizophrenia.* New York: Viking Press, 1977.

Derrida, Jacques. *Edmund Husserl's "Origin of Geometry": An Introduction.* 1978. Trans. John P. Leavey Jr. Lincoln: Univ. of Nebraska Press, 1989.

———. *Of Grammatology.* 1967. Trans. Gayatri Chakravorty Spivak. Baltimore: Johns Hopkins Univ. Press, 1976.

Dickson, Kwesi A., and Paul Ellingworth, ed. *Biblical Revelation and African Beliefs.* Maryknoll, NY: Orbis Books, 1969.

Doty, William G. *Mythography: The Study of Myths and Rituals.* Tuscaloosa: Univ. of Alabama Press, 1986.

Douglass, Frederick. *Narrative of the Life of Frederick Douglass, An American Slave; Written by Himself.* 1845. Rpt. New York: New American Library, 1968.

Duberman, Martin Bauml. "'Writhing Bedfellows': 1826: Two Young Men from Antebellum South Carolina's Ruling Elite Share 'Extravagant Delight.'" *Journal of Homosexuality* 6, nos. 1–2 (Fall–Winter 1980–81): 85–101.

Du Bois, W. E. B. *The Souls of Black Folk: Essays and Sketches.* 1903. Rpt. 7th ed. Chicago: A. C. McClurg, 1907.

Due, Tananarive. *The Living Blood.* New York: Pocket Books, 2001.

———. *My Soul to Keep.* New York: HarperCollins, 1997.

Dunbar, Paul Laurence. *The Sport of the Gods.* 1902. Rpt. New York: Collier Books, 1970.

Eliade, Mircea. *Myth and Reality.* New York: Harper & Row, 1963.

Ellison, Ralph. *Invisible Man.* New York: Random House, 1952.

Equiano, Olaudah. *The Interesting Narrative of the Life of Olaudah Equiano, or Gustavus Vassa, the African, Written by Himself.* Ed. Werner Sollors. New York: W. W. Norton, 2001.

Erdrich, Louise. *Tracks.* New York: Henry Holt, 1988.

Ezeanya, Stephen. "God, Spirits and the Spirit World." In Dickson and Ellingworth, *Biblical Revelation and African Beliefs,* 30–46.

Faulkner, William. *Absalom, Absalom!* 1936. Rpt. New York: Vintage, 1972.

Fogel, Robert William, and Stanley L. Engerman. *Time on the Cross: The Economics of American Negro Slavery.* Boston: Little, Brown, 1974.

———. *Time on the Cross: Evidence and Methods, A Supplement.* Boston: Little, Brown, 1974.

Gaines, Ernest J. *The Autobiography of Miss Jane Pittman.* New York: Dial Press, 1971.

———. *A Gathering of Old Men.* New York: Alfred A. Knopf, 1983.

Gayle, Addison, Jr., ed. *The Black Aesthetic.* Garden City, NY: Doubleday, 1971.

Gerald, Carolyn F. "The Black Writer and His Role." In Gayle Jr., *Black Aesthetic,* 370–78.

Gilbert, Olive, comp. *Narrative of Sojourner Truth; A Bondswoman of Olden Time, Emancipated by the New York Legislature in the Early Part of the Present Century; With a History of Her Labors and Correspondence Drawn from Her "Book of Life."* 1878. Rpt. New York: Arno Press, 1968.

Greene, Alison de Lima. "John Biggers: American Muralist." In Wardlaw, *Art of John Biggers,* 16–75.

Greene, J. Lee. *Blacks in Eden: The African American Novel's First Century.* Charlottesville: Univ. Press of Virginia, 1996.

Griggs, Sutton E. *The Hindered Hand; or, The Reign of the Repressionist.* 3rd ed. 1905. Rpt. New York: AMS Press, 1969.

Gross, Seymour L., ed. *A "Benito Cereno" Handbook.* Belmont, CA: Wadsworth Publishing, 1965.

Grosz, Elizabeth, ed. *Becomings: Explorations in Time, Memory, and Futures.* Ithaca, NY: Cornell Univ. Press, 1999.

Hammond, James Henry. *Secret and Sacred: The Diaries of James Henry Hammond, a Southern Slaveholder.* Ed. Carol Bleser. New York: Oxford Univ. Press, 1988.

Harper, Frances E. W. *Iola Leroy, or Shadows Uplifted.* 1883. Rpt. New York: AMS Press, 1971.

Harris, Middleton A., ed. *The Black Book.* New York: Random House, 1974.

Heidish, Marcy. *A Woman Called Moses.* Boston: Houghton Mifflin, 1976.

Hildreth, Richard. *Archie Moore, the White Slave; or, Memoirs of a Fugitive.* 1836. Rpt. Edited with an introduction by Richard Hildreth. New York: Augustus M. Kelley, 1971.

Holloway, Karla F. C. *Moorings and Metaphors: Figures of Culture and Gender in Black Women's Literature.* New Brunswick, NJ: Rutgers Univ. Press, 1992.

Horvitz, Deborah. "Nameless Ghosts: Possession and Dispossession in *Beloved.*" *Studies in American Fiction* 17 (Autumn 1989): 157–67.

Howard, James H. W. *Bond and Free: A True Tale of Slave Times.* 1886. Rpt. College Park, MD: McGrath Publishing, 1969.

Hurston, Zora Neale. "Characteristics of Negro Expression." In Napier, *African American Literary Theory,* 31–44.

——. *Their Eyes Were Watching God.* 1937. Rpt. New York: HarperCollins, 2000.

Hutcheon, Linda. *A Poetics of Postmodernism: History, Theory, Fiction.* 1988. Rpt. New York: Routledge, 1989.

Jacobs, Harriet. *Incidents in the Life of a Slave Girl.* 1861. Rpt. Ed. Nellie Y. McKay and Frances Smith Foster. New York: W. W. Norton, 2001.

Jessee, Sharon. "'Tell me your earrings': Time and the Marvelous in Toni Morrison's *Beloved.*" In *Memory, Narrative, and Identity: New Essays in Ethnic American Literatures,* ed. Amritjit Singh, Joseph Skerrett Jr., and Robert E. Hogan, 198–211. Boston: Northeastern Univ. Press, 1984.

Johnson, Charles. *Being and Race: Black Writing since 1970.* 1988. Rpt. Bloomington: Indiana Univ. Press, 1990.

———. "The Education of Mingo." In *The Sorcerer's Apprentice: Tales and Conjurations.* 1986. New York: Penquin Books, 1987.

———. *Middle Passage.* New York: Atheneum, 1990.

———. *Oxherding Tale.* Bloomington: Indiana Univ. Press, 1982.

Johnson, James Weldon. *The Autobiography of an Ex-Coloured Man.* 1912. Garden City, NY: Garden City Publishing, 1927.

———. *God's Trombones: Seven Negro Sermons in Verse.* New York: Viking Press, 1927.

Jones, Absalom, and Richard Allen. *A Narrative of the Proceedings of the Black People During the Late Awful Calamity in Philadelphia in the Year 1793, and a Refutation of Some Censures Thrown Upon Them in Some Late Publications.* 1794. Rpt. Philadephia: Rhistoric Publications, 1969.

Jones, Gayl. *Corregidora.* New York: Random House, 1975.

Jones, J. McHenry. *Hearts of Gold.* 1896. Rpt. College Park, MD: McGrath Publishing, 1969.

Jones, Robert B. *Jean Toomer and the Prison-House of Thought: A Phenomenology of the Spirit.* Amherst: Univ. of Massachusetts Press, 1993.

Kafka, Franz. *The Great Wall of China: Stories and Reflections.* 1946. Trans. Willa and Edwin Muir. New York: Schocken Books, 1970.

Katz, Jonathan. *Gay American History: Lesbian and Gay Men in the U.S.A., A Documentary History.* Rev. ed. New York: Meridian Books, 1992.

Keizer, Arlene R. *Black Subjects: Identity Formation in the Contemporary Narrative of Slavery.* Ithaca, NY: Cornell Univ. Press, 2004.

Kelly, William Melvin. *dem.* Garden City, NY: Doubleday, 1967.

Kennedy, John Pendleton. *Swallow Barn, or a Sojourn in the Old Dominion.* 1832. Ed. William Osbourne. New York: Hafner Publishing, 1962.

Kerman, Cynthia Earl, and Richard Eldridge. *The Lives of Jean Toomer: A Hunger for Wholeness.* Baton Rouge: Louisiana State Univ. Press, 1987.

Kincaid, Jamaica. *The Autobiography of My Mother.* New York: Farrar, Strauss & Giroux, 1996.

Kirschke, Amy Helene. *Aaron Douglas: Art, Race, and the Harlem Renaissance.* Berkeley: Univ. of California Press, 1997.

Knight, Etheridge. *Black Voices from Prison.* Edited with an introduction by Roberto Giammanco. New York: Pathfinder Press, 1970.

Kutzinski, Vera. "Johnson Revises Johnson: *Oxherding Tale* and *The Autobiography of an Ex-Coloured Man.*" In Byrd, *I Call Myself an Artist,* 279–87.

LaCapra, Dominick. *History and Criticism.* Ithaca, NY: Cornell Univ. Press, 1985.

Larsen, Nella. *Passing.* 1929. Rpt. New York: Collier Books, 1971.

Lévi-Strauss, Claude. *The Raw and the Cooked.* Trans. Johns and Doreen Weightman. New York: Harper & Row, 1969.

Little, Jonathan. *Charles Johnson's Spiritual Imagination.* Columbia: Univ. of Missouri Press, 1997.

———. "An Interview with Charles Johnson." In Byrd, *I Call Myself an Artist,* 225–43.

Locke, Alain, ed. *The New Negro: An Interpretation.* New York: Albert & Charles Boni, 1925.

Lovelace, Earl. *Salt.* 1996. New York: Persea Books, 1997.
Marshall, Paule. *Praisesong for the Widow.* New York: G. P. Putnam's Sons, 1983.
Martin, Valerie. *Property.* Rpt. New York: Vintage Books, 2003.
Mbiti, John S. *African Religions and Philosophy.* 1969. Rpt. Garden City, NY: Anchor Books, 1970.
McKoy, Sheila Smith. "The Limbo Contest: Diaspora Temporality and Its Reflection in *Praisesong for the Widow* and *Daughters of the Dust.*" *Callaloo* 22, no. 1 (Winter 1999): 208–22.
Miller, Arthur. *The Crucible: A Play in Four Acts.* 1953. New York: Penguin Books, 1995.
Miller, Laura. "The *Salon* Interview: John Edgar Wideman." http://www.salon.com/nov96/interview961111.html.
Mitchell, Angelyn. *The Freedom to Remember: Narrative, Slavery, and Gender in Contemporary Black Women's Fiction.* New Brunswick, NJ: Rutgers Univ. Press, 2002.
Mitchell, Margaret. *Gone with the Wind.* New York: Macmillan, 1936.
Momaday, N. Scott. *House Made of Dawn.* 1968. Rpt. New York: Perennial Classics, 1999.
Morrison, Toni. *Beloved.* New York: Alfred A. Knopf, 1987.
———. *Jazz.* New York: Alfred A. Knopf, 1992.
———. *Playing in the Dark: Whiteness and the Literary Imagination.* Cambridge, MA: Harvard Univ. Press, 1992.
———. "Rootedness: The Ancestor as Foundation." In *Black Women Writers (1950–1980): A Critical Evaluation,* ed. Mari Evans, 339–45. Garden City, NY: Doubleday, 1984.
———. "The Site of Memory." In *Inventing the Truth: The Art and Craft of Memoir,* ed. William Zinsser, 101–24. Boston: Houghton Mifflin, 1987.
———. *Song of Solomon.* New York: Alfred A. Knopf, 1977.
———. *Sula.* New York: Alfred A. Knopf, 1973.
Muhammad, Elijah. *Message to the Blackman in America.* 1965. Rpt. Chicago: Final Call, n.d.
Mulago, Vincent. "Vital Participation: The Cohesive Principle of the Bantu Community." In Dickson and Ellingworth, *Biblical Revelation and African Beliefs,* 137–58.
Napier, Winston, ed. *African American Literary Theory: A Reader.* New York: New York Univ. Press, 2000.
Naylor, Gloria. *Linden Hills.* 1985. Rpt. New York: Penguin, 1986.
———. *The Women of Brewster Place.* New York: Viking Press, 1982.
Neely, Mark E., Jr., Harold Holzer, and Gabor S. Boritt. *The Confederate Image: Prints of the Lost Cause.* Chapel Hill: Univ. of North Carolina Press, 1987.
Obiego, Cosmas Okechukwu. *African Image of the Ultimate Reality: An Analysis of Igbo Ideas of Life and Death in Relation to Chukwu-God.* Frankfurt: Peter Lang, 1984.
Oduyọye, Modupẹ. "Man's Self and Its Spiritual Double." In Adegbola, *Traditional Religion in West Africa,* 273–88.
Ogunyemi, Chilewenye Okonjo. "An Abiku-Ogbanje Atlas: A Pre-text for Rereading Soyinka's *Aké* and Morrison's *Beloved.*" *African American Review* 36, no. 4 (Winter 2002): 663–78.
Okonkwo, Christopher N. "A Critical Divination: Reading *Sula* as Ogbanje-Abiku." *African American Review* 38, no. 4 (Winter 2004): 651–68.
Okuda, Akiyo Ito. "Literary Re-Constructionists: The Makers and Makings of Charles

Chesnutt's *The Marrow of Tradition*, Thomas Dixon's *The Leopard's Spots*, and Walter Hines Page's *The Southerner*." PhD diss., Univ. of North Carolina at Chapel Hill, 2005.

Onyewuenyi, Innocent. "Is There an African Philosophy?" In Serequeberhan, *African Philosophy*, 29–46.

———. "A Philosophical Reappraisal of African Belief in Reincarnation." *International Philosophical Quarterly* 22, no. 3 (1982): 157–68.

Ottenheimer, Martin. *Forbidden Relatives: The American Myth of Cousin Marriage*. Urbana: Univ. of Illinois Press, 1996.

Panger, Daniel. *Ol' Prophet Nat*. Winston-Salem, NC: John F. Blair, 1967.

Pattanaik, Devdutt. *The Man Who Was a Woman and Other Queer Tales from Hindu Lore*. New York: Harrington Park Press, 2002.

Parrinder, G. *West African Psychology: A Comparative Study of Psychological and Religious Thought*. 1951. Rpt. New York: AMS Press, 1976.

Paynter, John M. *Fugitives of the Pearl*. 1930. Rpt. New York: AMS Press, 1971.

Peires, J. B. *The Dead Will Arise: Nongqawuse and the Great Xhosa Cattle-Killing Movement of 1856–57*. Bloomington: Indiana Univ. Press, 1989.

Perry, Phyllis Alesia. *Stigmata*. 1998. Rpt. New York: Anchor Books, 1999.

Petry, Ann Lane. *Tituba of Salem Village*. New York: Crowell, 1964.

Phelan, James. "Toward a Rhetorical Reader-Response Criticism: The Difficult, the Stubborn, and the Ending of *Beloved*." *Modern Fiction Studies* 39 (1993): 709–28.

Phillips, Caryl. *Cambridge*. 1991. New York: Alfred A. Knopf, 1992.

———. *Crossing the River*. 1993. New York: Alfred A. Knopf, 1994.

———. *The European Tribe*. London: Fabre & Fabre, 1987.

———. *Higher Ground*. New York: Viking Penguin, 1989.

Plato. *Symposium*. In *Great Dialogues of Plato*, ed. Eric H. Warmington and Philip G. Rouse, trans. Philip G. Rouse, 69–117. New York: Mentor Books, 1956.

Powell, J. H. [John Harvey]. *Bring Out Your Dead: The Great Plague of Yellow Fever in Philadelphia in 1793*. 1949. Rpt. with a new introduction by Kenneth R. Foster, Mary F. Jenkins, and Anne Coxe Toogood. Philadelphia: Univ. of Pennsylvania Press, 1993.

Powell, Richard J., ed. *The Blues Aesthetic: Black Culture and Modernism*. Washington, DC: Washington Project for the Arts, 1989.

———. *Rhapsodies in Black: Art of the Harlem Renaissance*. Berkeley: Univ. of California Press, 1997.

Prince, Mary. *The History of Mary Prince, a West Indian Slave, Related by Herself*. 1831. Rpt. Ed. Moira Ferguson. Rev. ed. Ann Arbor: Univ. of Michigan Press, 1998.

Reed, Ishmael. *Flight to Canada*. 1976. Rpt. New York: Atheneum, 1989.

———. *Mumbo Jumbo*. Garden City, NY: Doubleday, 1972.

———. *Writin' Is Fightin': Thirty-Seven Years of Boxing on Paper*. New York: Atheneum, 1988.

Reyes, Angelita. *Mothering across Cultures: Postcolonial Representations*. Minneapolis: Univ. of Minnesota Press, 2002.

Rogers, Joseph A. *World's Great Men of Color*. 2 vols. 1947. Ed. John Henrik Clarke. New York: Collier Books, 1972.

Rubin, Louis D., Jr. *The Wary Fugitives: Four Poets and the South*. Baton Rouge: Louisiana State Univ. Press, 1978.

Rusch, Frederik L., ed. *A Jean Toomer Reader: Selected Unpublished Writings.* New York: Oxford Univ. Press, 1993.

Rushdy, Ashraf H. A. "Daughters Signifyin(g) History: The Example of Toni Morrison's *Beloved.*" *American Literature* 64 (1992): 567–97.

———. "Neo-Slave Narrative." In *The Oxford Companion to African American Literature,* ed. William L. Andrews, Frances Smith Foster, and Trudier Harris, 533–35. New York: Oxford Univ. Press, 1997.

———. *Neo-slave Narratives: Studies in the Social Logic of a Literary Form.* New York: Oxford Univ. Press, 1999.

———. "The Phenomenology of the Allmuseri: Charles Johnson and the Subject of the Narrative of Slavery." *African American Review* 26 (Autumn 1992): 373–94.

Said, Edward W. *The World, the Text, and the Critic.* Cambridge, MA: Harvard Univ. Press, 1983.

Sartre, Jean-Paul. *Black Orpheus.* 1948. Trans. S. W. Allen. Paris: Présence Africaine, 1976.

———. *The Emotions: Outline of a Theory.* Trans. Bernard Frechtman. New York: Philosophical Library, 1948.

Schneider, Michael S. *A Beginner's Guide to Constructing the Universe: The Mathematical Archetypes of Nature, Art, and Science.* 1994. Rpt. New York: HarperPerennial, 1995.

Schwartzman, Myron. *Romare Bearden: His Life and Art.* New York: Harry N. Abrams, 1990.

Selvon, Samuel. *The Lonely Londoners.* 1956. Rpt. Essex, UK: Longman, 1985.

———. *Moses Ascending.* 1975. Rpt. London: Heinemann, 1984.

———. *Moses Migrating.* 1983. Rpt. Washington, DC: Three Continents Press, 1992.

Senghor, Léopold Sédar. *The Foundations of "Africanité"; or Négritude and Arabité.* 1967. Trans. Mercer Cook. Paris: Présence Africaine, 1971.

———. "On Negrohood: Psychology of the African Negro." Trans. H. Kaal. *Diogenes* 37, no. 1 (1962): 1–15.

Serequeberhan, Tsenay, ed. *African Philosophy: The Essential Readings.* New York: Paragon House, 1991.

Setiloane, Gabriel M. *African Theology: An Introduction.* Johannesburg: Skotaville Publishers, 1986.

Shockley, Ann Allen. "The Mistress and the Slave Girl." In *The Black and White of It,* 105–13. Tallahassee, Fl: Naiad Press, 1987.

Sidhom, Swailem. "The Theological Estimate of Man." In Dickson and Ellingworth, *Biblical Revelation and African Beliefs,* 83–115.

Silverman, Kaja. *The Subject of Semiotics.* 1983. Rpt. New York: Oxford Univ. Press, 1984.

Sitter, Deborah Ayer. "The Making of a Man: Dialogic Meaning in *Beloved.*" *African American Review* 26 (Spring 1992): 17–29.

Smith, Paul. *Discerning the Subject.* Minneapolis: Univ. of Minnesota Press, 1988.

Sollors, Werner. *Beyond Ethnicity: Consent and Descent in American Culture.* New York: Oxford Univ. Press, 1986.

Sounds of Blackness. *Africa to America: The Journey of the Drum.* LP. Astoria, NY: Perspective Records, 1994.

Spaulding, A. Timothy. *Re-Forming the Past: History, the Fantastic, and the Postmodern Slave Narrative.* Columbus: Ohio State Univ. Press, 2005.

Spivak, Gayatri Chakravorty. Preface to Derrida, *Of Grammatology,* ix–lxxxvii.

Starobin, Robert S., ed. *Blacks in Bondage: Letters of American Slaves.* New York: New Viewpoints, 1974.

Stevenson, Ian. "The Belief in Reincarnation among the Igbo of Nigeria." *Journal of Asian and African Studies* 20 (1985): 13–30.

Stowe, Harriett Beecher. *Uncle Tom's Cabin.* 1852. Rpt. with an introduction by Amanda Claybaugh. New York: Barnes & Noble, 2003.

Styron, William. *The Confessions of Nat Turner.* New York: Random House, 1967.

Tempels, Placide. *Bantu Philosophy.* 1959. Rpt. Paris: Présence Africaine, 1969.

Theisen, Olive Jensen. *A Life on Paper: The Drawings and Lithographs of John Thomas Biggers.* Denton: Univ. of North Texas Press, 2006.

Thompson, Robert Farris. "John Biggers's *Shotguns* of 1987: An American Classic." In Wardlaw, *Art of John Biggers,* 108–11.

Tolson, Melvin. *Harlem Gallery: Book I, The Curator.* New York: Twayne Publishers, 1965.

Toomer, Jean. *Cane.* 1923. Rpt. New York: Harper & Row, 1969.

———. *The Wayward and the Seeking: A Collection of Writings by Jean Toomer,* ed. Darwin T. Turner. Washington, DC: Howard Univ. Press, 1980.

Tripp, C. A. *The Intimate World of Abraham Lincoln.* Ed. Lewis Gannett. New York: Free Press, 2005.

Turpin, Waters Edward. *The Rootless.* New York: Vantage Press, 1957.

"The Uses of History in Fiction." *Southern Literary Journal* 1 (Spring 1969): 57–90.

Van Sertima, Ivan. "Egypto-Nubian Presences in Ancient Mexico." In *African Presence in Early America,* ed. Ivan Van Sertima. New Brunswick, NJ: Rutgers Univ. Press, 1987.

———. *They Came before Columbus: The African Presence in Ancient America.* New York: Random House, 1976.

Walcott, Derek. *Omeros.* New York: Farrar, Straus & Giroux, 1990.

Walker, Alice. "Beauty: When the Other Dancer Is the Self." In *In Search of our Mothers' Gardens,* 384–93.

———. *In Search of Our Mothers' Gardens.* San Diego: Harcourt, Brace, Jovanovich, 1983.

———. *Meridian.* New York: Harcourt, Brace, Jovanovich, 1976.

Walker, David. *David Walker's "Appeal, in Four Articles; Together with a Preamble, to the Coloured Citizens of the World, but in Particular, and Very Expressly, to Those of the United States of America."* 1829. Ed. Charles M. Wiltse. New York: Hill & Wang, 1965.

Walker, Margaret. *Jubilee.* Boston: Houghton Mifflin, 1966.

Walters, Wendy W. " 'One of dese mornings, bright and fair, / take my wings and cleave the air': The Legend of the Fying Africans and Diasporic Consciousness—Folklore as a Foundation for Literature." *Melus* 22 (Fall 1997): 3–29.

Wardlaw, Alvia J. "Metamorphosis: The Life and Art of John Biggers." In Wardlaw, *Art of John Biggers,* 16–75.

———, ed. *The Art of John Biggers: View from the Upper Room.* New York: Harry N. Abrams, 1995.

Webb, Frank J. *The Garies and Their Friends*. 1857. Rpt. New York: Arno, 1969.

Wesley, Charles H. *Richard Allen: Apostle of Freedom*. Washington, DC: Associated Publishers, 1935.

West, John Anthony. *Serpent in the Sky: The High Wisdom of Ancient Egypt*. New York: Harper & Row, 1979.

White, Hayden. *Tropics of Discourse: Essays in Cultural Criticism*. Baltimore: Johns Hopkins Univ. Press, 1978.

Wideman, John Edgar. *The Cattle Killing*. Boston: Houghton Mifflin, 1996.

Wiley, Bell I., ed. *Slaves No More: Letters from Liberia, 1833–1869*. Lexington: Univ. Press of Kentucky, 1980.

Williams, Sherley Anne. *Dessa Rose*. 1986. Rpt. New York: Berkley Books, 1987.

Wilson, Charles Reagan. *Baptized in Blood: The Religion of the Lost Cause, 1865–1920*. Athens: Univ. of Georgia Press, 1980.

Wilson, Harriet E. *Our Nig; or, Sketches from the Life of a Free Black, in a Two-Story White House, North, Showing That Slavery's Shadows Fall Even There*. 1859. Rpt. Edited with an introduction by Henry Louis Gates. New York: Random House, 1983.

Wright, Richard. "Blueprint for Negro Writing." *New Challenge II* (1937): 53–65.

———. *Native Son*. New York: Harper & Brothers, 1940.

Wyatt, Jean. "Giving Body to the Word: The Maternal Symbolic in Toni Morrison's *Beloved*." *PMLA* 108 (May 1993): 474–88.

Zubiri, Xavier. *Dynamic Structure of Reality*. Trans. Nelson R. Orringer. Urbana: Univ. of Illinois Press, 2003.

Index